ADVENTURES IN WOODTURNING

TECHNIQUES AND PROJECTS

ADVENTURES IN WOODTURNING

TECHNIQUES AND PROJECTS

David Springett

Guild of Master Craftsman Publications Ltd

First published 1994 by
Guild of Master Craftsman Publications Ltd,
166 High Street, Lewes, East Sussex BN7 lXU

The frontispiece is from *1800 Woodcuts by
Thomas Bewick and his School* edited by
Blanche Cirker; the illustration on page 3 is
from *L'Art du Tourneur* by Diderot; the
illustration on pages 15 and 150, and the
illustration on pages 177 and 180 (bottom)
are from *Manuel du Tourneur* by Hamelin
Bergeron; the illustration on page 179 is from
*Mechanick Exercises or the Doctrine of
Handy-Works* by Joseph Moxon; the
illustration on page 180 (top) is from *The
Principles and Practice of Ornamental or
Complex Turning* by John Jacob Holtzapffel.

Designed by Fineline Studios

Printed and bound in Great Britain by Hollen
Street Press

This book is for Bernard and Mary Springett,
my parents, with love and thanks

Acknowledgements

I would like to acknowledge the help given by many friends and to give them my thanks:

John Davenport who, like the magician he is, appeared at exactly the right moment.

Frank Dutton for always being so ready to help with odd mechanical parts so expertly engineered.

Yvonne Fawdrey for the enormous amount of typing.

Ian French for throwing in ideas and suggestions in barren times.

My wife, Christine, for being so reasonable when the bobbins that should have been made were not.

Bill Weprin for bringing light where there was darkness – improving the quality of some of my black and white photographs.

I would also like to thank those who helped by giving me wood, particularly on my last Australian trip:

Bill Botman for the Australian blackwood and many others.

Gordon Ward for that magnificent piece of sandalwood.

Len Smith of Woodsmith for introducing me to Tasmanian tiger and many others.

Harry Gates for that lovely white holly at such short notice.

Ian Jackson for that help with the padauk.

Contents

Foreword

What an incredible man is David Springett, for I am convinced that he must spend every waking moment – and a good number of sleepless nights too – puzzling out the solutions to these treats of woodturning. On first seeing the pieces he produces, the immediate reaction is that he must be the proud possessor of an ornamental lathe, but no, he simply uses a basic Myford ML8 woodturning lathe. However, he is well equipped with the most agile, questing and analytical mind.

David seeks his inspiration from the objects around him – antiques, pieces in museums – and reminds us of the ingenious examples of woodturning craftsmanship that earlier turners were producing 500 years ago. All were produced on comparatively simple machines but, like the author, these turners of yore were superb craftsmen, innovative and most numerate. Apart from the homely objects that so often help unravel problems, David Springett has researched early works from the 17th century onwards by Moxon, Bergeron and of course the ornamental turner's bible – Holtzapffel. Almost 40 years ago I was building up a specialist library encompassing the history of tools and technology, and I recall with great clarity the fascinating illustrations in these early works that David has found so illuminating.

Meticulous instructions are given for turning the projects, and when you add the making of chucks, jigs and specialist tools, this book will keep you happily tuned in to turning for a long time yet. Apart from the ability to turn accurately, readers will need woodworking ability and workshop facilities for constructing the various chucks and jigs David so ably describes – a happy combination. As he suggests in his introductory chapter, by all means use proprietary equipment, but do not overlook your own ability to be more self reliant – workshop-made chucks and jigs are easy to keep running and readily repaired.

Like the good schoolmaster he obviously was, we are encouraged and shown how to achieve what may at first appear to be the impossible: to progress and further experiment in 'turning with a difference'.

To quote from his first book, 'If someone else can do it, then so can I'.

John Haywood

Introduction

IT CAN BE A SOBERING EXPERIENCE LOOKING AT CERTAIN EARLY TURNED PIECES; THE TECHNIQUES WERE OFTEN REMARKABLY SOPHISTICATED, YET THE MACHINERY WITH WHICH THEY WERE PRODUCED WAS OFTEN SIMPLY MADE.

Today we rely so much on factory-made accessories to assist our work. The temptation to use them is irresistible. I use a four-jaw chuck for it is quick and easy, but then so is the newspaper and glue method, and so are bobbin chucks, jam chucks, directly turned wood Morse tapers and chucks specially made from wood. Use today's technology and beautifully engineered gadgets, but do not overlook your own ability to be more self-reliant. Those chucks and jigs simply made in the workshop are easy to keep running and readily repaired if problems arise.

We seem equally blinkered when considering the turning itself, for turning is thought by many to be worked either between centres or centred on a faceplate. Explore the varied pathways that can be taken across or around a rotating piece, particularly if the work is set away from the centre of rotation. You may be surprised by the result.

Imagine yourself as an eighteenth-century turner and ask how, with the more limited resources of that time, you would produce the piece, and maybe a more direct and more satisfying solution will present itself.

So, there's nothing new in this world, just new ways of using old ideas. A number of techniques described in this book are old, forgotten or just neglected. The projects used to demonstrate these techniques can be considered complete in themselves but I would rather it be that they become a stimulus to create new and interesting turned forms. It is far more exciting to develop than to duplicate.

When turning wood, there isn't a right or wrong way to work, but there are easier and more effective techniques which, if used, will allow wood to be cut more efficiently, quickly and cleanly. Although I consider it best to use these techniques, woodturning in most cases is followed purely for enjoyment and that enjoyment should not be spoiled if other methods are used.

I hope this book will help your continued enjoyment of woodturning by adding variety and increasing the range of turned objects that you can make in your own workshop.

Enjoy your woodturning!

Measurements – cautionary note

Although care has been taken to ensure that the imperial measurements are true and accurate, they are only conversions from metric. Throughout the book instances will be found where a metric measurement has fractionally varying imperial equivalents (or vice versa), usually within ⅟₁₆in either way. This is because in each particular case the *closest* imperial equivalent has been given, so that a measurement fractionally smaller will be rounded down to the nearest ⅟₁₆in and a measurement fractionally greater will be rounded up. For this reason it is recommended, particularly on the smaller projects, that a drawing is made of the work in imperial sizes to ensure that the measurements have not lost anything in the translation. (*See* also the Metric Conversion Table, page 227.)

Also, although the measurements given here are carefully calculated and are accurate, some variation may occur when pieces are hand turned, so care must be taken and adjustment may be necessary as the work progresses.

N.B. All dimensions within illustrations are in millimetres.

PART 1

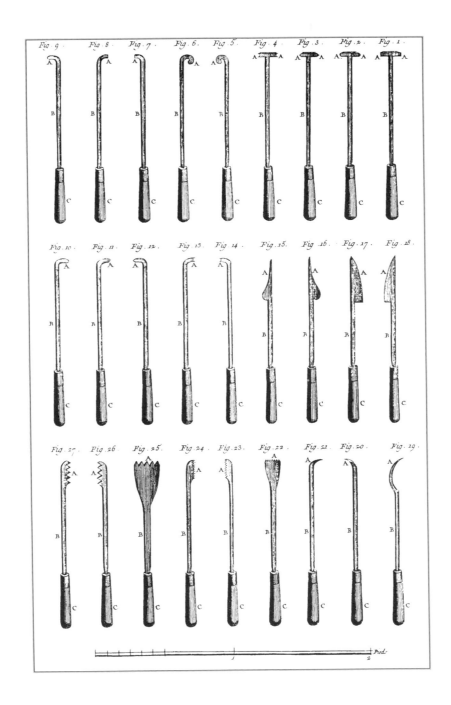

TOOLS, MATERIALS AND TECHNIQUES

CHAPTER 1

Woods

WHERE POSSIBLE I LIKE TO USE LOCALLY GROWN WOODS. IF I HEAR OF A TREE BEING FELLED OR SEE A TREE DOWN IN A GARDEN AFTER A STORM I MAKE AN ENQUIRY AND VERY OFTEN I AM OFFERED MORE WOOD THAN I CAN HANDLE.

To add a little zest to my turning life I use some exotic woods, a little like salt and pepper on a meal, just enough throughout the year to liven up those dull patches.

Recently I have discovered the enormous variety and quality of Australian timbers and was delighted when I discovered that a venture called Goldfield Timbers had begun in Western Australia. Run by Conservation and Land Management (CALM), they provide the local turners and woodworkers with a huge range of woods the equal of anywhere in the world. I understand it is intended that many of the timbers from this area are to be made available commercially throughout the world.

Australian timbers from other areas are already easily obtainable worldwide. The range and variety are such that there will always be one to suit the planned project.

Caring for timber

If you have gathered your own timber, most of it will be unseasoned and require drying. This process has to be started immediately because logs, if left, will split and decay may begin.

Fortunately most timber needed for turning does not need to be planed square, so small logs and even some larger branches may be used by turners.

Seasoning

◆ Cut logs or pieces into lengths that are easy to handle.

◆ All logs need to be sawn or split through the middle. This helps to relieve the tension, allowing the halves to dry and shrink more evenly.

◆ The end grain has to be sealed to slow down evaporation from those ends. This will encourage a slower moisture loss from the sides. Wax, PVA glue and certain paints are effective but use paint with care for the colour may be drawn into the end grain of some woods.

◆ Store the cut sections in a well-ventilated, waterproof, dry and shaded area. Allow air to circulate around the wood. Small 25mm (1in) sticks can be used to separate the stacked pieces to assist movement of air.

◆ If branchwood is chosen then beware, for in hardwoods the area above the central pith of the branch is larger than that beneath. This helps support the branch, the larger area above the pith being held under tension. This tension wood, when cut, will slowiy (sometimes rapidly) relax changing a sawn straight piece to a twisted curve in a very short time.

◆ Turning wet wood is a most pleasant experience. In fact once tried it is hard to return to the dry dusty woods, but the drawbacks are great. Cracks and distortion are almost inevitable unless the piece, once turned, is either dried with extreme care or that incredible technological leap of microwave seasoning is practised.

◆ Air seasoning is a slow process. As a rule it will take about one year for every 25mm (1in) of thickness, but this will vary. A narrower or partially turned piece (leave allowance for movement) will dry more quickly.

For further information about seasoning timber, read *Understanding Wood* by R. Bruce Hoadley (Taunton Press, 1985).

Woods used in the projects

English

ASH

A creamy-white, open-grained wood that turns very well. Ideal for drinking vessels for it imparts no smell or taste to a liquid it holds. A particularly good choice for the folding beaker (*see* Chapter 7) as the wood is reasonably flexible. This is an advantage when the turned rings are telescoped out and pulled tightly together.

BOXWOOD

This wonderful English hardwood, although only available in small sizes, is a perfect turning timber. It cuts cleanly, holds detail and is very stable when dry. It has a firm, close grain and is buff in colour. Unfortunately, because it is such a slow-growing timber and because it has been heavily harvested in the past, the best and larger pieces have already been used, leaving only poorer quality small billets available commercially.

ELM

A dull brown colour with exciting open grain patterns. It turns well. The main use that I found for it was chucks and their hold-down collars. It is a wood that I enjoy using but it does have a farmyard smell when cut and turned, though fortunately not too unpleasant.

HAWTHORN

I consider myself fortunate to have a good supply of this excellent English hardwood. It is usually only available in small pieces but it turns so well. Creamy white, close grained with an occasional dark flame through the heartwood. It can be turned very thin and then it takes on a marvellous amber translucency.

HOLLY

This is not a timber I have turned very often but the experience so far has been superb. A very white wood – if it has grey streaks it may be due to careless seasoning or old age – close grained and quite dense. It can be turned extremely thin and takes very fine detail. It accepts dyes well.

LABURNUM

King of English timbers. Golden ginger to dark brown with streaks of green that have a lustrous glow when well polished. It is worthwhile planting in the garden for it provides swags of yellow flowers which are set beautifully against light-green foliage in the spring. It not only provides brilliance in the garden but also a warm ginger-brown wood which has an occasional darker streak. Polished well, this wood shows a deep lustrous golden glow with flashes of muted yellows, greens, golds and ochre. Look out for some in your neighbourhood for it is susceptible to fungal attack, and if you see a tree in distress you can offer to help the owner with your tree-removal service.

OAK

I used this timber for the slides and bearers in the oval chuck (*see* Chapter 19), having noted that oak that had been soaked in oil was used as bearings in water- and windmills. I felt that those moving parts in the oval chuck would be a most suitable application for oiled oak. It is a very satisfying wood to work for it planes so well, providing a crisp surface and sharp edges; and that wonderful tannin smell which comes when the wood is worked is very pleasant.

SYCAMORE

Very much a utilitarian wood. Creamy white in colour, it turns well though occasionally may tear out, so tools have to be kept sharp. Ideal for drinking vessels for it imparts no smell, taste or colour. Sycamore has to be seasoned very carefully with all sawdust wiped from its surface, otherwise the delicate cream is splashed with blue. The grain pattern varies enormously from a very wide to a close almost indistinct patterning.

WALNUT

A lovely dark-brown wood which, when well figured, has black streaks and spectacular patterning. The joining of branches or the division of twin trunks provides marvellous flame patterns and ripple compressions which look superb when used in turnery. An excellent timber for turning; mild and easy to cut, it polishes extremely well.

Australian

I am sold on Australian timbers. The variety is so great and the quality is generally very fine. Of course they do have some poorer woods, but don't we all? I hope that Australian turners appreciate what they have on their doorstep.

AUSTRALIAN BLACKWOOD

Not black, more brown. Turns very well on spindle work but the end grain can be a little troublesome for bowl turning. It is a reasonable wood but not my favourite Australian timber.

COOKTOWN IRONWOOD

Every time I use this wood I remember David Uppfield Brown, who calls this 'organic steel'. It is such a perfect description. I enjoy turning this wood for it is relatively easy to work, compared to planing or chiselling or sawing the stuff. A dense wood with a rust-red colour, it made the perfect slide in the oval chuck (*see* Chapter 19).

GREY GUM BURR

Wow – such a tight burr. The pieces stay together when turned, no drop out, no break out, it is magnificent. This grey-brown swirling mass of tiny knobs and rivulets of wood is so easy to work, coming cleanly from sharp tools and finishing to perfection. Thank you Australia.

PINK MYRTLE

Well there was some pink in it but a lot of brown as well. The sapwood is very woolly, the heartwood less so, but even then it turns quite well. Sharp tools are needed to produce a really crisp finish. The pink comes as an attractive flame pattern in the wood and with careful polishing can be coaxed into life.

RED RIVER GUM

A brick-red wood which chips away from the tool leaving a good surface finish. Quite dense and easy to work; a good all-round timber.

SANDALWOOD

I carried back a piece of this Western Australian timber in my hand luggage. I was not trusting it to the hold. A dense, sandy-coloured wood with a very clear grain pattern. It turns so well, the equivalent of English boxwood but in much larger sizes. The delicate scent whilst turning seems to disappear after the first few minutes but for days afterwards, as soon as an outside door is opened and fresh air comes in, that scent magically reappears. A top-quality turning timber.

TASMANIAN TIGER OR BLACKHEART MYRTLE

What a wood! Such a varied grain pattern: an underlying brown with slashes, streaks and spots of black – real tiger stripes. There is even an elusive shimmering pattern of green beneath the surface, and it turns so very well. A real treat.

Exotics

In this section I have included mahogany and olivewood – they are neither English nor Australian, so where else could they go?

EBONY

Everyone has heard of ebony – that incredibly black wood that is not all black. Ebony does have some lighter brown streaks so do not feel cheated if you come upon a piece like that. With such a regular quality of density it is a treat to turn. Hard and firm, it cuts well, takes fine detail and blunts tools. It can be unforgiving. When a tool is presented at an incorrect angle or is blunt, it will grab or dig in or whip it away. So work cautiously until you get to know ebony.

MAHOGANY

There is such a variety of timbers available called mahogany of one sort or another, it is difficult to provide general working properties. The piece I used to make the headstock box for the oval chuck was from an old piece of table top (*see* Chapter 19). It was gentle to work and came cleanly from the tool, finishing extremely well. When sanding, no matter how carefully the dust was extracted, some managed to touch my lips and it was bitter. I have worked many forms of mahogany and some were no better than packing-case material, so I was grateful for the fine piece I chose here.

OLIVEWOOD

That warm, oily smell when turned provides only happy memories, for this wood is so gentle and easy to turn. The grain pattern can be wild and exuberant – browns, huge black swirling streaks, chocolate, buff, all shades mixing and twisting – yet even with the most contorted grain patterns it turns so well. Such a soft and rounded wood, it seems to hold the character of those warm and gentle olive groves from which it was harvested.

PADAUK

It can be brilliant red or a disappointing brown, so watch out. It has a custard powder smell when worked and it cuts and finishes well. A little open grained but who cares when you have a piece that's the colour of the setting sun.

PINK IVORY

Mystery and magic seem to have been woven around this wood. A good marketing technique or a good wood? When it's pink it's pink, when it's not it's a disappointment. Even when the colour is not there the wood is excellent to turn. Close grained and a little waxy, it takes fine detail and can be turned very thin. It was the perfect choice for the rose petals of the turned rosebud (*see* Chapter 13).

PURPLEHEART

A dense wood. A crisp finish straight from sharp tools. Excellent for turnery and that purple colour can be stunning, but use it sparingly; too much in a large area becomes overpowering.

CHAPTER 2

Tools and Toolmaking

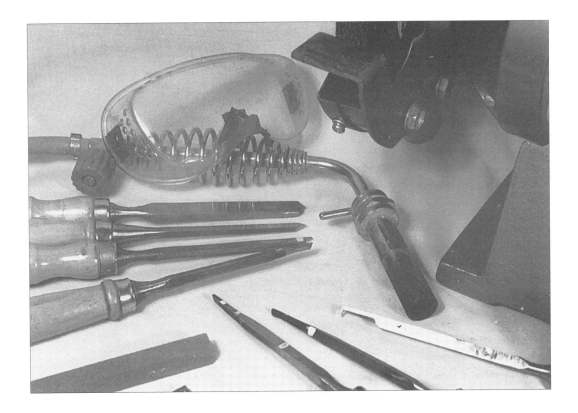

THE FEW EXTRA TOOLS NEEDED BEYOND THOSE GENERALLY AVAILABLE TO TURNERS WERE MADE FROM INEXPENSIVE WOOD CHISELS. THE REQUIRED SHAPE WAS MARKED UPON THEIR SURFACE AND THEN GROUND OUT.

These tools could equally easily be made from tool steel or gauge plate, then a handle turned to fit.

Making the tools

◆ Decide upon the shape of the tool and choose an inexpensive wood chisel of the correct width, or cut a piece of gauge plate to width and length.

◆ Paint the surface of the metal with typists' correction fluid or engineers' blue if you have some. This will allow the marking out on the surface to be seen more easily.

◆ Mark out the tool's shape.

◆ Carefully grind away the waste metal leaving the shape clear and clean.

◆ Grind the tool in small stages. Do not try

to grind too much too quickly.

◆ If the tool is overheated whilst grinding the metal may lose its temper. It will then need to be hardened and tempered.

Hardening and tempering

Hardening and tempering is a simple process in which the metal tool is heated with a gas torch. This alters the crystalline structure and its degree of hardness, enabling the tool to hold an edge once sharpened. The exact process is detailed below.

◆ The tool first needs to be annealed, i.e. brought back to a fully soft state. Heat to a bright red and allow to cool.

◆ The next process, hardening, requires the tool to be brought to bright red and then quenched immediately in water or a water/salt solution. When quenching, move the tool slowly in the brine. If it is moved around rapidly a thin sheath of steam bubbles clings firmly to the surface stopping it from being cooled satisfactorily. The hardening is complete but the tool now needs to be tempered, to be brought to the correct degree of hardness.

◆ Clean off the surface of the tool using emery paper until it is bright and shiny.

◆ Place the middle of the tool in a moderate gas-torch flame. Oxide colours will be seen to form on the heated area – pale straw to brown, to purple, to blue and onwards.

◆ Once the oxide colours begin to form, carefully and slowly encourage them to move along the tool towards the tip. Keep the bands of colour wide with slow heating.

◆ If the heat is moderate then the bands of oxide colour, which crudely denote the crystalline structure and hardness of the metal beneath, will be quite wide This is exactly what is needed.

◆ Encourage the wide bands of oxide colour towards the tip using the flame of the gas torch.

◆ Watch as the colours go to the tip and disappear – first straw, then brown, then purple, then blue. And that is what is required, a broad blue band at the tip.

◆ Quench in the brine. It is important to quench immediately. The tempering is complete.

◆ Carefully sharpen the tool.

If the tool loses its temper during turning by being overheated, or the tempered area is eventually sharpened away, then simply harden and temper again.

CHAPTER 3

Jigs and Chucks

 O NOT CONSIDER THE MAKING OF SPECIAL CHUCKS TEDIOUS FOR IT IS ALL PART OF PRODUCING THE FINISHED PIECE AND JUST AS NECESSARY AS THE SELECTION AND CUTTING OF THE WOOD.

For many of the projects I have relied upon the glue and paper method of holding work. It is a very efficient and easy method leaving no grip marks when the piece is finished.

Glue and paper method

◆ Cut the work piece to rough shape.
◆ Mount on a faceplate and turn true a piece of softwood larger than the work piece.
◆ Face off the softwood block flat and true.
◆ Apply PVA glue to the surface of the softwood.
◆ Press newspaper onto the glued surface then smooth out wrinkles and bubbles.
◆ Apply PVA glue to the undersurface of the work piece then press it against the newspaper glued to the softwood.
◆ Bring the tailstock forward holding a centre. This should be used to apply pressure whilst the glue sets but can also be used to ensure the work piece is centrally positioned. For this to work the centre of the work piece should be marked, and the tailstock centre can then be pressed against that point.
◆ Allow the glue to dry thoroughly, for if the turner is impatient the soft undried glue joint could easily pull apart.
◆ Turn the work and, when finished, use a

11

sharp knife to split the newspaper joint. The newspaper shears into two parts. Keep the knife edge slightly on the softwood side to avoid damage to the work. Once the paper begins to shear the joint will easily come apart.

I use PVA glue for this joint because it is a 'soft' glue, never drying so hard and brittle that it becomes difficult to remove from the base of the work or the softwood surface.

This method of holding work is not advised for long pieces or for pieces where heavy turning forces are applied.

Jam chuck

Used to hold pieces in a turned-out matching hollow.

◆ Take a piece of softwood larger than the work piece to be held and fix it to a faceplate.

◆ Turn the piece so it is round, true and flat faced.

◆ Turn a hollow into the face to accept the work piece. The work piece needs to fit tightly into the turned hollow.

◆ Ensure that the surface of the work piece runs true. Make adjustments by tapping high areas deeper into the hollow.

◆ Turn the surface of the work to the desired shape. It is important to begin with light cuts, keeping the tool sharp.

◆ Often the work piece can be pulled free of the jam chuck but occasionally the tolerances have been judged so finely that it can become stuck. If this is the case, carefully turn a trench close to the outer edge of the work to allow the piece to be loosened.

Other jigs and chucks specific to a project are dealt with in the relevant chapter.

CHAPTER 4

Finishing

I HAVE NEVER FOUND FINISHING AND POLISHING A PIECE OF TURNED WORK AS EASY AS THE TURNING ITSELF. I HAVE TRIED EVERY RECOMMENDED METHOD – FRICTION POLISH WITH THE LATHE RUNNING, TUNG OIL, DANISH OIL, POLYURETHANE VARNISH BRUSHED ON AND SPRAYED ON, VARIOUS WAXES, SHELLACS AND SANDING SEALERS – EVERY LAST ONE.

The choice of finish should depend upon the use that is to be made of the piece being finished. Each finish has its drawbacks. For example, waxes and shellacs eventually mark (if handled frequently), polyurethane can look superficial, and oils take a while to dry and often need repeat applications.

My requirements for a finish:

◆ The surface of the work must be sealed.
◆ The finish must be easy to apply.
◆ The wood is the most important part and needs to retain its natural look.
◆ The piece, if handled frequently, must not show signs of that handling.
◆ The natural lustre of the wood must be shown to advantage.

I decided to try one last time to find *my* perfect finish and this is the nearest I have come to succeeding.

◆ Finishing the work begins when the turning starts. Extremely heavy early cuts can sometimes break grain below the surface, so keep all cuts moderate.
◆ Turn the finish surface as finely as possible. Sharp tools and light finishing cuts can help to achieve this.
◆ Glasspaper the whole surface to bring it to the same quality. Start with heavier grades and move through to the finer grades.

I have come upon some excellent abrasive paper called Vitex, cloth-backed emery. Between the grit particles there is a filling of what appears to be a fine white powder like French chalk. This prevents the paper from clogging, allowing the grit to cut more freely and also extending its working life.

◆ Final glasspapering should be with the grain.
◆ Burnish the work with the shavings of the wood.
◆ Apply a thinned coat (two parts white spirit to one part polish) of matt polyurethane to the wood surface, rubbing in with a cloth.
◆ Allow to dry, then buff hard.
◆ Another coat of the same mixture of polish may need to be rubbed in depending upon the surface quality of the wood.
◆ Other 'top' finishes such as wax may be applied, but I have been very satisfied with the gentle sheen imparted by this finish.

Of course, finishes tend to be very personal and turners swear by the finish they have used successfully for years. If your finishing method works well then that's fine. If not, maybe the above information will be of help.

CHAPTER 5

Safety

THE PROJECTS DESCRIBED IN THE FOLLOWING CHAPTERS ARE FOR ENJOYMENT AND PLEASURE; IF SIMPLE COMMON-SENSE RULES ARE FOLLOWED, THAT PLEASURE SHOULD BE LASTING.

◆ Always wear eye protection when turning or grinding metal.

◆ Keep loose clothing away from the lathe when working.

◆ If you use a three- or four-jaw metal chuck, be aware of those spinning jaws. Before the chuck is used on the lathe remove the jaws and grind back the sharp external edges. If the jaws hit the hand whilst turning it may cause a bruise but with the sharp edges removed it will prevent a serious cut. In addition, if the ends of the jaws are painted white it makes them more visible when the lathe is operating.

◆ Make absolutely sure that any screws used in wooden chucks are fully tightened before turning on the lathe.

◆ It is good practice to revolve the work by hand to ensure that nothing catches before turning the lathe on.

◆ Have the lathe and lathe area well lit and if a deep cut is being made, arrange the light fitting so that it may be moved to illuminate the cut being worked.

◆ Do not overextend the tool for deep cuts; try to reposition the tool rest for maximum support.

◆ Keep all tools sharp.

◆ Safety is often thought of in terms of protecting fingers or eyes. Consider your lungs and protect them from the fine dusts produced when turning. There are some excellent masks available; the better types filter the air and blow clean, cool air across the face behind a protective visor.

Be sensible, take simple precautions, don't try to shortcut them. Enjoy turning in safety.

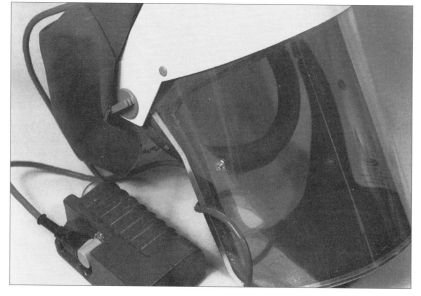

Fig 5.1 Visor and clean air in one.

PART 2

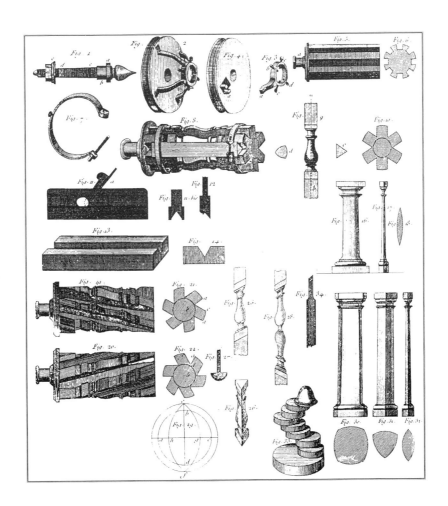

PROJECTS

CHAPTER 6

Combination Locking Box

I N THE PINTO COLLECTION OF TREEN THERE IS A DELIGHTFUL S O V E R E I G N BOX WITH A T U N B R I D G E STICKWARE PATTERNED TOP. AROUND ITS BARREL BODY IS A SERIES OF RINGS. UPON EACH OF THESE RINGS IS FIXED AN ALPHABET. WHEN THESE RINGS ARE TURNED THE LETTERS CAN BE ALIGNED TO SPELL A CODE WORD WHICH ALLOWS THE TOP TO BE LIFTED FROM THE BASE: A WOODEN COMBINATION LOCK.

The Pinto Collection box was made from yew but here I have chosen to work with ebony for it is much stronger in the finer sections required and there is a greater chance of success in the making. This box also has a plain turned top, although an inlaid patterned top can be substituted.

The box will hold a good quantity of coins, one pound coins from the UK, one and two dollar coins from Australia and the American quarter, but please, before filling it with coins and twisting the rings, write down that code word somewhere safe for it is a half-million-to-one chance that you will be able to reopen the box without knowing that code.

Preparation

◆ Select a piece of ebony or similar close-grain wood, 220mm (8⅝in) long by 60mm (2⅜in) square.

◆ It will be necessary to make a simple wooden chuck, so have ready a faceplate and a piece of softwood from which to cut a 90mm (3⁹⁄₁₆in) diameter disc 37mm (1½in) thick. Also have ready a thinner piece of hardwood about 6mm (¼in) thick, again by 90mm (3⁹⁄₁₆in) diameter, from which to make the collar for this simple chuck.

◆ Have available a 9mm (⅜in) cheap wood chisel so that a simply shaped tool may be ground (*see* Fig 6.2).

◆ Lathe speed should be around 1250rpm.

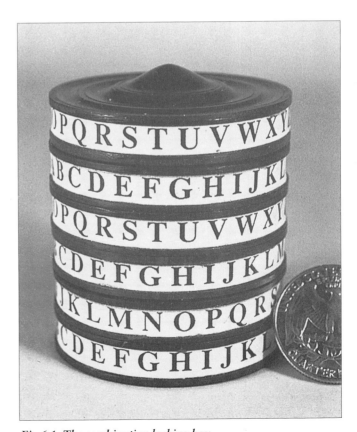

Fig 6.1 The combination locking box.

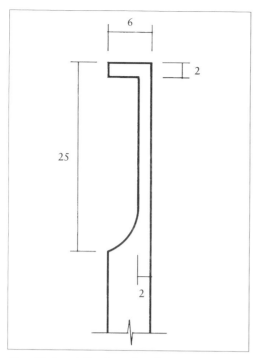

Fig 6.2 Specially shaped tool.

Turning the blank

◆ The dimensions of the turned blank are given in Fig 6.3.

◆ Take the 220mm (8⅝in) by 60mm (2⅜ in) square piece of ebony. Mark diagonals on its end and, using a centre punch or nail, mark the centres. This will help position the driving dog and revolving centre. At the end

into which the driving dog will be fixed, make sure that the centre is well punched, enabling the driving dog point to bite deeply and the dog to grip firmly.

◆ Turn the part using a large sharp gouge down to a precise 51mm (2in) diameter.

◆ Square off the end supported by the revolving centre.

◆ Measuring from the tailstock end towards the headstock, mark the first point 39mm (1½in) from the end. From that point, measure a further 9mm (⅜in). These two measurements constitute Part A.

◆ From that last position, measure 15mm (⅝in). This point will be the start of Part B. The gap between them will be turned down to a plug and used to hold Part A whilst turning later.

◆ From the start of Part B, measure 41mm (1⅝in) followed by a 9mm (⅜in) length. These two measurements constitute Part B.

◆ From the end of Part B, still towards the headstock, measure 15mm (⅝in). Again this section will be turned to a plug and used to hold Part B whilst turning later.

◆ Now begin measuring the four rings: a 9mm (⅜in) distance which is the width of the ring, followed by 7.5mm (⁵⁄₁₆in); a 9mm (⅜in) distance (the ring), followed by 7.5mm (⁵⁄₁₆in); a 9mm (⅜in) distance, followed by 7.5mm (⁵⁄₁₆in); then the final 9mm (⅜in) and

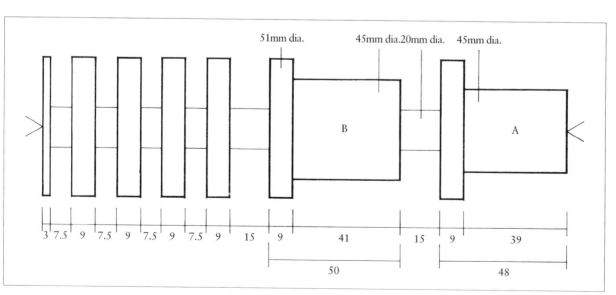

Fig 6.3 The turned blank.

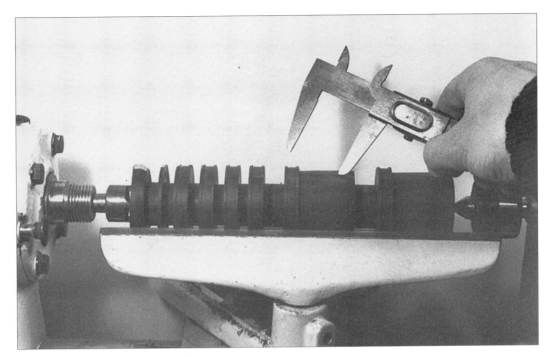

Fig 6.4 All parts turned on one piece.

7.5mm (⁵⁄₁₆in). Four rings and four gaps.

◆ To complete, mark a 3mm (⅛in) distance for the locking ring. The remaining wood will be unused.

◆ At each of the areas between Parts A and B and the rings – the two 15mm (⅝in) and 7.5mm (⁵⁄₁₆in) gaps plus the section on the headstock side of the locking ring – turn down to a 20mm (¾in) diameter using a parting tool that is narrower than the gap being cut to prevent gripping. Be careful to turn only on the waste side of the line, turning the rings and Parts A and B accurately to size.

◆ Turn the 39mm (1½in) measured part of A down to 45mm (1¾in), leaving the 9mm (⅜in) wide section at the full 51mm (2in) diameter.

◆ Turn the 41mm (1⅝in) measured part of B down to 45mm (1¾in), leaving the 9mm (⅜in) wide section the full 51mm (2in) diameter.

◆ Dealing with the 9mm (⅜in) parts only (that is the four rings turned closest to the headstock and the two marked on A and B), mark on each of these six parts a 1mm (¹⁄₂₄in) area on each edge which will remain unturned at the full 51mm (2in) diameter.

◆ Between these two marked lines, turn a 1mm (¹⁄₂₄in) deep groove using a square-end tool with the depth marked upon its blade.

The first part is now complete (*see* Fig 6.4) and the parts may be sawn apart with care. The following procedure must be adopted to allow the gripping areas to be left attached to the correct parts. Also, to ensure that the pieces fit together with colour and grain matching, mark each with an identifying number.

Cutting up the parts

◆ Part A needs to be sawn off so that it retains the 15mm (⅝in) long 20mm (¾in) diameter plug.

◆ Part B needs to be sawn off so that it retains the plug.

◆ The remaining rings may be sawn apart keeping what is left of the joining waste wood to one side only. Saw the locking ring free also.

◆ To prevent saw cuts marking the edges of these parts as they are cut, fix a small piece of masking tape on the edges at risk and take particular care.

◆ As preparation for turning Parts A and B,

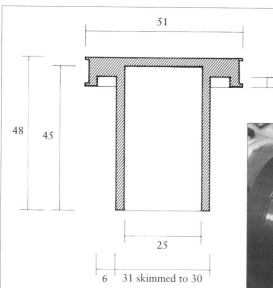

Fig 6.5 Part A.

Fig 6.6 Part A being drilled out.

turn three plugs from softwood to the following dimensions:

The first (to be used to support both A and B) is turned 30mm (1⁵⁄₂in) long with a 12mm (½in) length and 25mm (1in) diameter, followed by another 12mm (½in) length and 32mm (1¼in) diameter. The final 6mm (¼in) should be 35mm (1⅜in) in diameter.

The second plug is used solely to support Part A. It is 72mm (2¹³⁄₁₆in) long with the first 30mm (1⁵⁄₂in) being 25mm (1in) in diameter, followed by a 12mm (½in) section 30mm (1⁵⁄₂ in) in diameter and a further 30mm length 25mm (1in) in diameter.

The third plug is used only to support Part B. It is 72mm (2¹³⁄₁₆in) long, the first 30mm (1⁵⁄₂in) being 25mm (1in) in diameter, followed by a 12mm (½in) section of 30mm (1⁵⁄₂in) diameter, and the final 30mm (1⁵⁄₂in) being 32mm (1¼in) in diameter.

Turning Part A

◆ Begin working on Part A. See Fig 6.5 for the dimensions of Part A.
◆ Fit a three- or four-jaw chuck to the headstock.
◆ Grip the 20mm (¾in) diameter plug in the chuck. Bring up the tailstock holding the revolving centre to support the end. Make sure that the piece runs true and on centre, then turn the end square and true.
◆ Withdraw the tailstock. Replace the revolving centre with a drill chuck holding a 25mm (1in) drill.
◆ Mark a position on the drill shank 45mm (1¾in) away from the drill tip.
◆ Drill Part A to the marked depth (*see* Fig 6.6).
◆ When drilling, regularly clean out waste wood and allow the drill to cool. Do not allow it to overheat and lose its temper or allow the wood to overheat (which causes rapid drying and cracking).
◆ Withdraw the tailstock and replace the drill chuck with a revolving centre.
◆ Fit the first plug into the drilled hole, bringing up the revolving centre to support. Tighten down.
◆ Turn the lathe by hand first to ensure nothing catches.
◆ Leaving the 9mm (⅜in) ring section, turn the remaining part down to an outer

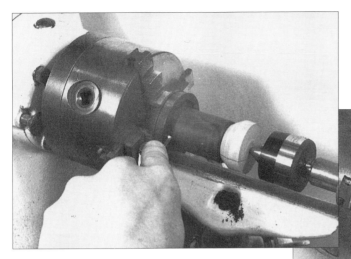

Fig 6.7 *Undercutting beneath the top of Part A.*

Fig 6.8 *Turning the top surface of Part A.*

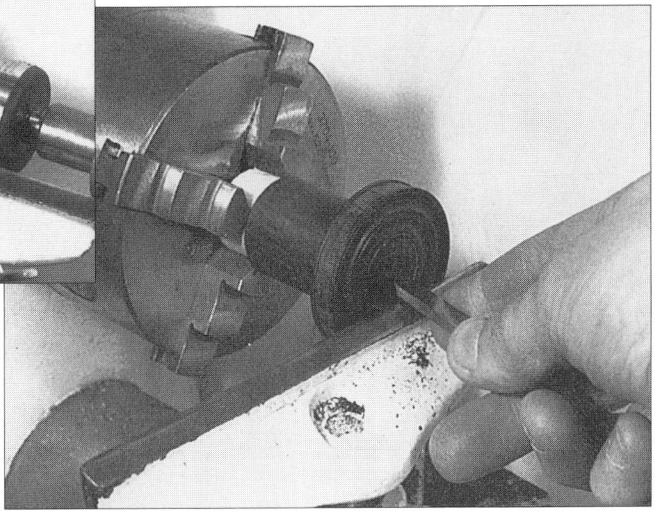

diameter of 31mm (1¼in). Turn the majority away with a gouge using a square-end tool to turn into the corner tight to the shoulder. Carefully turn a light chamfer on the end nearest the softwood plug.

◆ From a 9mm (⅜in) cheap wood chisel, grind a tool as shown in Fig 6.2. This tool will be used to undercut the 'ring' at the headstock end (*see* Fig 6.7). This undercut is a space to take the locking ring later to be fitted on top of Part B.

◆ Turn the undercut from the 31mm (1¼in) diameter of the barrel outwards 6mm (¼in) wide and 3mm (⅛in) deep.

◆ Clean up the piece thoroughly and remove from the lathe. Remove the first softwood plug.

◆ Carefully saw off the majority of the plug held in the chuck leaving 3mm (⅛in) showing.

◆ Fit the second softwood plug into the chuck, fitting the 25mm (1in) drilled hollow of A over the matching plug end. Bring the tailstock forward. Carefully centre the work, then tighten the centre in place.

◆ Turn the majority of the base of A with the revolving centre in position, removing it to make the final delicate cuts to the whole of the piece, erasing the mark left by the centre. The shaping of this part must be level with, if not lower than, the edges so that it will sit evenly when placed down (*see* Fig 6.8).

◆ Clean up the end and remove Part A and also the plug from the lathe. Set aside carefully.

Turning the rings

The next stage is to make a jam chuck plus collar to hold the rings so that the internal shaping may be worked. See Fig 6.9 for the rings' dimensions.

◆ Cut a 90mm (3⅞in) diameter by 37mm (1½in) thick piece from pine. Mount centrally on a faceplate, then turn the edge and face flat and true.

◆ For the collar, cut a 90mm (3⅞in) diameter by 6mm (¼in) thick piece of hardwood.

◆ Drill and countersink four equally spaced screwholes on an 85mm (3¹¹⁄₁₆in) diameter circle.

◆ Screw the disc centrally to the softwood

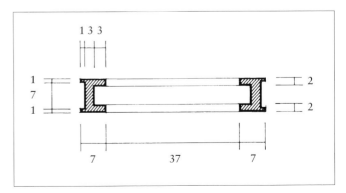

Fig 6.9 *The ring (four off).*

Fig 6.10 The jam chuck and collar being turned.

Fig 6.11 The ring blank fitted inside the jam chuck is first turned to thickness.

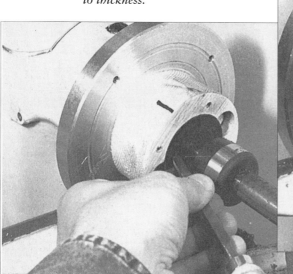

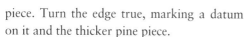

piece. Turn the edge true, marking a datum on it and the thicker pine piece.

◆ Turn through the collar at a diameter of 40mm (1⁹⁄₁₆in) until it touches the softwood surface (*see* Fig 6.10). Stop the lathe, undo

Fig 6.12 Turning the 'centre' out of the ring.

the screws and remove the collar.

◆ Turn into the softwood at a 50mm (2in) diameter 8mm (⁵⁄₁₆in) deep. Check the fit of the turned ring blanks. Slowly and carefully open up the turned hollow until it accepts the ring as a good fit but not so tight that it will be difficult to remove. If necessary, drill two release holes 15mm (⅝in) in diameter and 12mm (½in) deep either side of the turned hollow (*see* Fig 6.11).

◆ Using double-sided Sellotape, fix small pieces of fine glasspaper to the underside of the collar to help it grip the ring blanks.

◆ If any of the rings are greatly over thickness they may be held in the jam chuck without the collar, but use the tailstock holding a revolving centre to support the work whilst they are turned to size.

◆ Always keep the tools sharp.

◆ Taking each of the rings in turn, referring to the pencilled numbers marked earlier, use the following procedure to turn the inner hollow.

◆ Fit the ring into the chuck. Make sure it sits level. Tighten down the outer ring to hold it firmly in place.

◆ Mark in pencil a 37mm (1½in) diameter circle concentrically upon its surface whilst the lathe is running.

Fig 6.13 *The specially shaped tool ready to turn the inner groove on the ring.*

Fig 6.14 *Removing the finished ring from the jam chuck.*

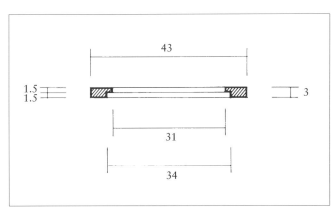

◆ Using a gouge, remove the majority of the wood inside the marked pencil circle taking care when breaking through into the back of the softwood chuck (*see* Fig 6.12).

◆ Using a square-end tool, turn the hollow to a precise 37mm (1½in) diameter checking with calipers to ensure accuracy. Also make sure that the cut edge is square to the surface.

◆ Take the specially ground chisel used earlier and mark a position on its blade 3mm (⅛in) away from its cutting edge.

◆ Leave a 1mm (¼in) section either side of the inner surface of the ring and, using the shaped tool, cut away the waste wood between to a depth of 3mm (⅛in) using the depth mark on the tool as a guide (*see* Fig 6.13).

◆ Having turned each ring satisfactorily, lay them on one side (*see* Fig 6.14).

Fig 6.15 *The locking ring.*

Preparing the locking ring

◆ See Fig 6.15 for the dimensions of the turned locking ring.

◆ Take the locking ring part, holding the stub end in the three- or four-jaw chuck. Ensure it runs true and on centre.

◆ Face off the front flat and true.

◆ Remove the piece from the chuck and the chuck from the headstock. Replace the chuck with a faceplate holding a softwood disc, to

be used as a glue and paper chuck.

◆ Fix the turned disc with its flat face to the softwood surface, first gluing a layer of newspaper, then fixing the disc to that. Ensure that it is fixed centrally. Bring the tailstock forward, holding the revolving centre, to press the disc firmly against the faceplate until the glue has set.

◆ When the glue has dried, withdraw the tailstock and bring the tool rest across the

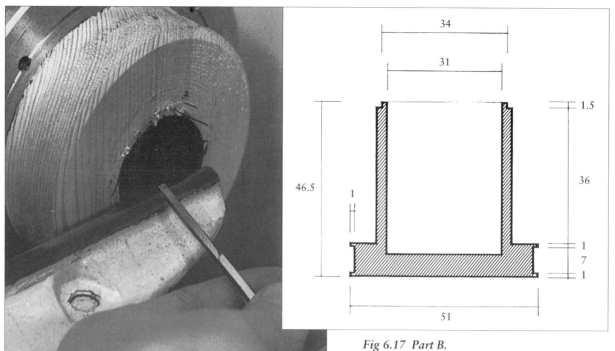

Fig 6.17 Part B.

Fig 6.16 The locking ring blank held on a newspaper and glue chuck.

face of the work. Turn the face flat and true and to a thickness of just a little under 3mm (⅛in)(*see* Fig 6.16).

◆ Turn the outside diameter fractionally under 43mm (1¾in) so that it will fit the undercut in Part A without jamming. Then

cut an inner hole of 31mm (1¼in) diameter. Turn this inner hole through until a cut is made in the softwood beneath.

◆ Finally, turn a 34mm (1⅜in) diameter step 1.5mm (¹⁄₁₆in) deep on the inside edge of the 31mm (1¼in) diameter hole.

◆ Leave this part fixed to the softwood faceplate to be checked for fit against Part B when it has been turned to match.

Fig 6.18 Drilling Part B to depth.

Turning Part B

◆ The dimensions for Part B are given in Fig 6.17.

◆ Hold Part B on the turned plug in a three- or four-jaw chuck. Make sure that it is running true and on centre.

◆ Bring up the tailstock with the revolving centre to support the work, then square off the end.

◆ Drill out using a 32mm (1¼in) diameter drill to a depth of 40mm (1⅝in) (*see* Fig 6.18). Remove the drill regularly to prevent overheating of both the drill and the work. Be aware when measuring the depth on the drill to allow for the centre point, because if it is long and the measurement is taken from the cutting edge of the drill, the point may pierce the top surface of the piece.

◆ Remove the drill and withdraw the tailstock. Take the prepared plug and fit it into the drilled hole. Bring the tailstock, now holding the revolving centre, back to support the plug. Tighten down.

◆ Turn the outer diameter of Part B – with the exception of the 9mm (⅜in) part closest to the chuck – down to 38mm (1½in) diameter (*see* Fig 6.19). Test the now hollowed rings upon this turned part. Turn until the rings are a relatively easy fit.

Fig 6.19 Turning the body of B to exact size.

◆ Fit all four rings upon Part B in correct order. Pack them tightly. Mark the position in pencil on B where the stack of four finishes. Add 1.5mm (¹⁄₁₆in) for the locking ring (joint part only) then add a further 1.5mm (¹⁄₁₆in) for movement between the parts. If all the parts are accurately made this will add up to 39mm (1¹³⁄₁₆in) Turn off at this point.

◆ Withdraw tailstock and plug.

◆ Upon that turned end of B, turn a small step 34mm (1⅜in) in diameter and 1.5mm (¹⁄₁₆in) deep (*see* Fig 6.20).

◆ Bring forward the softwood faceplate

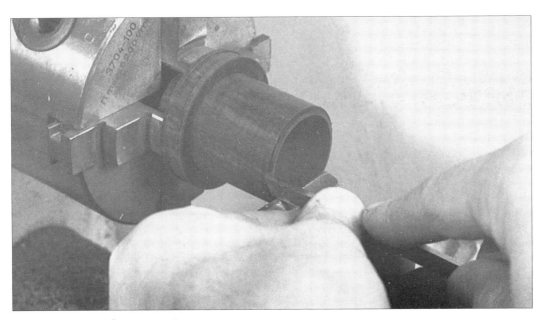

Fig 6.20 Turning the 'step' on B.

holding the turned locking ring and test for fit. If it fits, fine. If not, make adjustments.

◆ Remove Part B from the lathe. Saw off the majority of the plug that was held in the chuck on the end of B.

◆ Set the turned softwood plug prepared to hold B in the chuck, then fit the drilled-out section of B onto the plug.

◆ Bring the tailstock holding the revolving centre to support the end of B. Make sure all runs true and on centre. Begin turning the end face.

◆ Having turned as much of face B with the revolving centre in place, withdraw and finish with extremely light cuts.

◆ Remove the work from the plug and the plug from the chuck.

◆ Polish all the parts but do not polish the base of the six ring areas for this is where the alphabets need to be glued.

Fitting the alphabets in place

◆ Photocopy the set of six alphabets (*see* Fig 6.21).

◆ Use an acrylic varnish to cover the letters of the alphabets. This seals them without darkening the paper.

◆ Measure the gaps on each of the rings, four loose, one on A and one on B. They should be 7mm (⁵⁄₁₆in). Slice the alphabet to a width to fit each ring. Test one alphabet on one ring for length. If it is too long or too short use the magic of the photocopier to reduce or enlarge.

◆ Leave extra blank paper at the start of the alphabet but trim 'Z' close.

◆ Taking one ring, ensuring that it is the correct way round, apply a little PVA glue to the groove. Push the blank end of paper down onto it. Apply the glue sparingly in front of the paper, pressing down as it goes around until 'Z' is reached (*see* Fig 6.22). Do not apply glue ahead of this area; be careful that a good clean joint is made between 'Z' and 'A'.

◆ Repeat this process for each of the rings and also the top and bottom of A and B remembering to have the alphabet the right way up on both.

◆ If a mistake is made the letters can be scraped off cleanly and, using fresh photocopies, a new start can be made.

A B C D E F G H I J K L M N O P Q R S T U V W X Y Z

A B C D E F G H I J K L M N O P Q R S T U V W X Y Z

A B C D E F G H I J K L M N O P Q R S T U V W X Y Z

A B C D E F G H I J K L M N O P Q R S T U V W X Y Z

A B C D E F G H I J K L M N O P Q R S T U V W X Y Z

A B C D E F G H I J K L M N O P Q R S T U V W X Y Z

A B C D E F G H I J K L M N O P Q R S T U V W X Y Z

Fig 6.21 The alphabets. They must be reproduced this size to fit around the circumference of the rings.

Fig 6.22 Applying the alphabet to one of the rings.

Cutting cross grooves and fitting dowel pegs

◆ Decide on the six-letter code word to be used. In this case it is NICOLA.

◆ Taking Part B, move the piece around until 'N' is facing the front. A 4mm (⅙in) wide slot needs to be cut into the drilled-out body down its length and centred upon 'N' at the top.

◆ Mark out the slot in pencil and, using a fine blade in a junior hacksaw, saw down as far as possible. Be careful not to put saw marks into the fully turned collar at the end. The centre section between the saw cuts may be removed by drilling a small hole at the base of the cut sufficiently large to leave only two whiskers of wood supporting the central waste. It can now be broken away and the base of the slot cleaned out using wood chisels and needle files.

Cutting the slots in the rings

◆ Taking the rings in turn, identify the letter next to which the slot needs to be cut – 'I',

'C', 'O' and 'L'. Mark the 4mm (⅙in) width in pencil centrally against that letter on the ring's edge. Remove the blade from the junior hacksaw. Slip the blade through the ring. Replace the blade in the hacksaw

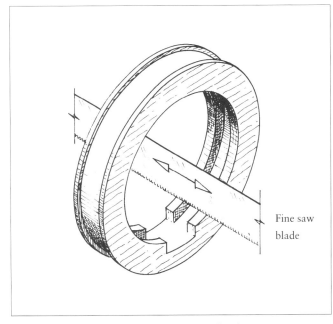

Fig 6.23 Cutting the slot across the inside of the loose rings.

Fine saw blade

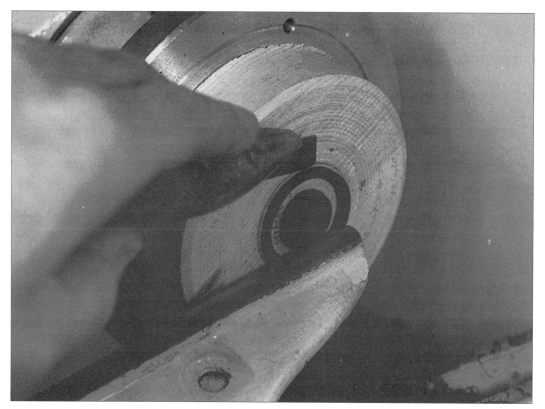

Fig 6.24 The locking ring, having been fully turned, is carefully split away from the newspaper/glue chuck.

frame. Lightly hold the ring in a vice, then saw down on the inside of the two marked lines to a depth of 3mm (⅛in) (*see* Fig 6.23). Cut further lines inside those first two to remove as much of the waste wood as possible. Remove the blade from the frame and the ring. Use chisels and needle files to clean out the groove.

◆ The next stage is to turn four small dowels. Each is 3mm (⅛in) in diameter and 6mm (¼in) long, the first 3mm (⅛in) being turned down to a 2mm (½in) diameter tenon. These small parts can first be roughed down from a slightly larger part of 9mm (⅜in) diameter, turned between centres. It can then be re-turned and refined whilst being held in a drill chuck set in the headstock. Work on a 9mm (⅜in) length can safely be turned overhanging from the drill chuck without support of a centre. Light cuts are required.

◆ Part A now needs to be worked upon. Choose the final letter of the code word from around its rim. In this case it is 'A'. Mark a vertical pencil line from the centre of the letter up the turned barrel.

◆ From the end of the collar (or alphabet ring) measure 4.5mm (⅛in). Mark that point on the vertical pencil line. Then from that point measure 9mm (⅜in) and mark it, then another 9mm (⅜in) and mark it, followed by the last 9mm (⅜in) and mark that. These are the points at which to drill 2mm (½in) diameter holes.

◆ Re-fit the turned softwood plug to support the inside of the drilled hole whilst it is being drilled through.

◆ At these four marked points drill through using a 2mm (½in) drill.

◆ Remove the plug, tidy up the holes, then carefully glue the four pegs, one into each hole. Allow the glue to set.

◆ Finally, take the softwood faceplate holding the locking ring and very, very carefully split it away from the newspaper and glue joint using a very thin-bladed knife (*see* Fig 6.24).

◆ Clean off the back of the ring, rubbing it across flat, fine glasspaper.

◆ Into its edge cut a 4mm (⅛in) gap, but again, do this with extreme care for until it is glued in place it is very delicate.

◆ Take each of the loose alphabet rings and slip them into place on Part B having first lightly rubbed the barrel with candle wax, avoiding the joint end. Make sure that they are in the correct order. Glue the locking ring in place with its cut gap in line with the cut in B (*see* Fig 6.25). Fit a small weight on top and leave to dry.

When the part is dry this wonderful combination locking box is ready to be put together and tested. Once satisfied, lock a coin inside and hand to a friend, asking them to crack the code.

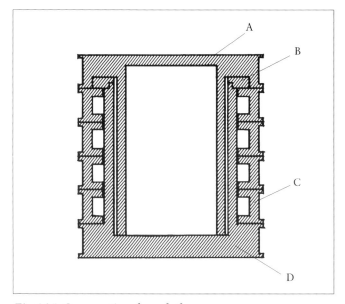

Fig 6.25 *Cross section through the combination locking box.*
A *Top*
B *Locking ring*
C *Rotating rings (four in number)*
D *Base*

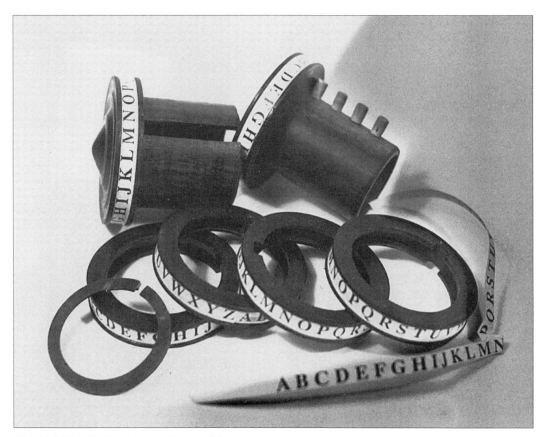

Fig 6.26 *The finished parts of the combination locking box.*

CHAPTER 7

Folding Beaker

 HAVE SEEN MANY FOLDING BEAKERS BUT NEARLY ALL WERE MADE FROM METAL. IN FACT I HAVE A LOVELY COLLAPSIBLE METAL BEAKER WHICH FITS NEATLY INTO THE BACK OF A POCKET WATCH. THE WATCH HAS BEEN EMPTIED OF THE WORKS TO ACCOMMODATE THE BEAKER AND LOOKS QUITE INNOCENT, YET IT HOLDS THE MEANS FOR A QUIET DRINK WHEN NO ONE IS LOOKING.

I first saw a wooden folding beaker made from ash in the Pinto Collection at Birmingham Museum. It had a series of concentric turned rings which telescoped out to make the beaker but it also had a foot on which it stood. The foot ensured that the rings stayed together, none being large enough to slip over the end.

Many woods may be chosen for a piece like this but they should be reasonably close grained – ash being the limit. If the beaker is to be used for drinking and not just for show the wood must impart no taste or colour to the liquid being held. Boxwood, sycamore or ash would work well. For one of the pieces shown in the colour section (between pages 200 and 201) I have used laburnum, but that was purely for the quality of grain pattern and colour.

The top rim of this beaker is turned to a minutely smaller diameter than the inside of the cover so that as the cover is removed the top ring clings lightly to the internal sides, telescoping magically to reveal a complete and open beaker.

Fig 7.1 The folding beaker.

Preparation

◆ Cut a piece of suitable wood 200mm (8in) long by 60mm (2⅜in) square.

◆ Take a 6mm (¼in) cheap chisel and grind a 25mm (1in) length 2mm (½in) wide (*see* Fig 7.2). It may be necessary to harden and temper this tool after grinding. If so, refer to Chapter 2 on toolmaking.

◆ Lathe speed should be 1250rpm

Turning the blank for the beaker

◆ The dimensions of the turned blank are given in Fig 7.3.

◆ Take the prepared piece of wood and set between centres. Turn to an exact 55mm (2⅛in) diameter.

◆ Measuring from the tailstock end, mark a position at 30mm (l½in). This part is to be turned down to a 35mm (1⅜in) diameter and will be used as a spigot held in the chuck whilst turning the base.

◆ The base is measured a further 30mm (1½in) from that end of the spigot. This area remains the full diameter.

◆ From the end of the base, measure 10mm (⅜in). This section will be initially turned down to 25mm (1in) diameter and once all

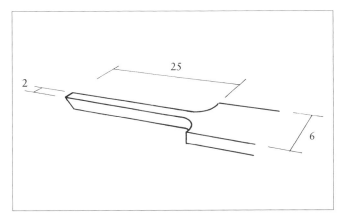

Fig 7.2 Specially ground tool.

parts have been completed this cylinder will be sawn or parted through, cutting the base from the top.

◆ The top joins this waste area and measures 40mm (1⅝in) from that gap towards the headstock and remains the full diameter.

◆ Attached to the top is a 30mm (1½in) length to be turned down to a 35mm (1⅜ in) diameter. Again this part will act as a spigot to be held in the chuck whilst turning the top.

◆ The remaining 60mm (2⅜in) can be divided into a 40mm (1⅝in) length left full diameter and the final 20mm (1³⁄₁₆in) turned down to a 35mm (1⅜in) diameter, again as a holding part. This last section will act as a jam chuck for the final turning.

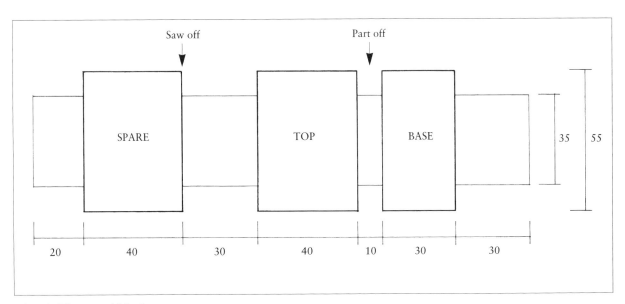

Fig 7.3 The turned blank.

Fig 7.4 The parts turned from one piece, waiting to be cut apart.

Making the folding beaker

◆ The dimensions of the beaker are given in Fig 7.5.

◆ Saw the pieces apart, leaving the holding spigots attached to the required parts.

◆ Fit a three- or four-jaw chuck onto the headstock.

◆ Take the base part and fix the 35mm (1⅜in) diameter spigot in the jaws of the chuck. Make sure the piece runs true and on centre. Adjust if necessary.

◆ Bring the tool rest across the face of the work and turn off flat and square to the sides.

◆ Adjust the tool rest so that the cutting edge of the 2mm (½in) square-end tool is at centre height.

◆ Mark in pencil on the squared-off face of the work a series of concentric circles of the

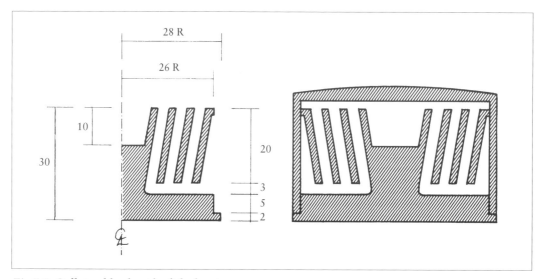

Fig 7.5 Collapsed beaker plus lid, showing dimensions.

following diameters: 16mm (⅝in), 20mm (¹³⁄₁₆in), 26mm (1in), 30mm (1½in), 36mm (1⅜in), 40mm (1⅝in), 46mm (1¹³⁄₁₆in) and 50mm (2in) (*see* Fig 7.6).

◆ Make sure that the edge of the tool rest is set parallel to the face of the work. On the edge of the tool rest fix a piece of masking tape. Using a protractor, draw a series of lines on the masking tape in ink at 10° to the centre line of the lathe set towards the turner.

◆ Take the 2mm (½in) wide tool. Mark a position on its blade 20mm (¹³⁄₁₆in) from the cutting edge.

◆ Position the tool facing the 3mm (⅛in) gap between the line drawn on the 46mm (1¹³⁄₁₆in) diameter and the 40mm (1⅝in) diameter.

◆ Hold the tool horizontally, then move the handle towards the turner until it is set at 10° to the centre line. Judge this setting against the line marked upon the masking tape. The tool will be used to cut a channel 3mm (⅛in) wide (*see* Fig 7.7). The tool, being 2mm (½in) wide, will have to be moved

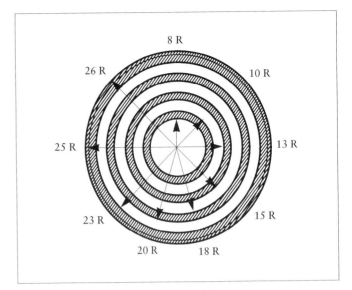

Fig 7.6 Concentric circles to be pencil drawn on base part, showing required radii of each circle.

from side to side, maintaining the 10° angle to create the wider groove. This will ensure that the tool is not gripped by the work and pulled in.

◆ Cut the groove until the 20mm (¹³⁄₁₆in) depth mark is reached.

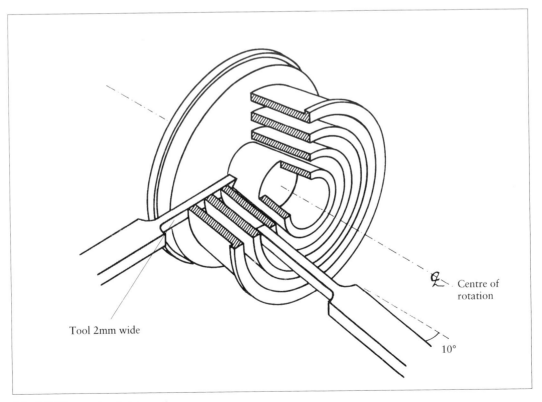

Fig 7.7 The angle of approach.

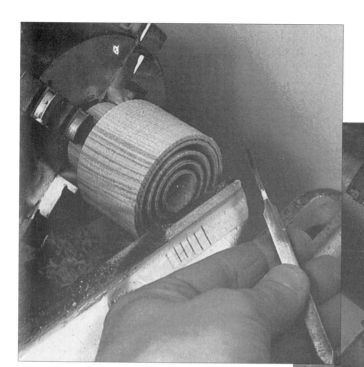

Fig 7.8 *The specially ground tool used to cut the pathways between the beaker walls.*

Fig 7.9 *The 10° marking which helps guide the tool can be seen on the tool rest.*

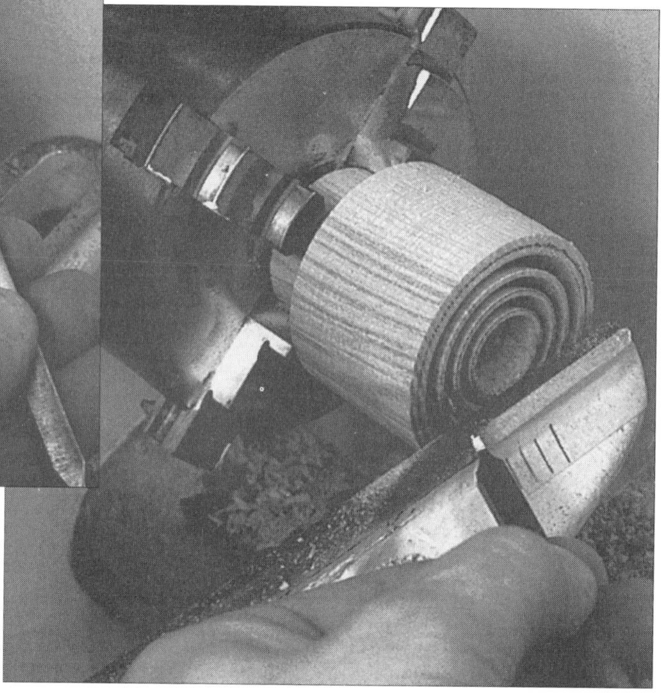

◆ Withdraw the tool and move to the next gap between the line drawn on the 36mm (1⅜in) diameter and the 30mm (1⁵⁄₃₂in) diameter.

◆ Set the tool to the 10° angle and cut the groove until the 20mm (¹³⁄₁₆in) depth mark is reached. Widen the groove as the cutting progresses but maintain the angle. Withdraw the tool (*see* Figs 7.8 and 7.9).

◆ It is most important to keep the tool sharp. Check the depth mark and widen the groove to the correct size as it is cut. Again, for safety, it will be noticed that the wider groove cannot grip the tool and drag it in.

◆ Move the tool to the next gap between the line drawn on the 26mm (1in) diameter and the 20mm (¹³⁄₁₆in) diameter.

◆ Set the tool to the 10° angle and cut the groove until the correct depth is reached. Widen the groove as the cut is made.

◆ Finally, set the tool to the inside of the 16mm (⅝in) diameter pencilled circle at the 10° angle.

◆ Carefully turn out the whole of the centre, flattening the base. It may not be necessary to cut to the full 20mm (¹³⁄₁₆in) depth, but this judgement will need to be made at the time of turning.

◆ Having completed all the grooves and the inner hollowing, withdraw the tool.

◆ Return to the edge of the work and again hold the tool at the set angle to the outer edge of the outer circle (50mm [2in]

Fig 7.10 *Cutting away the outer waste ring.*

diameter). Move 1mm (¼₄in) further out so that the outer wall thickness will be a constant 3mm (⅛in).

◆ Turn off the lathe and bring the tool rest around parallel to the lathe bed and close to the work.

◆ Measure from the face of the work 20mm (¹³⁄₁₆in) towards the headstock. If the 2mm (½in) square-end tool now cuts on the headstock side of this line, the waste wood – the remaining flat edge – can be cut into until it becomes a loose ring on the work. It can then be broken away (*see* Fig 7.10).

◆ The outer angled wall must now be turned down from 3mm (⅛in) to 2mm (½in) thick to match the other rings. A 3mm (⅛in) rounded bead is left at the top.

◆ Remember to keep the tool sharp.

◆ Continue cutting in with the square-end tool at a point 20mm (¹³⁄₁₆in) measured from the face towards the headstock, and part off the first complete ring on the headstock side of that line (*see* Fig 7.11).

◆ Pull the ring forward and hold it forward and out of the way of the cutting tool by binding it with masking tape (*see* Fig 7.12).

Fig 7.11 Beginning the cut to separate the first ring of the beaker.

◆ Continue to cut through with care, loosening the second and the third rings. Be particularly careful cutting through the last ring as too much forward pressure could cause the tool to cut into the stem of the beaker.

◆ Keep the rings out of the way of the work whilst a 6mm (¼in) wide by 52mm (2½in) diameter step is turned on the edge of the base. This will be the joint on which the top fits.

◆ Take this opportunity to turn a decorative

Fig 7.12 Masking tape holds the loosened rings whilst successive rings are cut free.

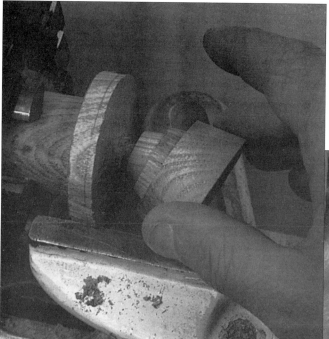

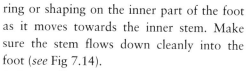

ring or shaping on the inner part of the foot as it moves towards the inner stem. Make sure the stem flows down cleanly into the foot (*see* Fig 7.14).

◆ Part off *under* the whole foot of the beaker but not too close. The base will be remounted and fully turned.

Fig 7.13 All the rings have been cut free.

Fig 7.14 The rings have been pulled up to form the beaker, allowing the turned foot to be viewed.

Fig 7.15 The top is held in the chuck so it may be turned.

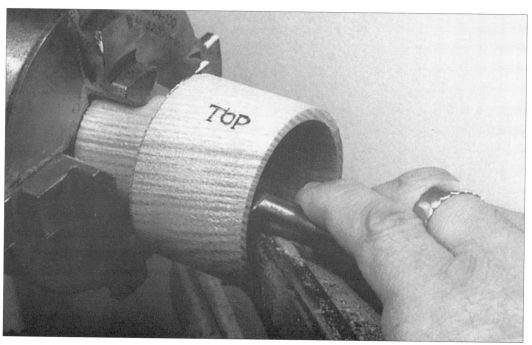

Turning the lid

◆ Take the lid section and hold the 30mm (1½in) long 35mm (1⅜in) diameter spigot in the chuck (*see* Fig 7.15).

◆ Turn the face flat and true.

◆ Turn into the top a hollow a little under 52mm (2½in) diameter and 30mm (1½in) deep. The diameter of this hollow relates to the outer diameter of the largest ring. If the hollow is a little under size it can be turned out to fit, so test the beaker occasionally inside the hollow, slowly opening until a good nip fit is achieved on the turned step and rim of the outer ring. It will need to be quite a tight fit for it is initially to be used as a jam chuck to turn the base (*see* Fig 7.16).

◆ Support the base of the beaker when fitted into the hollow with the revolving centre held in the tailstock. This will prevent any damage caused if the piece were to fly loose. Turn the underside of the base flat and true so that it will sit well, leaving the final centre pip supported by the revolving centre until after the outer edge of the top is turned so that the base and side become fluent.

◆ Withdraw the tailstock and turn away that final pip with light cuts. Make absolutely sure the base is flat, even a little concave, so that it will stand well.

◆ Remove the beaker from inside the lid. Open out the inner diameter just a little so that the lid will lift on and off more easily.

◆ Part off the lid leaving sufficient to turn the top away cleanly (*see* Fig 7.17).

◆ Take the last piece from the original turned length and hold it in the chuck on the spigot.

◆ Turn the outer diameter to a tight 52mm (2½in) so that the lid can jam upon it.

◆ Turn the top of the lid with a gentle dome.

◆ Remove the lid from the jam chuck then carefully polish the top, edge and base of the beaker but not the rings. The beaker becomes watertight as the rings swell. If the rings are polished they cannot absorb any liquid.

To test the beaker, pull up the rings tightly. There should be no gaps if turned well. Fill with liquid and drink away. When finished, do not try to collapse the beaker for the joints will have swelled and tightened. Shake out well and allow a little time to dry. Then pack away. Good health.

Fig 7.16 *If the base is 'jammed' into the top, it may be turned.*

Fig 7.17 *Parting off the top.*

CHAPTER 8

Necklace and Rattlesnake

THE BALL-AND-SOCKET JOINT HAS ALWAYS HELD A FASCINATION FOR ME. IT ALLOWS MOVEMENT IN ALL DIRECTIONS, YET THE JOINT STAYS TOGETHER THROUGHOUT THOSE MOVEMENTS. I COULD SEE HOW A JOINT LIKE THIS COULD BE USED IN INTERESTING WAYS – SO HOW WOULD A BALL-AND-SOCKET JOINT BE TURNED?

I remember a development in fashion jewellery which was exciting at the time but now seems forgotten. A set of colourful plastic beads called Poppets were introduced. They had a hole at one end of the spherical bead and a stem with a rounded head at the other. The rounded head on the stem was slightly larger than the hole so a string of these beads could be made by 'popping' heads into holes. If this principle were used in turnery the relationship between head and hole would need to be precise so that the work would not be split when pushing the

Fig 8.1 The necklace.

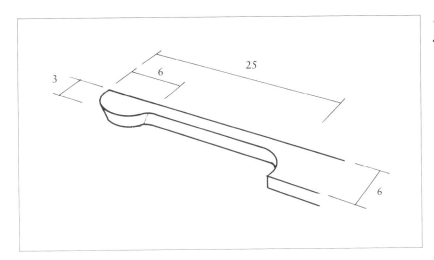

Fig 8.2 Specially ground tool.

Fig 8.3 V-ground tool.

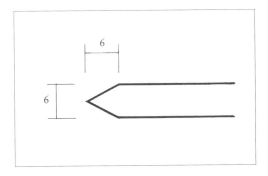

pieces together, or fall apart from being too loose. The size of head to hole will vary from wood to wood so this will have to be decided by experiment, but an approximation of the size can be made initially to reduce the amount of experimentation needed.

Obviously a necklace can be made using this technique, the beads being turned to any shape as long as head and hole fit well, but the rattlesnake was a fun discovery made apparent when the first few wood beads were 'popped' together and acted in a sinuous snake-like manner.

Preparation

◆ Cut a 200mm (8in) by 45mm (1¾in) square of purpleheart.

◆ Cut fourteen pieces of padauk 140mm (5½in) by 22mm (⅞in) square.

◆ Take a 6mm (¼in) cheap wood chisel and grind to a spoon shape as shown in Fig 8.2. Be careful not to overheat and cause the tool to lose its temper. If this happens, refer to the section on hardening and tempering on page 10.

◆ Take a 6mm (¼in) wide cheap wood chisel and grind the end to a V point (see Fig 8.3). This will be used to cut grooves into the spherical padauk beads.

◆ Lathe speed for the larger purpleheart pieces should be 1500rpm, and for the smaller diameter padauk beads 1750rpm

NECKLACE

Turning the blanks

◆ Set the purpleheart between centres and turn to a precise 40mm (1⁹⁄₁₆in) diameter.

◆ Square off the work at the tailstock end.

◆ From that squared-off end, measure 12mm (½in) followed by 20mm (¹³⁄₁₆in). Repeat these measurements five more times so that there are six areas in all, each 12mm (½in) wide separated by six areas 20mm (¹³⁄₁₆in) wide, plus a final waste piece at the headstock end.

◆ At each of the 20mm (¹³⁄₁₆in) wide areas, turn down to a 9mm (⅜in) diameter (*see* Fig 8.4).

◆ Remove the purpleheart piece from the lathe.

◆ Cut the purpleheart piece into sections so that there are six pieces 32mm (1³⁄₁₆in) long, each with a 12mm (½in) length full diameter

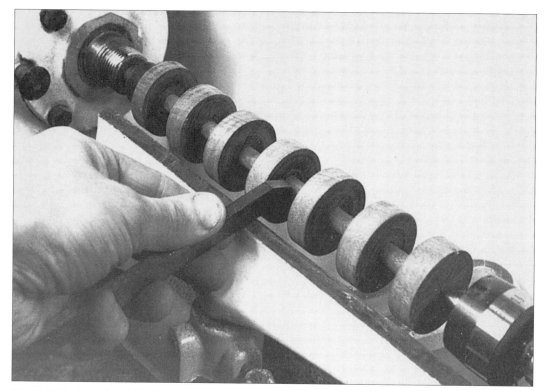

Fig 8.4 The large bead blanks are turned on one spindle.

and an attached 20mm (¹³⁄₁₆in) length of 9mm (⅜in) diameter (*see* Fig 8.5).

◆ Set the purpleheart pieces to one side.

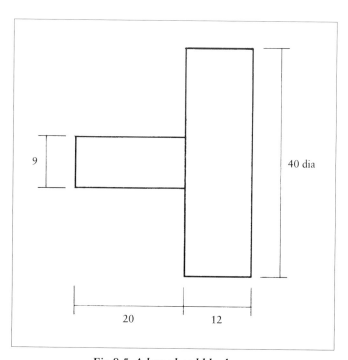

Fig 8.5 A large bead blank.

As the padauk in such small sizes would be likely to split if a driving dog were used when turning, a lace bobbin centre seems a more appropriate holding method. If you do not own a lace bobbin centre then one may easily be turned.

◆ From a block of suitable size, turn a Morse taper on one end to fit the size in your lathe headstock. Leave a larger block on the end, say 35mm (1⅜in) in diameter and the same length. Drill a 19mm (¾in) hole 15mm (⅝in) deep into the squared-off end whilst it is held in the headstock on its morse taper. Remove the piece from the lathe and, using a sharp 6mm (¼in) chisel, with care, open out the round hole into a square tapered hollow (*see* Fig 8.6). If there is concern that the outer edge of the wood might split, take a strip of cloth 25mm (1in) wide and 102mm (4in) long, cover the cloth with PVA glue then wrap around the turned end of the centre. Leave to dry and the cloth will bond the wood firmly, preventing the possibility of splitting.

The six pieces of padauk are turned in the following manner:

◆ Take the square section of padauk, trim one end to a tapered 19mm (¾in) square over a 16mm (⅝in) length.
◆ Fit the tapered section into the lace bobbin centre. Bring up the tailstock holding the revolving centre to support the end.
◆ Turn to an accurate 13mm (½in) diameter.
◆ Square off at the tailstock end.
◆ Measure from that squared-off end towards the headstock 13mm (½in) followed by 19mm (¾in).
◆ Repeat these measurements twice more so that there are three sections in all, each 13mm (½in) long followed by 19mm (¾in). There will be a small length of waste wood close to the headstock.
◆ At each of the 19mm (¾in) long sections, turn down to a 9mm (⅜in) diameter.
◆ Remove from the lathe and cut the six pieces so that there are eighteen pieces in all, each with a 13mm (½in) section of 13mm (½in) diameter and an attached 19mm (¾in) length of 9mm (⅜in) diameter.

Now take seven more pieces of padauk, taper the ends and turn in the following manner:

◆ Turn down to an accurate 19mm (¾in) diameter.
◆ Square off the end closest to the tailstock.
◆ Measure from the tailstock towards the headstock 19mm (¾in), mark that point, then measure a further 19mm (¾in).
◆ Repeat the measurements twice more.
◆ Turn the second, fourth and sixth sections down to 9mm (⅜in) diameter.
◆ Having turned all seven pieces in this way, cut them so that there are twenty-one pieces in all, each with a 19mm (¾in) long piece of 19mm (¾in) diameter, followed by an attached 19mm (¾in) length 9mm (⅜in) in diameter (see Fig 8.7).

Now take the remaining three pieces of padauk, trim the ends to fit the bobbin chuck and turn as follows:

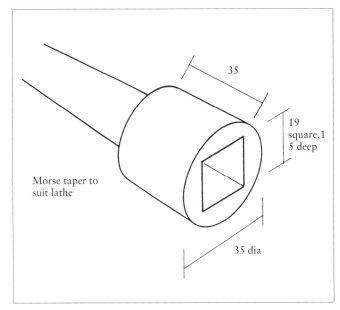

Fig 8.6 A bobbin chuck turned from wood.

◆ Turn down to an accurate 22mm (⅞in) diameter and square off at the tailstock end.
◆ Measure from that end and mark a point 22mm (⅞in) away. Measure a further 19mm (¾in) from that point. Repeat so that there are three sections in all marked in this manner.
◆ Leave the 22mm (⅞in) sections full diameter, and turn down the 19mm (¾in) sections to 9mm (⅜in) diameter.
◆ Having turned all three pieces in this way, cut into nine parts, each part with a 22mm (⅞in) section full diameter and a 19mm (¾in) section of 9mm (⅜in) diameter.
◆ One or two spare pieces have been

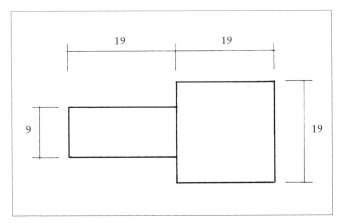

Fig 8.7 A small bead blank.

Fig 8.8 A large bead is drilled out while held in the chuck.

Fig 8.9 The spoon-shaped tool is used to shape the drilled hole.

allowed in each of the three sizes of padauk and purpleheart so do not be fearful of making mistakes.

Turning the beads

When producing these beads, develop a system so that once started they can be rattled out; but even while working quickly remember to work with care, particularly when drilling the hole and opening the hole to accept the shaped head, and when shaping that head. The following process applies to all the beads, all sizes and all wood types:

◆ Fit a three- or four-jaw chuck onto the headstock. A Jacobs chuck would work equally well but a drill chuck will be needed when drilling the bead.

◆ Take the bead blank and fit into the chuck the 9mm (⅜in) diameter section. Push the work into the chuck until the shoulder is firmly against the chuck jaws.

◆ Bring the tool rest across the face of the work, then turn the work flat and true.

◆ Remove the tool rest. Fit a drill chuck into the tailstock and into that chuck fit a 6mm (¼in) drill.

◆ Mark a position on the drill a bare 9mm (⅜in) from its tip.

◆ Drill into the bead. Withdraw the tailstock (*see* Fig 8.8).

◆ Bring the tool rest back across the face of the work.

◆ Bring the special spoon-shaped tool to the work (*see* Fig 8.9). Adjust the tool rest so that the cutting edge of the tool is at centre height.

◆ Mark on the tool a position a bare 9mm (⅜in) from its tip.

◆ Turn on the lathe. Push the tool into the

Fig 8.10 Turning the head of the large bead.

opening avoiding any contact with the edges. Move the tool inside the work to the left so that a larger internal opening is excavated.

◆ Use judgement to ensure that the inside hollow is sufficiently large to take the soon-to-be-turned head (no larger than 6.5mm, or just over ¼in).

◆ When satisfied, remove the tool, turn off the lathe, remove the bead and move on to the next one.

◆ Prepare them all in this manner.

Having rattled carefully through this first process, now work on each group of bead blanks in turn, beginning with the purpleheart.

◆ Remove the chuck from the headstock. Replace with the Jacobs drill chuck.

◆ Hold a 6mm (¼in) length of the 9mm (⅜in) section in the drill chuck. Support the drilled end with the revolving centre.

◆ Turn a fine central groove, 2mm (½₂in) wide around the large diameter of the purpleheart disc.

◆ Turn down either side of that groove, curving on one side to the revolving centre and on the other to the turned stem. Make

sure the shape on either side matches.

◆ Now begin work on the stem.

The size of the head in this case is 6.3mm (just over ¼in), but this will vary according to the hardness or softness of wood being used. Make sure by experiment that the correct size is decided upon.

◆ Turn down the stem to a precise 6.3mm (just over ¼in).

◆ Measure 12mm (½in) from the side of the bead towards the headstock.

◆ The first 6mm (¼in) can be turned to about 5mm (⅛in approx.)(*see* Fig 8.10). The last 6mm (¼in) is rounded over, leaving a small part at full diameter (*see* Fig 8.11).

◆ Once the bead is shaped and the stem and head are accurately cut, part off on the headstock side of the turned head. Repeat for all the purpleheart pieces.

The reason for the shaping is that the head shape helps the bead into the hole with only a small amount full diameter – only a small amount to compress and spring back once inside the hole. The turned-away section closest to the bead allows for the

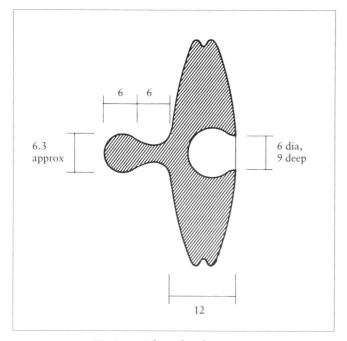

Fig 8.11 A large bead.

Fig 8.12 Grinding the V tool, which will be used to cut the surface decoration on the padauk bead.

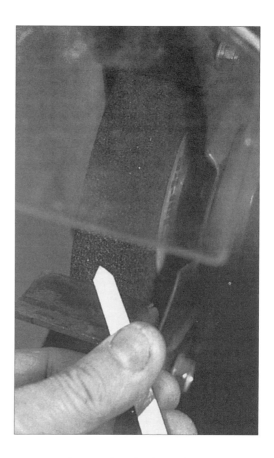

roll-around movement of the ball-and-socket joint.

Now move on to the seven 22mm (⅞in) diameter padauk beads. Work each in the following manner:

◆ Again hold a 6mm (¼in) section of the stem in the Jacobs chuck and support the drilled end with the revolving centre.

◆ Turn the large section into a spherical bead.

◆ Take the tool ground to a V point (see Fig 8.12) and, by eye, cut a series of equally spaced grooves. Begin at the centre top and work down to the left. Then from the centre,

Fig 8.13 The V tool in use.

cut down to the right (*see* Fig 8.13).

◆ Turn the stem and head as described earlier (*see* Fig 8.14). Part off on the headstock side of the shaped head.

◆ Next, work the twenty 19mm (¾in) diameter padauk beads. These will be turned smooth and fully rounded. Turn the stem and head as before, parting off on the headstock side of the head.

◆ Finally, turn the fifteen 13mm (½in) diameter padauk beads so they are smooth and fully rounded, turning the stem and head as before and parting off carefully on the headstock side of the head.

Some points of which to be aware:

◆ Do not turn into the edge of the hole when shaping the bead close to the revolving centre.

◆ Do not overtighten the revolving centre into the drilled hole as this could open it out.

◆ Experiment first to ensure that the size of the head fits the hole without splitting and without falling out. Turn a full bead so that account is taken of the full pressure in the centre hole on the whole bead.

◆ Turn spare beads as there will be some failures.

◆ Make sure the beads are clean and ready to polish before they are parted off – it is too late afterwards.

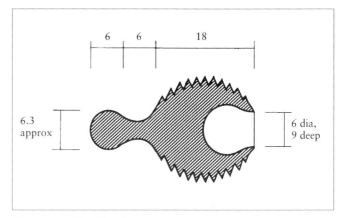

Fig 8.14 *Ridged bead.*

◆ One important final tip. Rub a little candle wax onto the rounded heads – this will help when pushing the beads together.

Padauk and purpleheart. It really is quite splendid to see the vibrant shavings from the two woods mingling and to smell the custard powder scent from the padauk.

Finishing

Once all the beads are completed, do not be tempted to pop them together. First polish. Polyurethane again works well – nice and crisp as a finish and also hard wearing, but two coats are needed with tedious rubbing down between coats. Fit the beads on pins to

Fig 8.15 *Polished beads drying.*

Fig 8.16 'Popping' the necklace together.

dry (*see* Fig 8.15). Leave to dry thoroughly as they will receive heavy handling when 'popping' together (*see* Fig 8.16). Remember the candle wax and be careful when 'popping' to keep the pieces lined up, for a sideways movement could cause splitting.

In the necklace shown in Fig 8.1 there are six purpleheart disc beads surrounded by seven grooved padauk beads – ten smooth on either side and the remaining smaller smooth beads at the top.

RATTLESNAKE

This rattlesnake, which really does rattle, consists of a head, eight segments and a tail. The head has a turned stem and head, the segments have drilled holes, stems and heads, and the tail only has a drilled hole.

Having understood the basic principle of turning the stem and head the only extra part to note here is that there is a taper leading into the hole and a taper on the head and the segments leading to the stem. These allow the snake's body to move freely without showing the joint.

The wood I used for this snake was Australian blackwood which turned beautifully.

Preparing the blanks

◆ For the head section, cut a piece 90mm (3⁹⁄₁₆in) long by 19mm (¾in) square.

◆ Taper to fit into the bobbin centre and turn a piece 75mm (3in) long and 16mm (⅝in) in diameter. Of this piece 50mm (2in) remains full diameter, while the remaining 25mm (1in) is turned to a 9mm (⅜in) diameter. It is cut to the 75mm (3in) length.

◆ For the segments, cut four pieces 110mm (4⁵⁄₁₆in) long by 19mm (¾in) square. Taper the ends.

◆ Turn each to a 16mm (⅝in) diameter.

◆ Mark on each piece two segments, each 44mm (1¾in) long, 19mm (¾in) of which remains full diameter. The remaining 25mm (1in) is turned down to 9mm (⅜in).

◆ Cut and turn these segments so that there are eight in all (*see* Fig 8.18).

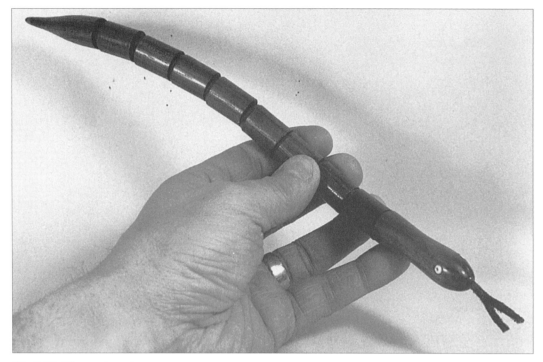

Fig 8.17 The rattlesnake.

◆ Finally the tail section – 55mm (2³⁄₁₆in) by 19mm (¾in) square – is turned down to 16mm (⅝in) diameter.

◆ Turn so that a 9mm (⅜in) length has a 9mm (⅜in) diameter (for holding) and a further 30mm (1³⁄₁₆in) remains full diameter.

The tail

◆ For the dimensions of the finished tail, refer to Fig 8.19.

◆ Remove the bobbin chuck and replace with a Jacobs chuck.

Fig 8.18 Turning the snake segments.

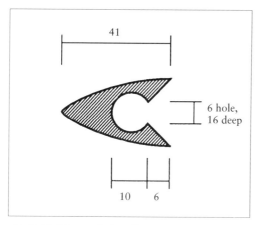

Fig 8.19 The snake's tail.

Fig 8.20 Parting off the finished tail, which is held in a drill chuck.

◆ Hold on the 9mm (⅜in) diameter section. Drill with a 6mm (¼in) drill to a depth of 16mm (⅝in).

◆ Next, taper the hole. Work from the outer edge into the hole for a 6mm (¼in) depth.

◆ Take the spoon-shaped tool and undercut the inside of the hole being careful not to open out the hole where it meets the taper. Open out well to improve the snake's movement.

◆ Bring up the tailstock with the revolving centre. Push the centre into the tapered hole for support. Turn the end of the tail in a long slow taper. Clean up before parting off to a length of 41mm (1⅝ in) (*see* Fig 8.20).

The body

◆ For the dimensions of the eight body segments, refer to Fig 8.21.

◆ Each of the eight segments is turned in the following manner:

◆ Hold the stem in the Jacobs chuck. Drill out with a 6mm (¼in) drill to a depth of 16mm (⅝in).

◆ Taper the hole from the outer edge into the hole for a depth of 6mm (¼in) (*see* Fig 8.22).

◆ Take the spoon-shaped tool and undercut the inside of the hole, being careful not to open out the hole where it meets the turned taper. It is best to open out the inside well for

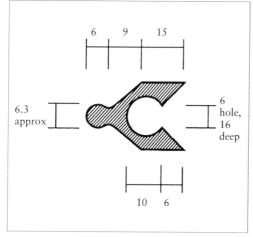

Fig 8.21 A segment of the snake's body.

a good amount of movement in the snake.

◆ Loosen the chuck, slide out the stem so that it is held on a 6mm (¼in) end of the stem. Tighten the chuck.

◆ Bring up the revolving centre held in the tailstock and push it into the tapered hole for support.

◆ Carefully turn the stem so that the first 6mm (¼in) closest to the main bulk of the segment is about 5mm (⅛in) diameter, certainly smaller than the drill hole diameter. Turn the rounded head to a 6.3mm (just over ¼in) diameter on the next 9mm (⅜in) of the stem.

◆ Before parting off, turn a taper on that part of the segment closest to the stem 3mm (⅛in) wide and 3mm (⅛in) deep.

The precise shape of stem, head, internal tapers and external tapers will need to be discovered by practice. The measurements given here are guidelines which worked for the piece shown here. It produced a snake that had good flexibility without the joints opening too wide. Experiment to ensure your snake works well.

◆ Clean up the segment and part off on the headstock side of the rounded head (see Fig 8.23).

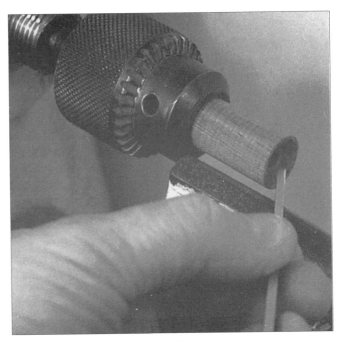

Fig 8.22 Turning the taper inside a segment.

The head

◆ For the dimensions of the completed head, refer to Fig 8.24.

◆ Hold in exactly the same manner as the segments, though of course there will be no drilling. Support with the revolving centre.

Fig 8.23 The head end of the segment is turned, then the piece is parted off close to the drill chuck.

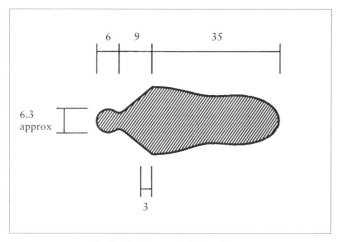

Fig 8.24 The snake's head.

The point made by the centre on the front of the head will be used to centre the drill when drilling the pilot hole to hold the forked leather tongue.

◆ Turn the stem and rounded head as before.

◆ Turn the curved shaping of the head and round over the nose to the revolving centre (*see* Fig 8.25).

◆ Clean up and part off on the headstock side of the rounded head.

◆ Cut a forked tongue from leather. Drill a 2mm (½in) hole at the point where the revolving centre touched.

◆ Choose two small white glass beads for the eyes. Measure 13mm (½in) from the nose along the head. Drill two holes of a size to take the beads 16mm (⅝in) apart at that distance in.

Finishing

◆ Apply two coats of polyurethane to all the parts, rubbing down between coats.

◆ Fit the leather tongue in place. Use a little glue and hammer in a small wooden dowel to fit it firmly.

◆ Glue the two glass bead eyes using epoxy resin glue. Leave the bead holes uppermost so its pupils show, beady and snake eyed.

◆ The final act is to rub paraffin wax on the rounded head's joint and push the pieces together.

A good snake should be nice and flexible but not too loose, and of course should make a good rattling sound.

Fig 8.25 Completing the head.

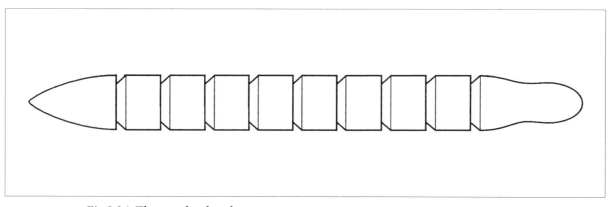

Fig 8.26 The completed snake.

CHAPTER 9

The Bottle Trick

SOME YEARS AGO ON TELEVISION I SAW AN INTRIGUING PIECE SENT IN BY A VIEWER. IT WAS A BOTTLE WITH A WOODEN BAR PUSHED DOWN THROUGH THE NECK AND INTO THE CENTRE OF THE BOTTLE. CROSSWAYS THROUGH THIS WOODEN BAR WERE FIXED TWO HEAVY NAILS. NOW THEY COULD NOT HAVE BEEN HAMMERED INTO PLACE BECAUSE THE GLASS BOTTLE SURROUNDED THEM. THEY COULD NOT HAVE BEEN PUSHED THROUGH THE WOOD FIRST AND THEN FED INTO THE BOTTLE BECAUSE THE NECK WAS TOO SMALL. JUST LIKE THE SHIP IN THE BOTTLE, THE BOTTLE SHOWN ON TELEVISION WAS A CLEVER TRICK THAT WOULD BE DIFFICULT TO SOLVE.

(Incidentally, the most memorable event was not seeing this bottle trickery but watching the bottle, as the television presenter placed it on the table in front of himself, roll slowly away. The presenter was so hooked up with microphones and earphones that he could not move quickly enough to stop the bottle's progress. It moved out of view of the camera and crashed to the floor. There followed a shot of the shattered glass surrounding the wooden bar and nails then back to an embarrassed and apologizing presenter.)

It has taken me all these years to work out how the nails were fixed through the bar inside the bottle. Here I will show the method but in place of the nails are two turned pieces which, to make life a little more interesting, are inlaid. The main wooden bar is fully turned with a turned 'handle' and stopper.

Preparation

◆ Buy two one-metre (3.28ft) lengths of different inlay bandings.

◆ Cut a 150mm (6in) length of 25mm (1in) square hardwood. My choice is English walnut for the central turned bar.

◆ For the handle and stopper, cut a further length of 30mm (1⅛in) square by 150mm (6in) long hardwood of the same variety as the centre bar.

◆ Have ready a 200mm (8in) long by at least 12mm (½in) wide by 6mm (¼in) thick similar hardwood from which to cut the

Fig 9.1 The bottle trick.

cores for the inlaid sticks.

◆ A quantity of small elastic bands are needed.

◆ And, of course, a bottle. The choice of bottle is important. It must have a short neck. The sides below the neck must slope towards the edges. If any other shape is chosen it does not make the work impossible but it does make it very difficult. I found that a vinegar bottle worked very well and had the added benefit of being inexpensive.

◆ Lathe speed should be 1500rpm for the handle and centre bar, and 1750–2000rpm for the inlaid sticks.

Inlaying the sticks

This method of applying inlay bandings to a central core is quite simple but very messy. Either wear rubber gloves or be ready with the tap running and have a towel handy.

◆ Take the inlay banding and measure its width. Here I have purposely chosen two bandings of different widths.

◆ The first piece is 6.5mm (¼in plus) and the second is 5.5mm (⁷⁄₃₂in).

I chose these different widths so that the thickness of the finished turned sticks would vary. Only one stick would fit properly into one hole, making the problem even greater.

◆ Cut the core squares for these bandings one thickness of the banding less than the banding's width. Now this works easily for metric measurements so I will use that for demonstration: banding thickness – 1mm; banding width – 6.5mm. Cut the core 5.5mm square.

◆ So cut two core sizes, one 5.5mm (⁷⁄₃₂in) square and the other 4.5mm (just under ³⁄₁₆in) square, both 200mm (8in) long and cut from the prepared piece.

◆ Now take four 200mm (8in) lengths of the widest banding. Pick the widest core and a handful of elastic bands.

◆ Decide before starting exactly how the inlay bandings are to be matched one side to the other. Are they to be staggered, reversed or laid side by side (see Fig 9.2). Remember the chosen arrangement.

◆ Take one piece of banding and run PVA glue along one surface.

◆ Lay that glued surface against one side of the core so that the edge of the banding and the edge of the core line up. The other edge of the banding will project by the thickness of the banding.

◆ Take the second piece of banding and

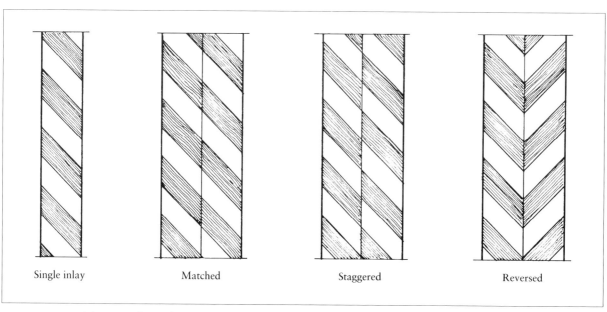

Single inlay   Matched   Staggered   Reversed

Fig 9.2 Inlay styles.

(without glue) lay it next to the overhung edge lining the pattern as required (a dry run).

◆ Apply glue to the face of the banding and replace in the decided position, butting the banding up to the first overhung edge. The edge of this second banding now overhangs.

◆ Make sure the first two bandings are correctly placed for the intended pattern before moving to the third banding.

◆ Place the third banding (without glue) next to the second, laying it up to the overhung edge and lining up the pattern as required.

◆ Apply glue to the banding and replace it in the correct position, butting it against the second overhung edge. The third band edge now overhangs.

◆ Make sure that the pattern is correctly placed before moving on to the fourth and final banding.

◆ Lay the fourth banding (without glue) on the remaining face, pushing it up to the overhung edge and lining up the pattern.

◆ Remove the piece and apply glue to its face. Replace it in the required position, push it up to the overhung edge and line up the pattern.

◆ The overhung edge of this final banding covers the first, covering the core completely.

◆ Make sure that the patterns are correctly positioned all round.

◆ Now fit the elastic bands as clamps.

◆ Run an elastic band on one end and twist it over several times until tight.

◆ Now move to the other end and repeat, but this time run the elastic band to the centre.

◆ Continue fitting elastic bands until half the stick is covered.

◆ Return to the first end. Roll the first wound band to the centre then continue fixing elastic bands until the second half is filled.

◆ Lay the first piece on one side then begin work on the second inlay stick, repeating the process.

◆ Now you will understand exactly what a messy job this is. If you have been using PVA glue a quick swill with water will remove all

Fig 9.3 *The inlaid sticks glued and elastic-band clamped.*

traces from the hands.

◆ Leave the bandings to dry (*see* Fig 9.3) and move on to turning the central spindle.

The central spindle

◆ Take the chosen bottle and a flexible tape measure.

◆ Push the tape down through the neck of the bottle to touch the inside base.

◆ Measure from the inside base to the start of the slope. In this case it is 115mm (4½in).

◆ Withdraw the tape and measure the neck opening. For this vinegar bottle it is 20mm ($^{13}/_{16}$in) in diameter.

◆ An allowance needs to be made to ensure that the central spindle can fit through the bottle neck. So here the central spindle will be made 18mm (¾in) in diameter. If you want to be really mean, turn the majority of the spindle to an 18mm (¾in) diameter and the last 1.5mm ($^1/_{16}$in) at the top can be left the smallest fraction over 20mm ($^{13}/_{16}$in) – the neck opening size. This slightly thicker section can be squeezed through the neck never to escape. (Don't make it too much larger or it may burst the neck.)

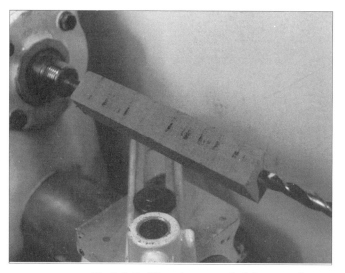

Fig 9.4 Drilling the top end of the central spindle.

◆ Take the 150mm (6in) long, 25mm (1in) square piece set aside for the central spindle and set this between centres making sure that the driving dog is small so that it will not split the work.

◆ Fit a 9mm (⅜in) diameter drill into the drill chuck held in the tailstock. Mark a position on the drill shank 15mm (⅝in) away from the cutting edge.

◆ Bring the drill centre up to the centre of the work. Turn on the lathe and drill to the marked depth (*see* Fig 9.4).

◆ Turn off the lathe. Withdraw the drill.

Remove the drill and chuck from the tailstock replacing it with a revolving centre.

◆ Push the revolving centre into the drilled hole for support.

◆ Turn the whole length down to an 18mm (¾in) diameter (or make an allowance for the thicker section if you are the mean type).

◆ Now mark upon a piece of card the shape of the central spindle which is 115mm (4½in) long. Mark all the important details, positions for drilled holes, coves and beads (*see* Figs 9.5 and 9.6).

◆ Turn to size and shape, undercutting the end so that it can be parted cleanly later.

◆ Clearly mark the positions to be drilled. The hole nearest the tailstock end will be smaller. The one nearer the headstock end will be larger. These two holes will be set at 90° to one another.

◆ Part off.

Turning the handle and the collar

The handle and the collar are made from the same piece of wood but are separate. The trick here is to make the two pieces, when fitted together, appear to be one. The handle is needed to manipulate the central spindle to juggle those inlaid sticks into position, but

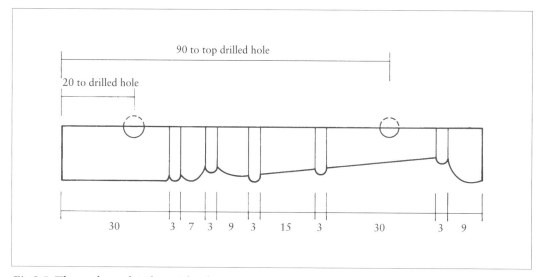

Fig 9.5 The card template layout for the central spindle.

with the collar attached it is just too short. Remove the collar and the handle becomes a useful tool. So make the collar and handle appear as one piece and make the collar hard to remove from the handle. Then the problem of fitting those inlaid sticks into the centre spindle becomes increasingly difficult.

◆ For the dimensions of the turned handle and collar, refer to Fig 9.7.
◆ Set the 150mm (6in) by 30mm (1¾in) square piece of walnut between centres. Again use a small driving dog to prevent splitting.
◆ Turn the whole piece down to 25mm (1in) diameter, which is the outside diameter of the bottle top.
◆ Measure 85mm (3⅜in) from the tailstock towards the headstock and mark this position in pencil. Turn this section down to an accurate 9mm (⅜in) diameter.
◆ Taper the end at the tailstock to 45° but not to a point.
◆ Make sure that the beginning and end of this turned section is a tight 9mm (⅜in) diameter so that the collar fits well at the top and the spindle hole is a good fit at the end. The middle section may be turned a little more easily.
◆ From the shoulder, measure 33mm (1¼in) towards the headstock and mark in pencil.

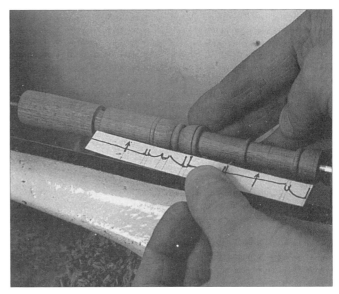

Fig 9.6 The card template held against the turned spindle.

◆ Turn this marked section to 18mm (¾in) diameter.
◆ This 33mm (1¼in) section is marked out in the following way starting from the shoulder: measure and mark in pencil 3mm (⅛in) towards the headstock followed by 12mm (½in), and a further 3mm (⅛in) and 15mm (⅝in) will remain.
◆ On the first 3mm (⅛in) section, turn a rounded bead.
◆ On the 12mm (½in) section, turn a nice

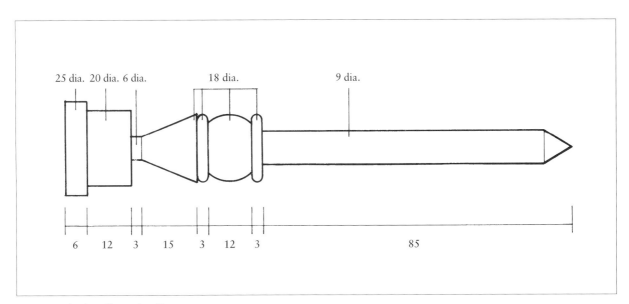

Fig 9.7 The handle and collar.

Fig 9.8 The handle and plug turned from one piece.

wide rounded piece.

◆ The second 3mm (⅛in) part is again turned to a well-shaped bead.

◆ The final 15mm (⅝in) length is turned to a conical point but not yet parted off.

◆ From the imagined end of that conical point, measure 3mm (⅛in). This will be waste wood and can be turned down to a 6mm

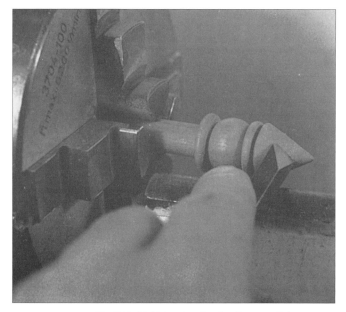

Fig 9.9 Held in the chuck, the top of the handle is fully turned.

(¼in) diameter.

◆ For the plug, measure from that line a 12mm (½in) length and turn this to an accurate 20mm (¾₆in) diameter to fit inside the neck of the bottle (*see* Fig 9.8).

◆ A further 6mm (¼in) is measured. This is left at the full 25mm (1in) diameter. A ridged pattern is turned upon its surface.

◆ Begin a parting cut on the headstock side of that line.

◆ Now cut through the waste section between the plug and the handle and cut away the parted section above the plug.

◆ Remove the driving dog, replacing it with a three- or four-jaw chuck.

◆ Hold the 9mm (⅜in) diameter section of the handle in the chuck leaving the part-turned conical end exposed.

◆ Complete the shaping on the conical end of the handle (*see* Fig 9.9).

◆ Remove the handle from the chuck and replace with the plug holding lightly on the 20mm (¹³⁄₁₆in) diameter section.

◆ Face off the end of the plug.

◆ Fit a 9mm (⅜in) drill in a drill chuck and fit the drill chuck onto the tailstock.

◆ Drill centrally through the plug (*see* Fig 9.10).

◆ Remove the finished plug from the chuck.

Turning the inlaid sticks

These sticks have been prepared much longer than necessary so that there is plenty of spare material that can be used if mistakes are made or pieces of inlay break out.

◆ The dimensions of the larger inlaid stick are given in Fig 9.11.
◆ Remove the elastic bands from the now-dried sticks.
◆ These pieces can be cut into convenient lengths for turning. So cut into two 100mm (4in) lengths.
◆ Hold a 6mm (¼in) length in the chuck, supporting the other end with a revolving centre held in the tailstock (*see* Fig 9.12).
◆ Turn down a short length closest to the tailstock then reverse the piece in the lathe holding the now-rounded part in the chuck.
◆ Turn the length fully round, the larger piece close to 6.5mm (¼in plus) diameter and the smaller to a 5.5mm (⁷⁄₃₂inch) diameter.

Before continuing with the turning the length of these crosspieces needs to be calculated.

◆ Measure the external diameter of the bottle at the position where the crosspiece will be held.

Fig 9.10 Having turned the plug it is drilled to accept the handle.

Fig 9.11 The larger inlaid stick.

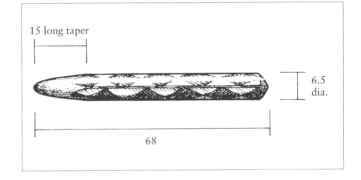

15 long taper

6.5 dia.

68

Fig 9.12 Diamond inlaid stick held in chuck.

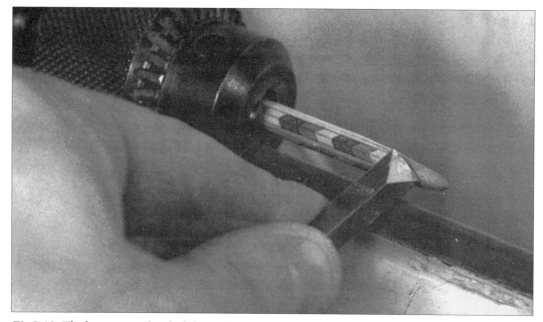

Fig 9.13 The long, tapered end of the stick being turned while held in a drill chuck.

◆ Judge the wall thickness of the bottle and take twice that away from the external diameter.

◆ Cut a piece of 6mm (¼in) dowel to that length.

◆ Turn both ends to a point or use a pencil sharpener to point the ends.

◆ Find the centre point of the dowel and drill a hole. The hole should be large enough to take a piece of string.

◆ Thread the string through the hole and knot off on the back.

◆ Lower the dowel into the bottle allowing it to hang horizontally at the position it should fit. Check its size. Cut down if necessary, or make a larger piece.

◆ The top, smaller-diameter inlaid crosspiece for the vinegar bottle shown in Fig 9.1 was 65mm (2½in) long. The lower, larger-diameter stick was 68mm (2¾in) long.

◆ Returning to the lathe, measure 9mm (⅜in) from the tailstock end and mark a pencil line. This section will be parted off later.

◆ From that pencil line, measure the correct length for the diameter of the piece being turned – 65mm (2½in) or 68mm (2¾in) long.

◆ Begin turning a long point over a 12mm (½in) length closest to the tailstock and a more obtuse angle at the end away from the tailstock.

◆ Part off at the marked lines. Complete the shaping of these pieces whilst held in a large chuck or even a drill chuck.

◆ Turn the obtuse angle firmly away with a skew, cleaning up the end.

◆ For the longer point, turn down over a 12mm (½in) length (*see* Fig 9.13). This will allow sufficient freedom for the pointed end to slide into the drilled hole in the centre spindle.

◆ Make sure that the pointed end has a slight round to help it slip into that drilled hole.

Preparing the spindle to accept the crosspieces

◆ Before drilling through the spindle, measure the diameter of the crosspieces accurately and select a drill a fraction larger.

◆ Take the drill bit and drill a hole into scrap wood testing the inlaid crosspiece. When satisfied with the fit the spindle may be drilled.

◆ When drilling through the spindle at the

Fig 9.14 *The top part of the central spindle is drilled. Note the masking tape on the underside of the drilled hole to prevent splitting out.*

Fig 9.15 *Shaping the drilled hole with a file so that the inlaid stick will slide in more easily.*

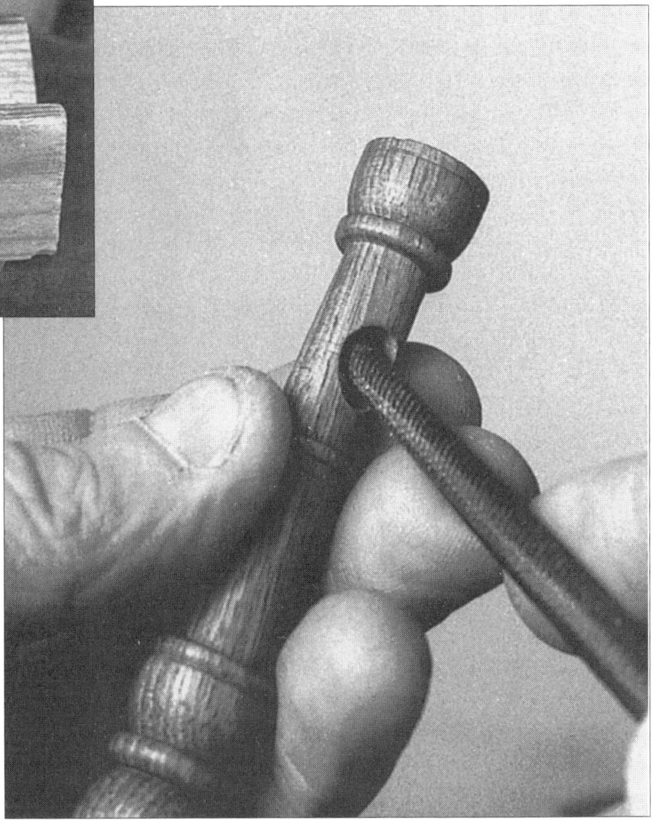

marked positions hold the piece in a wooden V block for support.

◆ To prevent the back surface splitting out, cover that area with masking tape. As an added precaution do not force the drill through; allow it to cut gently. This should leave a clean exit (*see* Fig 9.14).

◆ Once the holes have been drilled they need to be opened out slightly at one end to encourage the crosspieces in, so:

◆ Hold the spindle with the 9mm (⅜in) hole in its top at the top.

◆ Take a round file and rasp away a small ramp on the *lower* edge of *one side* of the top hole only (*see* Fig 9.15).

◆ Repeat for the lower hole and this should be enough to help the crosspieces slip in.

◆ All the pieces have now been completed and can now be polished. Do not increase the diameter of the crosspieces with thick layers of polish.

Fitting the inlaid crosspieces into the centre spindle

◆ Hold the bottle, neck down.

◆ Push the thickest crosspiece into the

bottle, blunt end first.

◆ Fit the handle, without the collar, into the drilled hole at the end of the stem.

◆ With the bottle held at a slight angle, push the stem into the bottle until the first, largest hole is at the inner slope of the neck.

◆ Angle the bottle a little more so that the crosspiece comes thin point first towards the hole and is lying on the sloping shoulder of the bottle.

◆ Allow the point to slide into the hole (*see* Fig 9.16).

◆ Keeping the bottle at the same angle, push the stem into the bottle. The point of the crosspiece stays in the hole but all of the

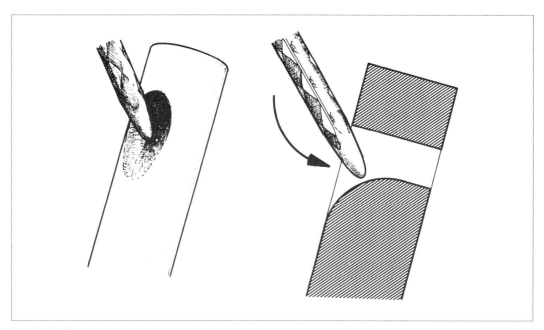

Fig 9.16 Slipping the crosspiece into the hole in the spindle.

Fig 9.17 The central spindle is eased upwards, keeping the inlaid stick point in the hole.

Fig 9.18 Sliding the spindle further up into the bottle – the inlaid stick is raised with it.

crosspiece is raised upwards with the stem (*see* Figs 9.17 and 9.18). The blunt end of the crosspiece rests against the inside of the bottle as it moves up.

◆ As the blunt end touches the inner corner (where the side of the bottle meets its base), allow the stem to move slowly away (*see* Fig 9.19). This then allows the angle of the crosspiece to the stem to lessen and the crosspiece begins to drop into the hole.

◆ Once the crosspiece is part way into the hole the wall of the bottle can be used to push the end against, forcing the crosspiece fully into the hole (*see* Fig 9.20).

◆ The second crosspiece is a little more difficult because there is no top corner to push against and allowance for the first piece held in the stem must be made. With care and persistence it will drop into the hole as the first did.

◆ When fitting the second inlaid piece it is necessary for the drilled end of the centre spindle to move all the way across to the opposite edge of the bottle. It may be necessary to loosen the grip of the 9mm (⅜in) end of the handle slightly in the drilled hole in the spindle's end.

◆ When both pieces are in place turn the bottle upright and pull out the handle. Fit the collar on the handle and replace.

If you want a little more fun with this bottle, spindle and crosspiece, then substitute a nail, a pencil or even a drill bit for the inlaid sticks and that should look really perplexing.

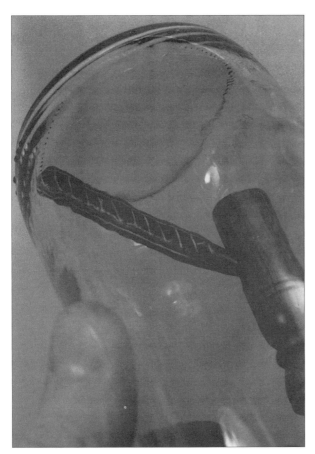

Fig 9.19 *The blunt end of the inlaid stick reaches the 'corner' of the bottle forcing it further into the hole.*

Fig 9.20 *Hey presto! It slides across into the hole in the central spindle.*

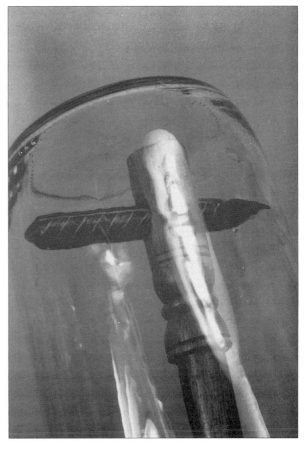

CHAPTER 10

Barrel

THE LID OF THIS BARREL IS LOOSE BUT IT WILL NOT COME OFF. PUSH, PULL, TWIST, PRESS THE SMALL BLACK BUNG AT THE BASE, TURN IT UPSIDE DOWN AND STILL IT WILL NOT COME OFF. IT WILL NOT COME OFF UNTIL THE WHOLE BARREL IS SPUN ROUND LIKE A TOP, FOR ACROSS THE LOWER PART IS A DRILLED HOLE – THE BUNG HIDES IT.

In that drilled hole are two small metal pins. Attached to the lid is a long dowel which reaches down into the barrel and into a drilled hole in its base. Crossways through that dowel is a drilled hole matching the one that holds the metal pins. This crossways hole through the dowel is also located at the same height as the pin hole so that no matter which way the barrel is moved at least one of the pins falls into the hole through the dowel, locking it in place. The centrifugal force of the spinning barrel throws the pins outwards, releasing the centre dowel and allowing the top to be lifted. It really is a most obscure trick which could be applied to a variety of shapes but here a simple barrel is used.

I chose to turn this piece from olivewood with a wild grain, which occasionally provided some wild turning. That soft warm oily smell of olivewood is so welcoming and the sweet shavings that curl off are so pleasing that the wood is rapidly becoming my favourite.

Fig 10.1 The barrel and its stand.

Preparation

◆ Cut a piece of olivewood 135mm (5⅜in) long by 60mm (2⅜in) square for the barrel.

◆ Cut a second piece of olivewood 12mm (½in) thick by 60mm (2⅜in) diameter for the stand.

◆ Have ready a 50mm (2in) length of 3mm (⅛in) diameter silver steel or a nail or panel pin or brass rod of the same diameter. The precise diameter is not important but it needs to be close to that size to be sufficiently strong.

◆ A 75mm (3in) length of 12mm (½in) square piece of olivewood is needed from which to turn a dowel.

◆ The usual selection of lathe tools and drills are necessary.

◆ Lathe speed should be 1250rpm for the barrel and 1750rpm for the dowel.

Turning the barrel blank

◆ Refer to Fig 10.2 for the dimensions of the turned blank.

◆ Fit between centres the 135mm (5⅜in) long by 60mm (2⅜in) square piece of olivewood.

◆ Turn down to a 55mm (2³⁄₁₆in) diameter.

◆ Measure from the shoulder at the tailstock towards the headstock 20mm (¹³⁄₁₆in) and mark a pencil line at that point.

◆ Turn down that marked 20mm (¹³⁄₁₆in) section to a 25mm (1in) diameter spigot.

◆ From that full diameter shoulder line measure again towards the headstock 15mm (⅝in) and mark a line.

◆ Leave this 15mm (⅝in) section full diameter.

◆ Measure 3mm (⅛in) from that last section and turn down to a precise 42mm (1¹¹⁄₁₆in) diameter.

◆ From that 3mm (⅛in) step measure, again towards the headstock, a further 6mm (¼in) and turn down to 20mm (¾in) diameter ready for parting off.

◆ From the headstock side of that 6mm (¼in) wide section, measure 65mm (2½in) towards the headstock. Leave this section full diameter.

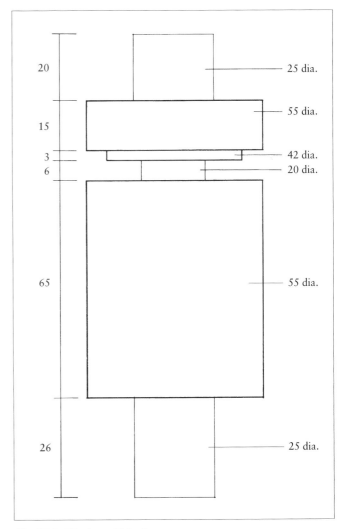

Fig 10.2 The barrel blank.

◆ The remaining section is turned down to a 25mm (1in) diameter spigot.

◆ The blank is now turned and the pieces are ready to be parted off (*see* Fig 10.3).

◆ The part on the headstock side of the parting off section is Piece A. The smaller part on the tailstock side of that parting off area is Piece B.

◆ Saw off or part off through the 6mm (¼in) wide parting off area separating Piece A from Piece B.

Turning the barrel

◆ For the dimensions of the turned barrel, refer to Fig 10.4.

◆ Remove the driving dog from the headstock and replace with a three- or four-

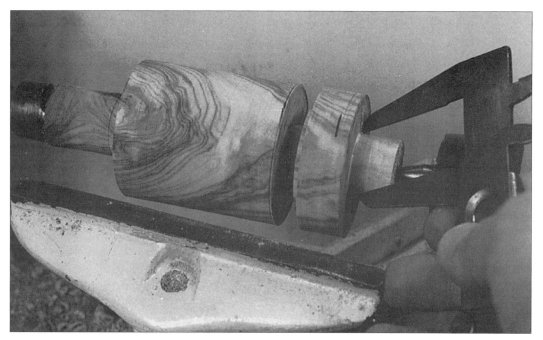

Fig 10.3 The barrel blank is turned with the top section waiting to be parted off.

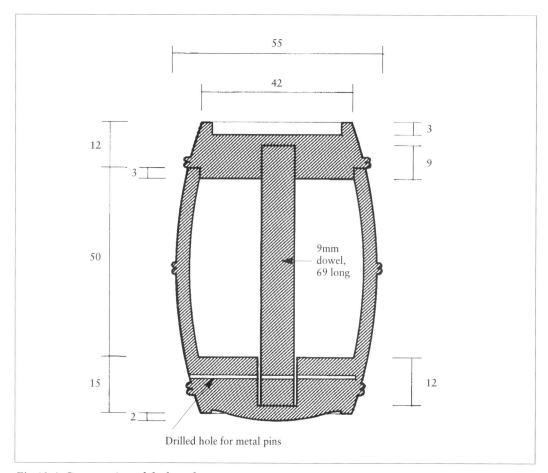

Fig 10.4 Cross section of the barrel.

Fig 10.5 The top is drilled whilst held in a chuck.

Fig 10.6 Turning out the inside of the barrel.

jaw chuck.

◆ Take Part B and grip the 25mm (1in) diameter spigot in the chuck jaws.

◆ Make sure the piece is running true and on centre before fully tightening the jaws. Once satisfied, lock lightly.

◆ Face off the exposed end so that it is flat and true but do not cut away any of the 42mm (1¹¹⁄₁₆in) diameter part if possible.

◆ Fit a 9mm (⅜in) diameter drill into a drill chuck fitted in the tailstock. Drill Piece B to a depth of 9mm (⅜in) (*see* Fig 10.5).

◆ Withdraw the drill and remove Part B from the chuck.

◆ Fit Part A into the chuck and hold the 25mm (1in) spigot in the chuck jaws.

◆ Make sure that the piece runs true and on centre.

◆ Bring the tool rest across the face of the work and face off the end flat and true.

◆ Mark on the end face in pencil a 42mm (1¹¹⁄₁₆in) diameter circle concentrically.

◆ On the inside of that line, turn out to at least 3mm (⅛in) deep. Turn off the lathe, move the tool rest away from the work and test Part B in the recess. Adjust until a good tight fit is achieved.

◆ Reset the tool rest and continue turning out the body to a depth of 50mm (2in)(*see* Fig 10.6). It may help if the majority of the wood is drilled away and the inside finish turned.

◆ The inside of this piece can be widened out in its middle to form more of a barrel shape, but leave the entrance diameter untouched.

◆ In a drill chuck fit a 9mm (⅜in) drill.

◆ Mark on its shank a position 62mm (2⁷⁄₁₆in) away from the cutting edge.

◆ Drill into the hollowed barrel and halt when the top surface of the barrel lines up with the marked point on the drill. A hole will then have been drilled 12mm (½in) deep into the internal base.

◆ Remove the drill and drill chuck.

◆ Loosen the jaws of the main chuck and pull Piece A a little away from the jaws. This will allow the end of the barrel to be turned without fear of striking the chuck jaws.

◆ Retighten the chuck. Make sure that Piece

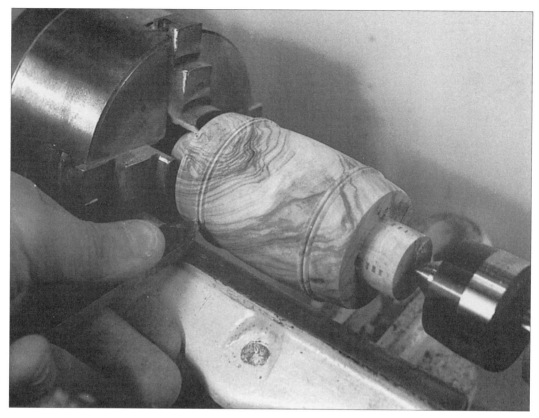

Fig 10.7 The top is fitted onto the base and
the whole barrel is turned to shape.

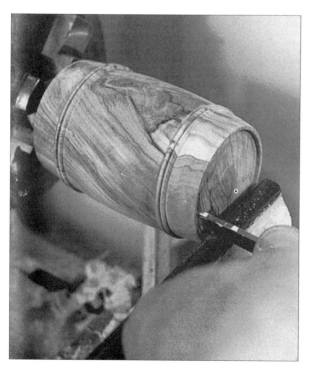

Fig 10.8 With the top 'jammed' onto the
base, it may be turned.

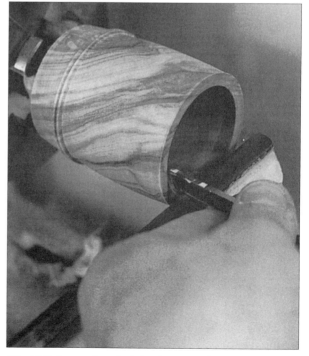

Fig 10.9 Loosening the joint between the top and the
base of the barrel.

Fig 10.10 The underside of the base is turned leaving a raised dimple upon which it will spin.

A is still running on centre, then fit Piece B in place.

◆ Bring the tailstock forward holding a revolving centre. Push the two parts together supporting Piece B with the centre.

◆ Turn the outer barrel shape with 'hoops' top and bottom (*see* Fig 10.7). The upper hoops disguise the joint, the lower hoops are set 15mm (⅝in) up from the base.

◆ The top and bottom of the barrel are turned to a 42mm (1¹¹⁄₁₆in) diameter. The centre remains full size.

◆ Carefully part off the waste wood spigot at the tailstock end. If the top of the barrel is a good jam fit then, using fine and light cuts, the top hollow may be turned (*see* Fig 10.8).

◆ If the top does not jam on sufficiently well a jam chuck will need to be turned later to complete this part.

◆ Remove the top and open out the 42mm (1¹¹⁄₁₆in) diameter opening so that the top will now fit on easily (*see* Fig 10.9).

◆ Remove the barrel base from the chuck.

◆ Turn a jam spindle from a piece of spare wood. The barrel body can then be pushed onto this piece allowing the end to be turned once the spigot has been sawn off. Do not cut the spigot too closely to the base; leave a little extra to be turned.

◆ Turn the end of the barrel so that a small rounded bump remains. This rounded bump must be raised higher than the surrounding edges of the barrel base for it is this bump upon which the barrel will spin (*see* Fig 10.10).

◆ Set aside the barrel.

Turning the dowel

◆ Set a piece of 75mm (3in) long by 12mm (½in) square olivewood between centres. Use a fine driving dog to prevent splitting.

◆ Turn this piece down to 9mm (⅜in) diameter for its full length.

◆ The part closest to the tailstock needs to be turned accurately for this part is to fit into the drilled hole in the barrel's top. The rest of

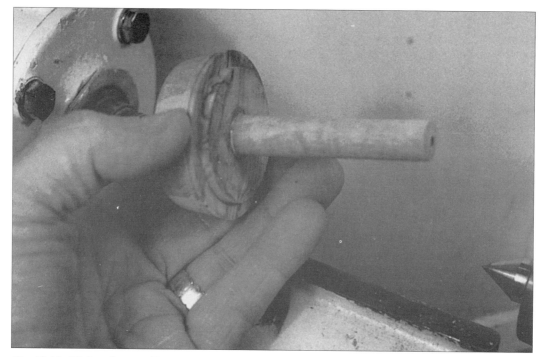

Fig 10.11 Gluing the spindle into the top once it has been cut to length.

the dowel may be turned slightly undersize.

◆ Measure from the tailstock end towards the headstock 69mm (2¾in). Mark in pencil.

◆ Remove the dowel from the lathe.

◆ Accurately saw across the marked line.

◆ Clean off the sawn end.

◆ Take the dowel. Apply glue to what was the tailstock end. Push this glued end into the drilled hole in the top of the barrel (*see* Fig 10.11).

◆ Place the top onto the barrel and test the fit of the dowel into the drilled hole beneath. If it sits well, fine. If it holds the lid high, either clean around the dowel end to reduce its diameter, allowing it to drop into the drilled hole, or trim a little off its length.

◆ When the dowel fits well, set on one side.

Making the stand

◆ For the dimensions of the finished stand, refer to Fig 10.12.

◆ Fit a piece of softwood to a faceplate to make the beginnings of a glue and paper chuck. Face off the softwood.

◆ Take the 60mm (2⅜in) diameter, 12mm (½in) thick piece of olivewood and fix it centrally upon the softwood surface using glue and newspaper as a joint.

◆ Using the tailstock holding a revolving centre, lock it down firmly until the glue has dried.

◆ Turn the edge square and true to a 50mm (2in) diameter.

◆ On the edge, turn a rim top and bottom, and in the centre, turn 'hoops' to match those on the side of the barrel.

◆ Turn the shaping on the face for what will

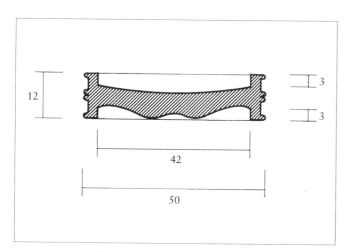

Fig 10.12 A cross section of the stand.

Fig 10.13 Turning the underside of the stand.

be the underside of the stand (*see* Fig 10.13). This shaping will complement the shaping on the barrel's base. A small raised section has a dimple turned into it so that the bump on the underside of the barrel can sit in it and revolve easily. Around the edge of this base is a raised 1.5mm (¹⁄₁₆in) high band. The centre of the piece should be no higher than this raised edge.

◆ Clean up well then remove from the glue

Fig 10.14 Turning a hollow into the softwood to act as a jam chuck to hold the base and turn the top side.

chuck using an old kitchen knife to break the newspaper joint.

◆ Clean up the face of the softwood disc, then turn a 50mm (2in) diameter hollow to match the outer diameter of the base, 9mm (⅜in) deep (*see* Fig 10.14).

◆ Jam the base with its turned face into the hollow and, when satisfied that it is held firmly and fixed level, continue to turn the exposed face.

◆ Leave a 1.5mm (¹⁄₁₆in) wide raised outer edge, turning the inside hollow to accept the barrel base, but this time shape the piece so that it sits firmly without rocking.

◆ Test the barrel base in the shaped area and, when satisfied, remove the piece from the glue chuck.

The base of the barrel is so shaped that when set on the firm side it will not spin and gives no clue to solving the problem. Flip the base over and it can be used to help the barrel to spin.

Fig 10.15 Supporting the barrel in a V block and drilling through the barrel and into the spindle.

Fitting the metal pins

◆ The pins can be made from good-quality nails with clean round shanks, pieces of silver steel, brass rod or anything of the correct diameter that comes to hand.

◆ The bung hole – the disguised entrance of the metal pin hole – will be positioned 10mm (⅜in) up from the base at any point around the rim. Mark the position to be drilled clearly.

◆ Use a bradawl or pointed awl to make the start point for the drill.

◆ Fit the lid onto the barrel, lining up the grain precisely. Use masking tape to hold the lid in position.

◆ Lay the barrel in a wooden V block set on the drill stand.

◆ Fit a 3.5mm (just over ⅛in) drill into the chuck or a drill 0.5mm (¹⁄₅₀in) larger than the metal pins if the size is different from those shown in Fig 10.15.

◆ Support the barrel in the V block so that it will not rock whilst being drilled. Bring the drill directly over the position to be drilled.

◆ The drill must cut precisely down through the centre of the work on a 'diameter' line.

◆ Mark on the drill a position 40mm (1⁹⁄₁₆in) away from its cutting tip.

◆ Drill through the barrel until the depth mark is reached, no deeper.

◆ The dowel held in the barrel's base will also be drilled through so be aware that there will be an uneven patch halfway through.

◆ Remove the piece from the drill making sure that the drilled hole is clear, then set aside.

◆ The drilled hole will be 2mm (¹⁄₁₂in) away from breaking through the opposite wall. Do not be worried if the drill does break through, for a second bung can be turned to fit into the hole to cover the mistake, but avoid the problem if possible.

Calculating the length of the pins

◆ The pin length should be greater than the diameter of the dowel so that when the pin slips into the drilled hole through the dowel there will always be some part held locked

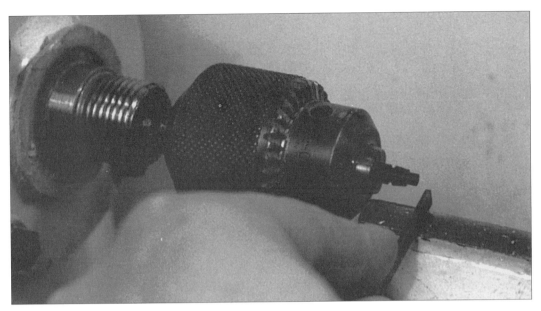

Fig 10.16 *The small bung is turned whilst held in a drill chuck.*

against the outer drilled holes.

◆ The length of the drilled hole is 40mm (1¹⁵⁄₁₆in). The bung depth will be 2.5mm (almost ⅛in), leaving a hole 37.5mm (just over 1⁷⁄₁₆in) long. Take away 9mm (⅜in) for the drilled hole. This leaves 28.5mm (around 1⅛in). Divided by two, this gives 14.25mm (⁹⁄₁₆in). The pins should be cut to this length but make a little allowance for wood dust or raised grain at the ends of the holes, so cut the two pins about 13.5mm metric or ½in imperial (yes, it's smaller).

◆ The ends of the pins will have a slight burr left from the cutting so grind the edges lightly. When grinding these small pieces hold them firmly in mole grips or a similar tool.

◆ From a piece of dark hardwood, turn a small bung 5mm (¼in) long, 2.5mm (just under ⅛in) of which will be turned down to match the drill diameter used to drill the pin hole (*see* Fig 10.16). The remaining length is turned to 4mm (⁵⁄₃₂in) diameter.

◆ This small bung may be turned by holding a small section of wood in a drill chuck held in the headstock.

◆ The end of this piece can be turned without support from the tailstock, but do not leave too great a length unsupported.

◆ Lightly turn the end, nibbling away using fine cuts. Work with either a fine skew chisel or a square-end tool. The exposed end should be turned to fit into the drilled hole. The area closest to the chuck should form the bung end.

◆ Part off closest to the chuck to make a neat end on the bung.

◆ To finish the piece, fit the top onto the barrel with the grain aligned. This will ensure that the drilled hole through the barrel and the dowel will be in line. Turn the barrel on its side with the drilled hole uppermost, then drop in the two metal pins. Push the bung in place but do not glue yet. If necessary hold the bung in position using masking tape. Now try removing the top. It should be firmly held. Spin it and the pins should fly to the ends of their holes. If there are problems make adjustments; clean out the holes, shorten the pins, whatever is necessary. Once the system works well, glue the bung in place. When gluing the bung, apply glue only to the edges of the dowel, not the end, for glue on the end could block or shorten the pin hole. Clean excess glue from around the bung.

Allow the glue to dry. Take the piece apart and polish, and whilst the polish dries think of all those who will shortly be tearing their hair out in frustration!

CHAPTER 11

Chess Set

LIKE MOST TURNERS I HAVE WANTED TO MAKE A CHESS SET BUT HAVE BEEN DISCOURAGED PARTLY BECAUSE I COULD NEVER FIND A GOOD-LOOKING SET I REALLY WANTED TO TURN. HOWEVER, THE MAIN REASON FOR NOT ATTEMPTING A SET WAS THAT MAKING THE KNIGHT ALWAYS POSED A PROBLEM. ARE THE KNIGHT SHAPES CUT ON A FRETSAW? THEN, DO THEY ALL MATCH? ARE THEY FULLY CARVED FROM A SINGLE BLOCK OR IS A COMPROMISE REACHED WHERE THEY ARE TURNED TO SOME REPRESENTATIONAL SHAPE

AND SO DO NOT LOOK HORSE-LIKE? IN THE LATTER CASE, EVERY TIME THE SET IS USED A LENGTHY EXPLANATION HAS TO FOLLOW THAT THE ODD-LOOKING PIECE REALLY IS A KNIGHT.

Well here is the answer. A traditional method of turning is used in a new way: ring or hoop turning, a technique practised in Germany and East European countries for mass-producing wooden toys and animals. A profiled ring is turned, much like a circular picture frame, and each time a slice is taken across the ring an exact copy of that first slice is produced.

Adapting this method, those awkward knights can be turned. By splicing two different coloured woods together to form a block before turning, matching knights for

Fig 11.1 The chess set.

both sides of the chessboard can be produced in one go.

Traditionally the rings or hoops were turned with the grain running vertically. This helped when the pieces were separated by splitting. Here, the grain can run horizontally as the parts can be band sawn apart. This means that the turning will be similar to turning the inside and outside of a bowl.

The chess set design is taken from a set which was recovered from the wreck of the ship *James Matthews* which sank in Cockburn Sound, south of Freemantle on the west coast of Australia in 1841.

Preparation

◆ Cut two blanks of walnut and sycamore each 200mm (8in) long by 90mm (3%₁₆in) wide by 35mm (1⅜in) thick.

◆ For the pawns, cut eight sycamore and eight walnut pieces 60mm (2⅜in) long by 13mm (½in) square.

◆ For the castles, cut two sycamore and two walnut pieces 80mm (3³⁄₁₆in) long by 25mm (1in) square.

◆ For the stems of the knights, cut two sycamore and two walnut pieces 50mm (2in) long by 25mm (1in) square.

◆ For the bishops, cut two sycamore and two walnut pieces 70mm (2¾in) long by 19mm (¾in) square.

◆ For the queens, cut one sycamore and one walnut piece 90mm (3⁹⁄₁₆in) long by 25mm (1in) square.

◆ For the kings, cut one sycamore and one walnut piece 90mm (3⁹⁄₁₆in) long by 25mm (1in) square.

◆ For the bases, cut one sycamore and one walnut piece 600mm (2ft) long by 100mm (4in) wide by 6mm (¼in) thick.

Although walnut and sycamore have been chosen, any two dark and light good-quality hardwoods could be used. Have available the following equipment:

◆ A 100mm (4in) long by 6mm (¼in) Allen bolt and matching nut.

◆ A 3mm (⅛in) square-end tool.

◆ A 9mm (⅜in) skew chisel.

◆ A small gouge.

◆ A 13mm (½in) cheap wood chisel ready to grind to shape. This will be needed to reach awkward areas on the ring-turned knight.

◆ Lathe speed should be 1000rpm for ring turning, and 1750rpm for turning the chess pieces.

THE KNIGHT

Preparing the blank for ring turning

◆ On the 200mm (8in) long walnut and sycamore pieces, using a router, cut a joint down their length 16mm (⅝in) wide and 17.5mm (¹¹⁄₁₆in) deep. NOTE: this joint is placed so that the 35mm (1⅜in) thickness is divided in two.

◆ Glue and clamp these two pieces together. They should now produce one continuous piece 165mm (6½in) wide and 200mm (8in) long.

◆ When the glue has fully set, mark the centre of the glued up block, making sure that the centre exactly straddles the joint (*see* Fig 11.2).

◆ Mark a 160mm (6⁵⁄₁₆in) diameter circle about the centre and cut out on a band saw.

◆ Drill a 6mm (¼in) hole through that centre and counterbore it to accept the head of the Allen bolt.

◆ Fit a pine block 160mm (6⁵⁄₁₆in) in diameter and 50mm (2in) thick onto a faceplate.

◆ Turn the face and edge of the pine block flat and square.

◆ Drill the centre of the block 6mm (¼in) in diameter to accept the Allen bolt.

◆ Remove the block from the faceplate, flip it over and counterbore the back to accept the nut that fits the Allen bolt.

◆ Use epoxy glue to fix the nut into place in the pine block, being very careful when holding it on the Allen bolt to ensure it is aligned and that none of the glue makes contact with the threads.

◆ When the glue has set, flip the block back over and refix to the faceplate and refix the

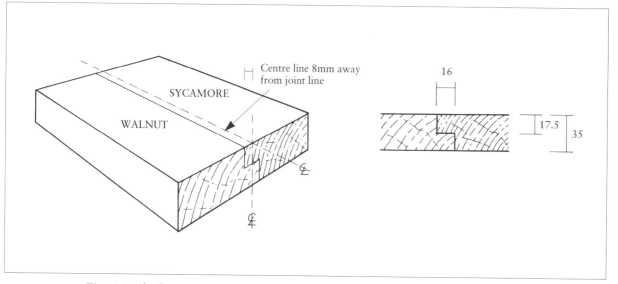

Fig 11.2 Blank construction.

faceplate to the lathe.

◆ Fix the sycamore/walnut joined disc to the softwood using the Allen bolt (*see* Fig 11.3). Lock it firmly in place. Make sure that it is firmly fitted onto the softwood disc all the way around.

◆ If the sycamore/walnut does not run true and on centre, turn so that it runs concentrically to the bolt and the softwood disc.

Marking out and rough shaping of the blank

◆ The knight will stand upright upon the pine block, so the top of its head will be facing towards the tailstock.

◆ As a datum from which to work, mark

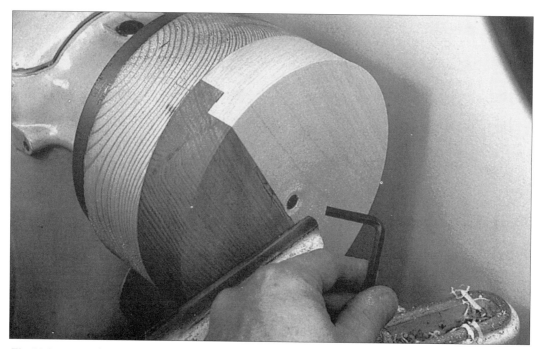

Fig 11.3 Fitting the blank to the softwood base plate using a central bolt hole.

Fig 11.4 *Marking out the lines showing the cutting positions for the top shaping of the knight.*

the top position of the ears 'Line A'. This will be a pencil line drawn with the lathe running, 10mm (⅜in) in from the outer edge.

◆ The pencil circles marked on the face of the block are temporary guides and will be marked Line A, Line B, Line C, etc. These circles are situated directly above the marked positions which bear the same indicator letter, e.g. Position C will be located 9mm (⅜in) directly below the pencil circle, Line C, on the face of the work.

◆ Measure 15mm (⅝in) in from the edge towards the centre and mark a further pencil line – Line B (*see* Fig 11.4).

◆ Measure 27mm (1¹⁄₁₆in) in from the edge to the centre and mark a pencil line – Line C.

◆ Measure 30mm (1³⁄₁₆in) in from the edge to the centre. Mark a pencil line – Line D.

◆ Use a 3mm (⅛in) square-end tool to cut grooves to depth as marking positions (*see* Fig 11.5). To mark the depth on the tool use typist's correction fluid (*see* Fig 11.6). Widen the groove slightly when cutting so that it is not gripped in the cut.

◆ Starting at Line B, cut on the outside of that line away from the centre to a depth of 3mm (⅛in). This marks the top of the

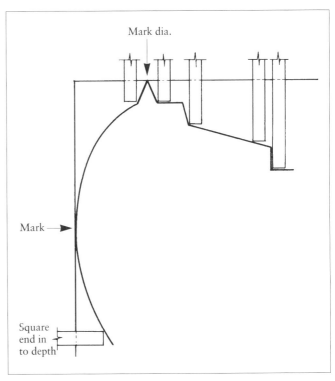

Fig 11.5 *The position of the lines and the grooves on the blank.*

forehead – Position B.

◆ On the centre side of that same line, cut to a depth of 6mm (¼in). This marks the flat front of the eyes and touches the beginning of the long snout – Position B1.

Fig 11.6 Turning into the block on the marked positions to the prescribed depth.

◆ On the centre side of Line C, cut down to a depth of 9mm (⅜in). This marks the front of the nose – Position C.

◆ On the centre side of Line C, cut down to a depth of 12mm (½in). This marks the extent of the lip – Position D.

◆ On the outer edge of the sycamore/walnut disc where it meets the pine disc, cut in to a depth of 5mm (just under ¼in) – Position E.

◆ Finally, measure from the top of the disc down along its outer edge towards the headstock 18mm (¾in) and mark a pencil line with the lathe running. This marks the point where the curve of the knight's back touches the outer wall of the disc (the knight faces towards the centre). This line marks Position F.

◆ Remember always to widen the groove slightly as it is being cut to prevent it being gripped and pulled in. Being nervous helps because that slight tremble of the hand is sufficient to widen the groove. These cuts mark positions at their bases to act as guides when turning. Cut card templates to match the knight's shape to assist in the turning – one of the whole knight's back, one of the

ear to the lip, and one of the lower lip to the base of the chest.

Shaping the outer profile of the knight

Now that all points on the top side are marked out, the turning can begin. Most, if not all, is turned using a gouge. It is very much like turning a bowl, only far more precise. Occasionally the square-end tool may be needed to sharpen up an internal corner.

◆ For the dimensions of the outer profile of the knight, refer to Fig 11.7.

◆ Begin with the ears. Measure 1.5mm (¹⁄₁₆in) either side of the ear datum – Line A. Turn from that line out to those lines 1.5mm (¹⁄₁₆in) away to a depth of 3mm (⅛in) so that slopes are formed and the pointed ear shows.

◆ Now turn from Line F on the side up to the base of the ear in a good, clean, fluent curve (*see* Fig 11.8).

◆ Then cut from F down to Position E at

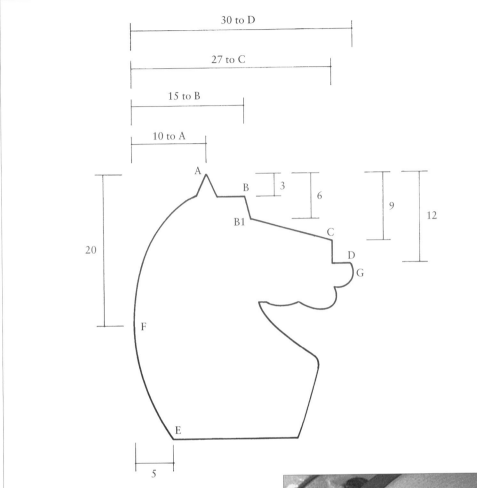

Fig 11.7 *The ring-turned knight, showing the dimensions of the outer profile.*

the junction of the two discs. Again a good fluent curve.

◆ Check the shape of the back against the card template and adjust if necessary.

It is important to cut cleanly from the gouge and to check the work against the template as the work progresses. It is very difficult to judge how the knight is shaping up from external appearances. The template is the only true method of testing the accuracy of the shape.

◆ Now cut the forehead from the base of the ear to Position B.

◆ Turn a clean flat from Position B down to Position C. By now the crisp cutting of both the sycamore and walnut will be apparent.

Fig 11.8 *Turning the outer shape.*

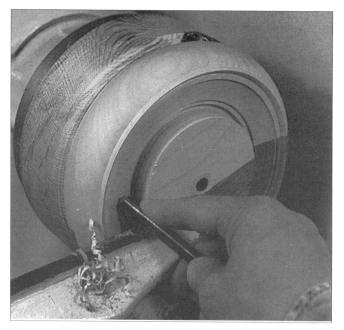

Fig 11.9 *Completing the top shaping.*

the precise shaping of the top of the knight.

◆ Before turning over check that all turning is clean and crisp. Check that the templates fit well to make sure the piece is accurate. Once turned over the top cannot be reworked.

◆ So, still on the top, cut Position G which is a deep cut past the front of the nose at Position D. It is 15mm (⅝in) deep and cut wider towards the centre of the blank. This is made to accept the parting cut from the other side once it is flipped over.

◆ Once satisfied that the top has been accurately finished, undo the Allen bolt and remove the blank from the softwood disc (*see* Fig 11.10).

Also by now any poorly chosen substitutes will be made apparent, so choose the woods with care.

◆ Turn the front lip to Position D. Clean up where necessary and test with the template for

Removing the centre portion

◆ Turn a V groove indent into the pine disc to match the V of the ear on top of the turned ring. Make sure that the diameters are precise.

◆ Fit the blank, now upside down, onto the

Fig 11.10 *Removing the part-turned disc.*

Fig 11.11 Turning out the centre core.

softwood disc. Lock down with the Allen bolt. It does not matter that the Allen bolt head now stands proud. The V groove in the softwood disc and the tightened Allen bolt ensure concentricity.

Shapes other than this knight could be securely fitted to a jam chuck to allow the underside to be turned, but because the knight's back is so well curved this is not an easy proposition. An easy way to make sure that the knight is firmly fixed once the centre and its locking bolt is turned through and removed is to screw the ring to the softwood. The joint between the sycamore and walnut is the most appropriate position to fix the screw because this area will be of little use as a chess piece.

So, drill and countersink on the joint. The screws should go through the centre section of the knight – it's no good fixing a piece that will later be removed – straight down through the ears and into the pine disc. They should be fully countersunk, if not slightly counterbored, so that no metal is showing. These screws are fixed on a line that will not be turned and will therefore be safe. The block will now remain fully secure even when the ring is parted through and the centre portion removed.

◆ Once the knight is positioned, measure 22mm (⅞in) in from the outer edge to the centre. This is Position H, the base of the chest.
◆ Measure 25mm (1in) from the outer edge to the centre, then cut 10mm (⅜inch) deep to mark Position L, the front of the chest.
◆ Also on that 25mm (1in) line, cut 17mm (⅝in) deep for Position J, the underside of the jaw.
◆ At 32mm (1¼in), cut 20mm (¾in) deep to Position K, the underside of the lip.
◆ Remember to keep tools sharp and to widen the grooves when cutting deep.
◆ Now part through at 37mm (1½in) measured from the edge to the centre. Cut until Position G is met.
◆ Turn off the lathe. Withdraw the Allen bolt and remove the centre portion (*see* Fig 11.11).

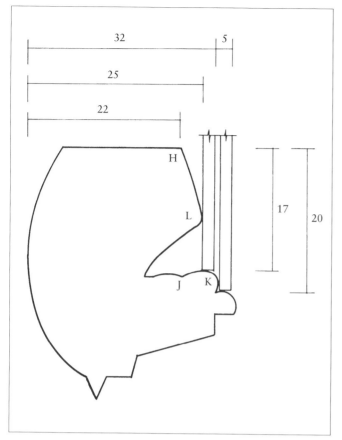

Fig 11.12 The ring-turned knight, showing the dimensions of the inner profile.

Shaping the inner profile of the knight

◆ Now the inner profile of the knight may be turned. For the dimensions, refer to Fig 11.12. Move the tool rest into the work so that the tools are more fully supported.

◆ Turn from Position H to Position J with a reasonable convex curve to shape the chest.

◆ Turn the underpart of the lip, opening the mouth slightly. Then turn the underside of the jaw.

◆ To reach into that area where the front of the chest meets the jaw, grind a suitable shape on the cheap 12mm (½in) wood chisel. Be careful when using this shaped tool to slice from the top and the underside so that the tool cuts rather than scrapes. The final cutting right into the corner between jaw and chest may have to be finished with a scraping action.

◆ Check the profile under the chin and chest by pushing plasticine or some other moulding material into the gap. Push the plasticine into the hollow, withdraw carefully so that the moulded shape is not distorted, check the profile and adjust if necessary.

Fig 11.13 Completing the internal shaping.

◆ When fully satisfied remove the ring – and still the profile cannot be seen (*see* Fig 11.14).

Remember, it is not essential to stick rigidly to the dimensions given. If a better shape can be seen or achieved when turning that's fine, but be sure it is a better shape as it is too late when it is being sliced later.

What is interesting about this turning is the degree of accuracy required to produce this meaningless series of ridges, grooves, coves and beads in order to create the shape within – a shape that cannot be seen until that exciting moment when it is too late to change, and the finished ring removed from the lathe lies on the band saw waiting to be cut.

So this is it. This smooth-ridged ring is ready for slicing. Each cut must be made towards the imagined centre of the ring. The nose faces the centre so that the knight's body will taper from its thicker, heavier back to the smaller, more pointed nose.

◆ Cut first through the main part of the walnut at a point 90° from the joint, all the way across the imagined centre and across through the sycamore. The two halves open up to reveal the shape – success or failure in

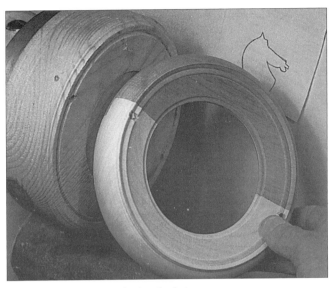

Fig 11.14 Removing the finished ring.

that one cut (*see* Fig 11.15).

◆ The next cut is made on the walnut 12mm (½in) away from the first, again towards the imagined centre, followed by another cut the same distance away.

◆ Repeat for the sycamore, and four knight profiles lie on the band saw table waiting to be cleaned up.

◆ Take a sheet of medium glasspaper and lay it upon a flat surface.

Fig 11.15 And that nerve-racking moment: cutting into the ring for the first time.

◆ Take one of the knights and lay it upon the glasspaper, cut side down. Rub until the surface is smooth, repeat for the other side and other pieces. The knight may be carved or left as a simple profile as you see in Fig 11.15.

TURNING THE REMAINING CHESSPIECES

I like to reduce my reliance on large pieces of equipment like the four-jaw chuck where I can. These pieces tend to impede the free movement of the tool and hand whilst turning. So in many cases I use the larger chuck to help hold pieces so that they may be roughed down to size or so that a holding spigot may be turned on one end. The piece may then be transferred to a small chuck such as a drill chuck, which can be held on its Morse taper in the headstock. This smaller chuck allows more movement around the work when turning the fine details.

◆ This is the best method when it comes to turning the chesspieces. All are turned round whilst held in the four-jaw chuck and then reversed so that the held end is turned round. The one end supported by the revolving centre is turned to a 6mm (¼in) diameter

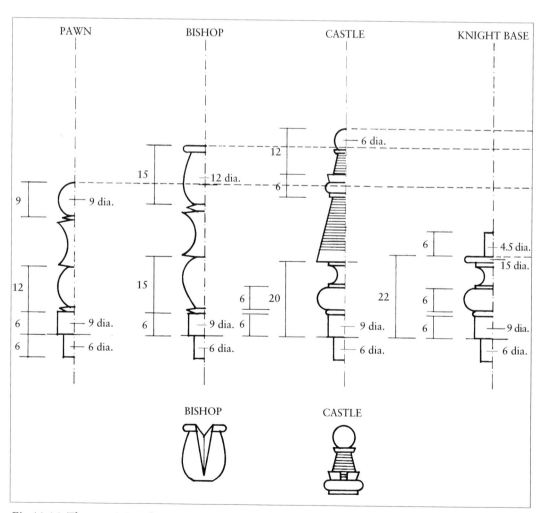

Fig 11.16 *The remaining chesspieces, showing dimensions.*

spigot 16mm (⅝in) long. This spigot is used to hold the work in the small chuck and also acts as the joint between the turned piece and the turned base.

◆ The bases are cut using a 38mm (1½in) plug cutter. Plugs of this diameter are cut from prepared walnut and sycamore 100mm (4in) wide and 6mm (¼in) thick. This seems the quickest and most efficient method of production. The centre of each plug is discovered by using a compass set to the radius of the plug. The point of the compass is then placed on the edge of the plug and an arc struck towards the centre. The point of the compass is moved to another point on the edge of the plug and a further arc is struck. Where the two arcs cross is the centre of the plug. Alternatively an engineers' centre

finder could be used. At the centre of each plug, drill through using a 6mm (¼in) drill.

◆ For the dimensions of the turned pieces, refer to Fig 11.16.

◆ All the pieces are turned using the following method:

◆ Hold the 6mm (¼in) diameter spigot in the drill chuck set in the headstock. Support the other end with a revolving centre.

◆ Turn the piece true and to the major diameter of the chesspiece being turned.

◆ Draw on card the shape of the piece, be it castle, knight stem, pawn, bishop, king or queen. Mark the major points on the card edge.

◆ With the lathe running, hold the template close to the revolving work. Transfer the major points from the template to the work

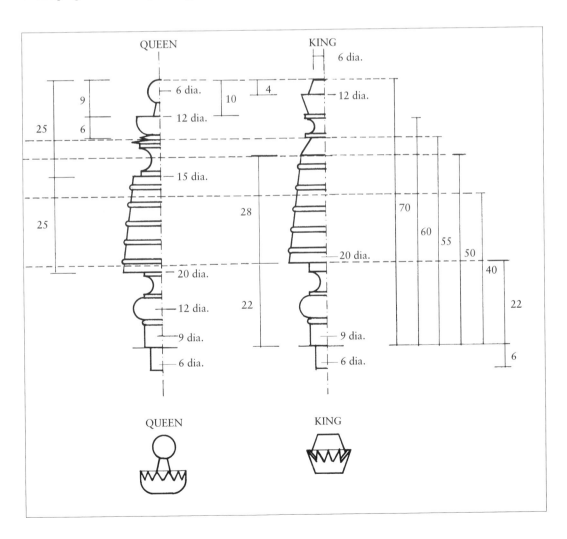

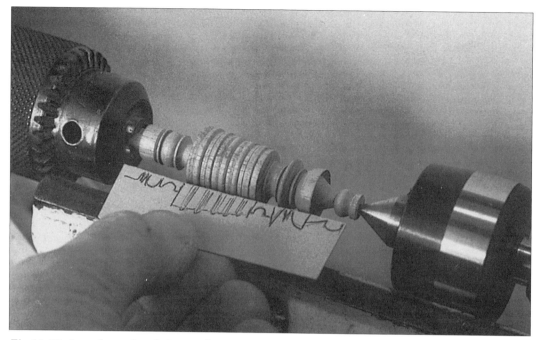

*Fig 11.17 A card template helps mark out
the king.*

(*see* Fig 11.17).

◆ The coves are turned using fine gouges. The convex curves and beads are turned using a fine 6mm (¼in) skew chisel which is made from square tool steel ground across the diagonal. Fine lines can be cut into the pieces using the corner of a square-end tool (*see* Figs 11.18, 11.19 and 11.20).

◆ With the exception of the stem for the knight, which has a 6mm (¼in) spigot turned at the tailstock end, all other pieces have to be parted off at the tailstock end and cleanly turned whilst supported only by the drill chuck. Use light fine cuts of course.

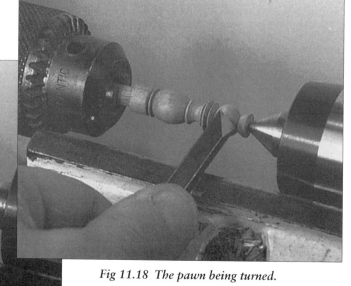

Fig 11.18 The pawn being turned.

*Fig 11.19 The tip of the square-end tool cuts
grooves into the castle sides.*

Fig 11.20 Using the small skew to cut details.

Turning the bases

◆ For the dimensions of the bases, refer to Fig 11.21.

◆ Fit a block of wood into the four-jaw chuck.

◆ Turn its face flat and true.

◆ Drill a 6mm (¼in) hole 9mm (⅜in) deep centrally into that face.

◆ Glue a 12mm (½in) length of 6mm (¼in) dowel into that hole and allow to dry. When dry, clean away any remaining glue from the surface between the dowel and the surrounding wood.

◆ Take a plug-cut piece. Apply some pieces of double-sided Sellotape to its underside, then press the hole on that side over the dowel to the block held in the chuck.

◆ Bring the tailstock up to support the work, pushing the revolving centre into the hole in the plug.

◆ Turn the outer edge to a true 35mm (1⅜in) diameter (*see* Fig 11.22).

◆ Turn the shaping on the foot leading up to a 12mm (½in) diameter part around the hole. Clean up thoroughly.

◆ Withdraw the tailstock and turn the top of the 12mm (½in) part around the hole perfectly flat so that it will make a good joint with the turned chesspiece. Take light cuts because the base is only held on the small dowel and double-sided Sellotape (*see* Fig 11.23).

◆ Remove from the dowel and move on to the next base.

Once all the bases are turned, carry out the finishing touches to the chesspieces. Cut the crenellations in the castles, the mitres in the bishops and the segments in the kings' and queens' crowns. These cuts may be made using a junior hacksaw and cleaned up with

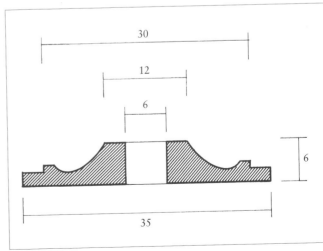

Fig 11.21 A cross section of the base for the chesspieces.

Fig 11.22 The base is turned whilst held between the centre and the small stub tenon.

Fig 11.23 Double-sided Sellotape holds the base long enough for the finishing turnery.

needle files. When cutting and cleaning these, fix masking tape to areas of the chesspieces where the saw or file may stray and cause damage. It is better to mark the masking tape, which can be removed and replaced, than to mark the chesspiece. Better still, apply the masking tape and plenty of concentration to avoid any stray cuts at all.

◆ Drill into the underside of the knight, centrally of course, to take the stem.
◆ Next, polish all the pieces, stems, bases, knights, tops and bottoms. It may have to be a production-line job.

And then all that remains is to cut the 6mm (¼in) round tenon accurately to length and glue the pieces together very carefully for a fully turned chess set.

CHAPTER 12

Balancing Egg

THIS NEAT LITTLE TRICK WAS SHOWN TO ME BY A MAGICIAN FRIEND. HE HANDED ME A SMALL PLASTIC EGG AND ASKED ME TO BALANCE IT UPON ITS END. AS EXPECTED I COULD NOT. IT JUST DID NOT WANT TO STAY UPRIGHT, YET EVERY TIME MY FRIEND TRIED, IT BALANCED PERFECTLY. HE HAD A SECOND SIMILAR PLASTIC EGG WITH A SLIGHT DIFFERENCE: THE TOP WAS MADE OF CLEAR PLASTIC AND THE TRICK COULD CLEARLY BE SEEN. A BALL BEARING RAN FREELY AROUND AN INNER RIM AND THIS SET THE EGG OFF BALANCE. THERE WAS A SMALL RAMP LEADING TO A CENTRALLY PLACED INDENT. BY CAREFULLY MOVING THE EGG, THE BALL BEARING COULD BE ENCOURAGED UP THE RAMP TO SETTLE IN THE INDENT WHERE IT WAS CENTRALLY PLACED, ALLOWING THE EGG TO BALANCE.

It was impressive to watch the almost unnoticeable movement of the 'magician' manipulating the egg so that it would balance and the equally neat move when handing it over to knock the ball bearing off its unseen perch.

So how would one be made in wood? If it were the size of the plastic egg the walls would have to be so thin that it would be too fragile. It would need to be larger. The walls of the egg would need to be turned reasonably thin so that the ball bearing would be sufficiently heavy to counter the weight opposing it.

Showy, well-figured woods are an ideal choice, for a feature in the grain can be used

Fig 12.1 The balancing egg.

to identify the location of the hidden internal ramp. I chose laburnum which had a patch of white sapwood showing and used that as the key.

The egg will be made up in three sections: the hollow base, the ramp turned as a cone and the hollow top.

Preparation

◆ Cut a piece of your chosen wood 200mm (8in) long by 90mm (3¾6in) square.
◆ Have ready a ball bearing of about 14mm (⅝6in) diameter.

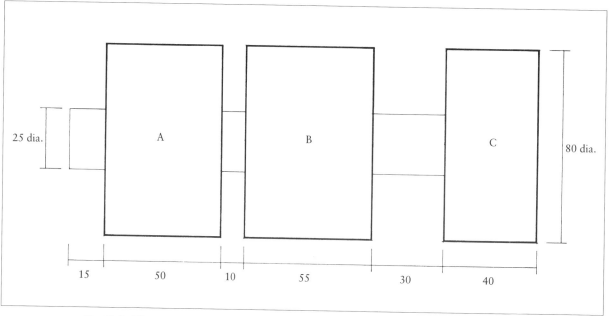

25 dia.

A

B

C

80 dia.

15   50   10   55   30   40

Fig 12.2 The turned blank.

◆ Have a piece of thick veneer ready about 2mm (¹⁄₂in) thick either band sawn or purchased.
◆ Have a 120mm (4¾in) diameter, 50mm (2in) thick piece of softwood set on a faceplate ready.
◆ Lathe speed 1500rpm

Turning the blank

◆ For the dimensions of the turned blank, refer to Fig 12.2.
◆ Fit the block between centres and turn to an 80mm (3³⁄₁₆in) diameter.
◆ Square off the work at the tailstock end.
◆ From that point, measure 40mm (1⁹⁄₁₆in) towards the headstock, followed by 30mm (1¹⁄₂in).
◆ This second section is to be turned down to a 25mm (1in) diameter.
◆ From that point, measure again towards the headstock 55mm (2³⁄₁₆in) followed by a further 10mm (³⁄₈in). This last narrow section is to be turned down to a 25mm (1in) diameter.
◆ From that point, measure 50mm (2in) again towards the headstock. The final 15mm (⁵⁄₈in) left, next to the driving dog, is turned down to a 25mm (1in) diameter.
◆ The three 80mm (3³⁄₁₆in) diameter parts are marked as follows: the part closest to the headstock is A, the middle part is B and the part closest to the tailstock is C (*see* Fig 12.3).
◆ Cut A and B apart. The 25mm (1in) spigot joining them should be turned or cut away from both pieces.
◆ The spigot at the headstock end will be used to hold A whilst turning.
◆ Cut the 25mm (1in) spigot joining B and C in half so each has a 15mm (⁵⁄₈in) length which may be held when turning B and C.
◆ Set A and B to one side.

Turning the egg

◆ Now make up six card templates for the inner and outer shapes of A, B and C (*see* Figs 12.4 –12.9).
◆ Fit a three- or four-jaw chuck to the headstock and grip the spigot on the end of C. Push the work hard up to the jaws to ensure that it runs true and on centre.
◆ Turn the end of C flat and true and to a diameter of 75mm (3in).
◆ Mark a pencil circle 66mm (2⅝in) in diameter concentrically on the face of C.
◆ Turn a step 3mm (⅛in) deep on the outside of that marked pencil circle. Make sure that the step is cut square and flat.
◆ Mark a second pencil circle 34mm (1¹¹⁄₃₂in) in diameter concentrically upon the face of C (*see* Fig 12.10).

Fig 12.3 *Parts A, B and C turned from one piece.*

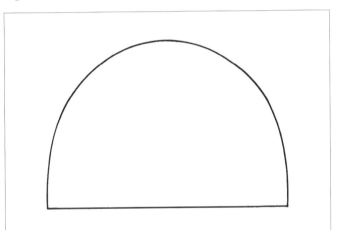

Fig 12.4 *The template for inner A.*

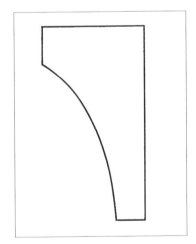

Fig 12.6 *The template for outer A.*

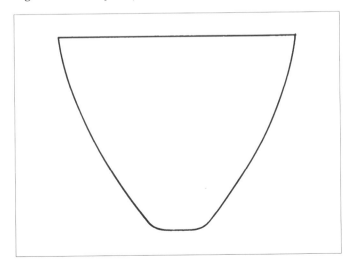

Fig 12.5 *The template for inner B.*

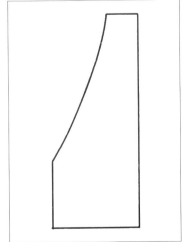

Fig 12.7 *The template for outer B.*

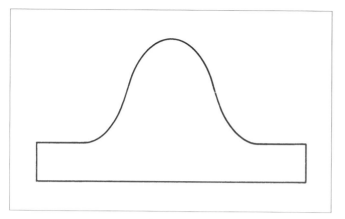

Fig 12.8 The template for inner C.

Fig 12.9 The template for outer C.

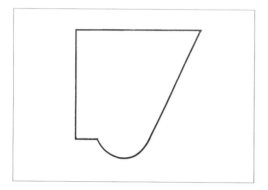

A Guide to Hollowing Out Forms to Match a Template

Before beginning the internal shaping, it is worth reading the following.

Look at the shape to be turned. Decide on its form. Is it rounded following a natural curve or is it more straight sided? Is the curve long and gentle or does it turn quickly? Follow the basic form that has been observed, testing the template against the shape. Sometimes a half-template can be more helpful.

It seems obvious, but turn wood away from those areas that are proud, i.e. the parts the template touches and is held up on, and leave the hollower parts, progressively moving deeper into the work, maintaining the basic shape and keeping the tool movement constant. This will ensure that the shape remains the same whilst becoming deeper and larger. Refine the shape towards the end of the process.

◆ Begin the internal shaping, cutting 26mm (1in) deep and checking the shape against the template (*see* Fig 12.11). Turn the majority

Fig 12.10 The underside of Part C being turned.

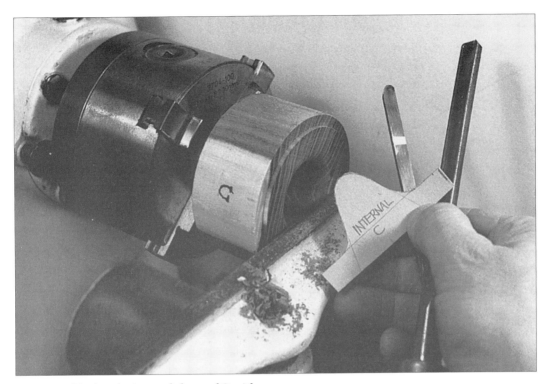

Fig 12.11 *Testing the internal shape of C with a template.*

out using a gouge. The final tight inner portion can be cleaned out using a small round-nosed tool.

◆ Only when you are fully satisfied that the inner shaping is correct and the work is fully cleaned up, can it be removed from the chuck and the spigot cut off.

◆ Remove the chuck and replace with the prepared faceplate and its attached softwood disc.

◆ Turn the softwood face flat and true and mark a 66mm (2⅝in) pencil circle.

◆ Turn inside the marked circle to a depth of 3mm (⅛in).

◆ Fit C onto the jam chuck, joint first, supporting the end with the revolving centre held in the tailstock.

◆ Measure 3mm (⅛in) up from the softwood. At that point and towards the tailstock, turn down to a 40mm (1⁹⁄₁₆in) diameter.

◆ Measure again from the face of the softwood 33mm (1¼in) towards the tailstock. At that point and towards the tailstock, turn down to a 15mm (⅝in) diameter.

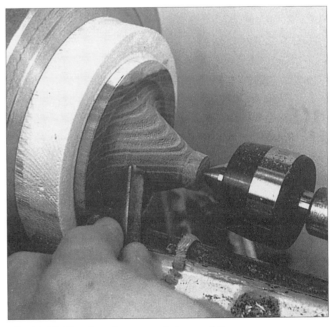

Fig 12.12 *Turning the external shape of C.*

◆ Join the start of the 40mm (1⁹⁄₁₆in) diameter to the start of the 15mm (⅝in) diameter so that it tapers towards the tailstock (*see* Fig 12.12).

◆ Next, turn out the groove in which the ball bearing will sit. The groove must allow the bearing to move freely and must not grip

Fig 12.13 *Testing the marble or ball bearing in place.*

it (*see* Fig 12.13). Consideration must be given to the gap left when the top is fitted over. There must be enough space in the turned groove so that the wall of the egg does not ram the ball bearing into the groove or against the conical side of the ramp.

◆ Mark a pencil circle of 69mm (2¾in) diameter concentrically on the outer edge of the ball groove.

◆ On the outside of this line, turn a 1.5mm (¹⁄₁₆in) deep step, making sure that it is square and flat.

Before moving on to the next stage, check that the jam chuck is firm. If it is loose then a newspaper and glue joint may be used but *only glue onto the horizontal outer surface;* do not let any glue into the step, otherwise the joint will be permanent. Also, make absolutely sure that there is newspaper separating the pieces.

◆ Measure 33mm (1¹¹⁄₃₂in) from the surface of the softwood towards the tailstock. At that point, on the tailstock side of the line, part off or cut off.

◆ Withdraw the tailstock.

Fig 12.14 *Testing the internal shape of A with a template.*

Fig 12.15 *Test C in Part A.*

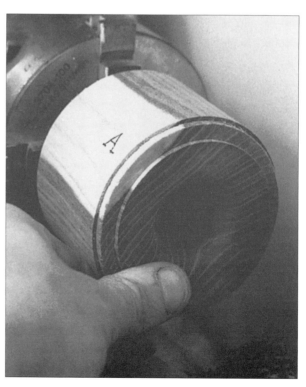

◆ On the now exposed top, turn a cup to hold the ball bearing about 6mm (¼in) deep and shaped to match the ball bearing curve. Clean up thoroughly.

◆ Remove the piece from the jam chuck. If glue and paper have been used, carefully scrape the remnants from the joint line.

◆ Remove the faceplate and replace with a three- or four-jaw chuck.

◆ Hold Part A in the chuck on the 25mm (1in) spigot.

◆ Square off the end face and then turn a step 1.5mm (¹⁄₁₆in) deep on the inside of a 69mm (2¾in) diameter pencil line to match the step on the top of C.

◆ Mark a 66mm (2⅝in) diameter pencil circle concentrically on the face of A and begin turning on the inside of that line to match the template.

◆ Turn out to a depth of 45mm (1¾in). Judgement is required to match the template shape (*see* Fig 12.14).

◆ The depth of A and height of C are critical, so once the inside has been satisfactorily turned, test C in place with the ball bearing Blu-tacked in place (*see* Fig 12.15). There should be sufficient space above the ball bearing, so place a small piece of Blu-tack on top. If the fit is good, fine; if not, adjust.

◆ Remove Part A from the chuck.

◆ Fit Part B in the chuck holding on the 25mm (1in) spigot. Make sure that it runs true and on centre, then turn the face flat and square.

◆ Mark a 66mm (2⅝in) diameter pencil circle concentrically on the face of B.

◆ Begin turning out B on the inside of that marked line to a depth of 50mm (2in). Ensure that the internal shape of B matches the template (*see* Fig 12.16).

◆ Fit the underside of C to B checking that the joint between the two is tight and accurate (*see* Fig 12.17). Adjust where necessary.

◆ Once Part B has been turned, leave it in the chuck and assemble all the pieces to check that the fit is satisfactory.

Fig 12.16 *Testing the internal shape of B with a template.*

Fig 12.17 *Fitting C into B.*

Fig 12.18 A fitted on top. The template length of the egg is marked.

Occasionally a surface of torn grain may be met close to the joint which, if turned away, could cause thinning and weakness at the joint. To firm an area such as this, rub with a little thinned-down glue. Leave to dry, then turn. The surface will have more strength, and less wood will need to be turned away to reach a clear strong surface. Use the glue sparingly for it can spread through the surface causing problems when applying the finish.

Good tight joints are a benefit. They will allow the assembled piece to be turned fully and easily. Try to ensure that tight joints are produced (*see* Fig 12.22). Loose-fitting joints can cause problems, allowing one piece to move off centre from another.

◆ Remove Part B from the chuck and the chuck from the headstock.
◆ Replace the chuck with the faceplate holding the softwood disc.
◆ Drill a 25mm (1in) diameter hole into the softwood. Glue the 25mm (1in) spigot attached to B into the hole. Fit C and A in place. Bring the tailstock holding the

revolving centre forward to apply pressure whilst the glue dries.
◆ Once the glue is dry, take the piece apart.
◆ Measure the precise depth of B – add 3mm (⅛in) for the wall thickness. It should then be 53mm (2⅛in).
◆ Mark a line on the outside of B, 53mm (2⅛in) away from the joint line.
◆ Measure the precise depth of A, adding 3mm (⅛in) for wall thickness. It should be 48mm (1⅞in) (*see* Fig 12.18).
◆ Mark a pencil line on the outside of A 48mm (1⅞in) away from the joint line.
◆ Measure the precise internal diameter of A at the joint line. Add two wall thicknesses, each 3mm (⅛in). It should make 72mm (2¹³⁄₁₆in). Make a clear note on paper and fit it to the lathe somewhere safe.
◆ Measure the precise internal diameter of B and add two wall thicknesses. It should be 72mm (2¹³⁄₁₆in) also. Make a note on that same piece of paper.
◆ These last two measurements should be the same but it is wise to check. If there is a discrepancy, take the larger size of the two.

Fig 12.19 Testing the external shape of the egg.

◆ Fit A and C back onto B. Bring up the tailstock holding the revolving centre to support, making sure the grain aligns.

◆ Turn the block to 72mm (2¹³⁄₁₆in) diameter.

◆ Measure from the joint line A/C 40mm (1⁹⁄₁₆in) towards the tailstock. At that point, turn down to a 40mm (1⁹⁄₁₆in) diameter on the tailstock side of the line.

◆ Now measure from the joint line B/C 38mm (1½in) towards the headstock and at that point turn down to a 40mm (1⁹⁄₁₆in) diameter on the headstock side of the line.

◆ These measurements and diameters were calculated by drawing the internal egg shape and then drawing the wall in place, then measuring along and down.

◆ Now very carefully turn the external shape. First turn Part B using the template to judge and the turned down section to work up to (*see* Fig 12.19).

This work can be a little nerve-racking because if you cut too deeply the tool will break into the internal hollow. Templates for inside and out must be marked out accurately and then the inside and out must be turned with equal accuracy.

◆ Now turn as close to the end shaping of both A and B as possible without parting off (*see* Fig 12.20).

◆ Make sure that the joint at C is turned fluently into the whole egg shape.

Fig 12.20 The partly finished shape.

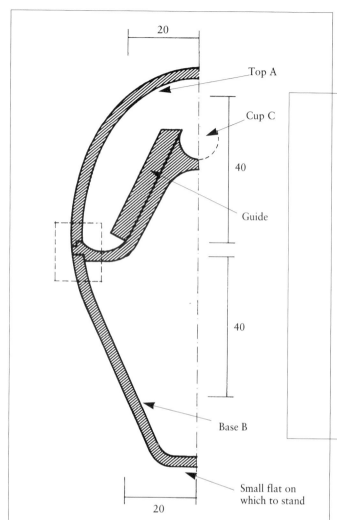

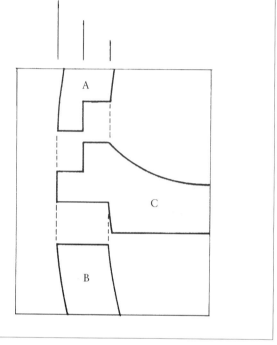

Fig 12.21 *A cross section through the balancing egg.*

Fig 12.22 *A detail of the joint.*

◆ All that remains is to make a jam chuck so that the ends of both A and B can be cleanly turned.

◆ The end of A is turned fully round like the top of an egg (*see* Fig 12.23).

◆ The end of B needs to be turned with a flat upon which it can stand (*see* Fig 12.24).

◆ Glue Part C into Part B, ramp uppermost. If the pieces are held in the lathe, pressed between the softwood faceplate and the revolving centre, pressure may be applied whilst the glue dries.

◆ Once the glue has dried, fit the ball bearing into the hollow and test that the half egg balances. Adjust the flat foot if necessary. It will be noticed that if the ball bearing is placed in the hollow at the base of the ramp it is impossible to balance the egg.

Making the ramp

◆ Cut two pieces of thick veneer to shape, calling them Guide A1 and Backstop B1 (*see* Fig 12.26).

Fig 12.23 *The end of A is finished in a jam chuck.*

Fig 12.24 The jam chuck base and turned end.

Fig 12.25 The finished parts.

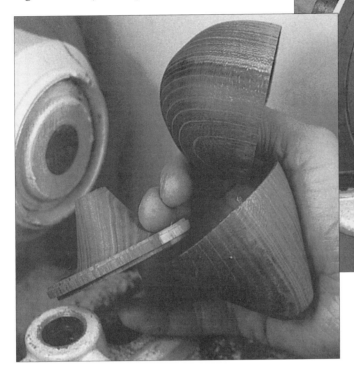

◆ Cut away half the side of the top cup (into which the ball bearing fits) to half its depth. File away a little of the ramp as a little encouragement (*see* Fig 12.27). This cut area should be positioned opposite a notable piece of patterned grain.

◆ Glue two small pieces of packing veneer at right angles to one another as shown in Fig 12.28. These will lift the veneer away from the top of the hollow allowing the ball bearing to drop into place more easily.

◆ Laminate the back of the veneer piece with paper to add strength.

◆ Drill and countersink a hole in both A1 and B1 to match the position of the veneer packing pieces.

◆ Drill pilot holes through the packing pieces to match the positions of the holes drilled in A1 and B1.

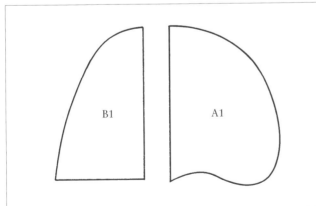

Fig 12.26 The templates for the veneer ramp guide and back stop.

Fig 12.27 The top of the cone with the hollow partially cut away to help the ball bearing to run in.

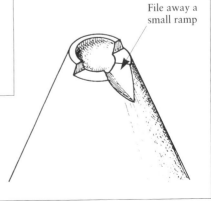

File away a small ramp

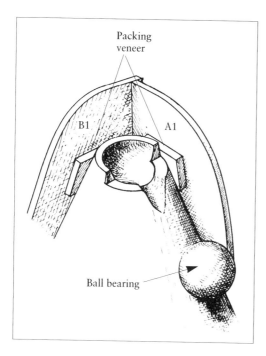

Packing
veneer

B1 · A1

Ball bearing

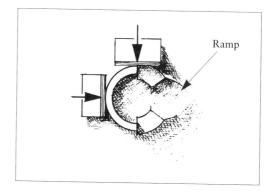

Fig 12.28 The top view of the hollow for the ball bearing, showing the position of the patches of veneer.

Fig 12.29 The guide and backstop fitted in place to help guide the ball bearing.

Ramp

◆ Screw A1 and B1 in place (*see* Figs 12.29 and 12.30).
◆ Check that the ball bearing is guided up the ramp into the top hollow correctly.
◆ Fit the top piece of the egg and check that the ball bearing will roll up the slope and that nothing snags and the egg balances.
◆ When satisfied, remove the top. Remove the screws from the veneer pieces, then screw

and glue them back in position.
◆ When the glue is dry, make an epoxy resin glue bandage for the back of the veneer to give added support. Remember that a heavy ball bearing rattling around inside could do damage. So cut a single piece of cotton material the shape of the two veneer pieces together.
◆ Mix epoxy resin glue and apply to the back of the veneer. Push the material onto the glue making sure that it works well into the weave.
◆ Allow the glue to dry fully before fitting the top.
◆ Do one more test run to check.
◆ Finally, before fixing the top, make a note of the ramp's position. See if there is some recognizable grain pattern close by so that when it is fully closed the trick can be worked.
◆ Once the position has been established the top may be glued in place but there are two last things to consider: firstly and most vitally, place the ball bearing inside; secondly, do not allow too much glue in the joint for it may squeeze out inside and, at the least, impede the ball bearing and, at worst, glue it firmly in place.
◆ With the glue in the joint and the ball bearing inside, press the pieces firmly together in the lathe between shaped wooden blocks.

Clean up the joint and, when dry, polish the piece. Then perplex someone.

Fig 12.30 The ramp veneers fitted in place.

CHAPTER 13

Opening Egg and Rosebud

THIS WOODEN EGG, WHEN OPENED, REVEALS A DELICATE WOODEN ROSE-BUD. ALTHOUGH INSPIRED BY A FABERGÉ EGG THE DESIGN DOES NOT SHARE THE GLITTER AND ORNAMENT OF THOSE FABULOUS AND BEJEWELLED ENAMEL EGGS. A LITTLE MORE REFINED WITH CLEAN LINES, IT IS MADE OF FOUR SYCAMORE SECTIONS. EACH SECTION IS DIVIDED BY A BAND OF SANDALWOOD.

The surprise is not the egg nor its rosewood hinge but the rosebud hidden inside. The sepals and stem are turned from holly – clean, white, with a delicate grain pattern. The petals are from pink ivory wood, a dusky rose pink – four separate petals which push against the holly sepals waiting to burst into flower.

I chose holly for, at first, I considered dyeing the stem and sepals green to make the rosebud more lifelike but, once turned, I found the delicate white far more satisfying, and why pretend? It is wood and should look like wood.

If a rose of a redder hue is required then try padauk or, for a deep purple bud, use purpleheart; a yellow rosebud is more difficult, though not impossible. Search for a thorny garden shrub called berberis or for mahonia which blossoms yellow over holly-type leaves midwinter. The scent from those yellow flowers is like lily of the valley – so out of place amongst the frost. Both of these woods provide brilliant canary yellow wood,

Fig 13.1. The egg with the rosebud inside.

but only in small sections.

If you want to make the eggshell more showy try finding and using some of that elusive quilted maple; now that would have the quality of a real Fabergé egg and provide a perfect and most unusual Easter gift.

Preparation

◆ Cut four pieces of sycamore 150mm (6in) long by 40mm (1⅟₁₆in) square.

◆ Cut a length of sandalwood 150mm (6in)

long by 85mm (3⅜in) wide by 3mm (⅛in) thick.

◆ Cut two pieces of sandalwood 150mm (6in) long by 40mm (1¹⁄₁₆in) wide by 3mm (⅛in) thick.

◆ These pieces of sandalwood are dividers, so will need to be planed both sides to ensure a good tight joint.

It will depend upon the quality of the blade in the band saw or circular saw blade used to cut the sycamore as to whether the cut surface should be planed or left as it is.

◆ Several pieces of dark veneer are needed. I chose walnut. Four pieces 150mm (6in) long by 40mm (1¹⁄₁₆in) wide and two pieces 150mm (6in) long by 85mm (3⅜in) wide.

◆ A piece of holly or similar close-grained hardwood 60mm (2⅜in) long by 35mm (1⁷⁄₁₆in) square is needed for the bud.

◆ A piece of pink ivory wood or substitute coloured hardwood 60mm (2⅜in) long by 35mm (1⁷⁄₁₆in) square is required for the petals .

◆ A small section of ebony or similar dense hardwood is required for the hinge.

◆ Two pieces of 90mm (3⅛in) square 6mm (¼in) thick applewood or similar hardwood are needed.

◆ Lathe speed should be 1250rpm for the egg, and 1750rpm for the rosebud.

THE EGG

Making and turning the blank

◆ For the dimensions of the turned blank, refer to Fig 13.2.

◆ Take four pieces of sycamore 150mm (6in) by 40mm (1¹⁄₁₆in) square.

◆ Make sure that one face of each of the pieces is planed flat, square and true.

◆ Take two of the blocks. Arrange them so that the grain is running in the same direction and the planed faces are opposite each other.

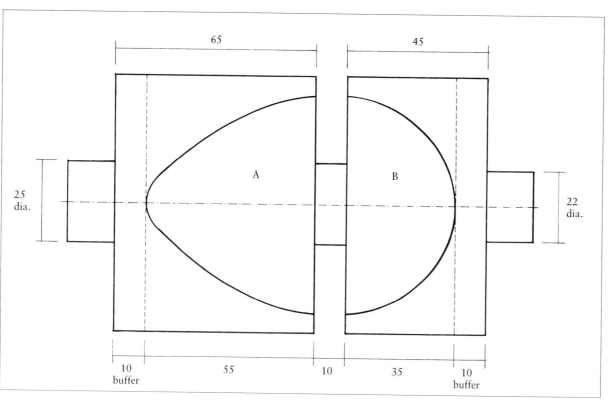

Fig 13.2 The turned blank.

Fig 13.3 The first part of the lamination.

Fig 13.4 All four parts accurately located and glued.

◆ Take two pieces of 40mm (1%₆in) wide walnut veneer and a similar piece of sandalwood.

◆ Make a sandwich of these pieces without glue first of all.

◆ The order should be: sycamore/walnut veneer/sandalwood/walnut veneer/sycamore – planed face to planed face.

◆ Cramp up with two or more G-cramps. This ensures (1) that the pieces fit well – adjust if necessary – and (2) that the cramps are set at the correct distance and are ready.

◆ Remove the cramps and separate the pieces, but lay them out in order.

◆ Using glue and a spreader, apply glue to the inner face of the first piece of sycamore, then lay the walnut veneer on top.

◆ Apply glue to the top surface of that walnut veneer and lay the sandalwood on top.

◆ Apply glue to the top surface of the sandalwood and lay the next walnut veneer on top.

◆ Apply glue to the top surface of the walnut veneer, then complete the sandwich by laying the sycamore planed edge down.

◆ Cramp up, making sure that the edges line up well without slippage, and leave to dry (*see* Fig 13.3).

◆ Prepare the second block in the same way.

◆ Once the glue in both blocks has dried, plane one side of the 85mm (3⅜in) wide

surfaces flat and true.

◆ Test the blocks together planed face to planed face and adjust until they fit perfectly.

◆ Now make a dry sandwich: one block with planed face up, walnut veneer on top, followed by a wide piece of sandalwood, followed by veneer and finally the block with planed face down.

◆ Cramp up firmly but make sure that the centre of the sandwich on both previously glued blocks lines up accurately each end. Mark datum lines to help relocation.

◆ Separate the pieces, laying them so that they can be replaced in sequence.

◆ Spread glue onto the planed surface of the block. Lay on the veneer.

◆ Glue the veneer surface. Lay on the sandalwood.

◆ Glue the sandalwood surface. Lay on the veneer.

◆ Glue the veneer surface. Lay on the block with planed side down.

◆ Now cramp up firmly and make *absolutely* sure that the centre of both blocks lines up accurately (*see* Fig 13.4). Once the glue has started to set it cannot be altered and a mistake in alignment will be there forever as a reminder.

◆ Leave the glue to dry.

◆ Once the glue is dry, set the block between centres making sure that both the driving dog and revolving centre are dead on the intersection of the sandalwood pieces.

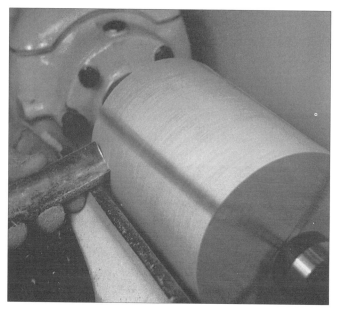

Fig 13.5 Turning the block to a round.

◆ Turn down to a 75mm (3in) diameter (*see* Fig 13.5).

◆ At the tailstock end, measure 15mm (⅝in) towards the headstock. Turn this area down to a 22mm (⅞in) diameter to match a drill of that size.

◆ From that 15mm (⅝in) line again towards the headstock, measure 45mm (1¾in). Mark a pencil line around at that point. From the tailstock to this line is Part B.

◆ Measure a 10mm (⅜in) gap and turn this section down to a 25mm (1in) diameter. This is the area where the two pieces will be parted.

◆ From the end of that gap, measure 65mm (2½in) still towards the headstock. This section, from the parting off area to the headstock, is Part A.

◆ The remaining 15mm (⅝in) closest to the headstock is turned down to 25mm (1in) to match a drill of that size.

◆ Mark a datum across A and B, then saw the two pieces apart through the 10mm (⅜in) wide gap (*see* Fig 13.6). Set the two pieces aside.

◆ Remove the driving dog from the headstock.

Fig 13.6 Spigots are turned at either end and a centre parting is cut.

Turning the applewood discs

◆ For the dimensions of the applewood discs, refer to Fig 13.7.

◆ On a faceplate, fit a softwood disc about 150mm (6in) in diameter, 50mm (2in) thick.

◆ Turn the softwood face flat and true and the edges square.

◆ Onto the softwood, fix concentrically an 80mm (3³⁄₁₆in) diameter, 6mm (¼in) thick piece of applewood, using newspaper and glue so that the piece may be split off once turned to shape.

◆ Bring the tailstock forward holding a revolving centre to apply pressure and to help centre the disc whilst the glue dries (*see* Fig 13.8).

◆ Once the glue has dried, turn the outside of the disc to an accurate 75mm (3in) diameter.

◆ Mark in pencil a 64mm (2½in) diameter circle on the face of the applewood disc.

◆ On the outside of that pencil line, turn a 2mm (³⁄₃₂in) deep step to the outer edge. Mark the depth on the face of the square-end tool to ensure accuracy.

◆ Mark a letter 'A' on the disc, for it will eventually fit Part A (*see* Fig 13.9).

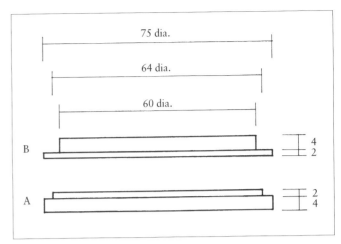

Fig 13.7 *Applewood dividers.*

◆ Split the applewood disc away from the softwood and set it to one side.

◆ Face off the softwood, then glue a second 80mm (3³⁄₁₆in) diameter applewood disc in place, again using the newspaper and glue technique.

◆ Turn the disc to an accurate 75mm (3in) diameter.

◆ Mark in pencil a 60mm (2⅜in) diameter circle and on the outside of that turn a 4mm

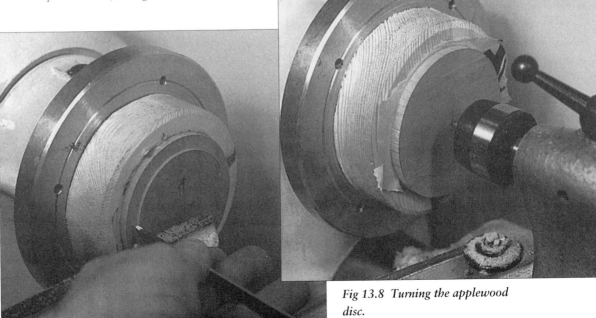

Fig 13.8 *Turning the applewood disc.*
Fig 13.9 *The letter A indicates into which side it will fit.*

(¾₆in) deep step, square and flat.

◆ Mark the letter 'B' on the disc then split it away from the softwood and set to one side.

◆ Mark a datum on the edge of each applewood disc to indicate similar grain direction so that they can be aligned with the datum mark on the blank laminated blocks.

Turning Parts A and B

◆ Face off the softwood disc. Drill a 22mm (⅞in) diameter hole, 15mm (⅝in) deep to accept the turned spigot on the end of Part B (*see* Fig 13.10).

◆ Glue around the spigot and the end face of B.

◆ Press the glued spigot into the drilled hole and bring forward the tailstock holding the revolving centre.

◆ Press the revolving centre into the face of B and tighten the tailstock to add pressure whilst the glue sets (*see* Fig 13.11).

◆ Once the glue has set, face off the end of B and mark upon that surface a 60mm (2⅜in) diameter pencil circle.

◆ On the inside of that circle, turn a 4mm (³₆in) deep step.

◆ Take the applewood disc marked B and check that the steps fit together. Adjust if necessary.

◆ Glue the step on the applewood. Align the

Fig 13.10 Drilling into the softwood to accept the spigot of Part B.

Fig 13.11 Part B is glued onto the softwood block.

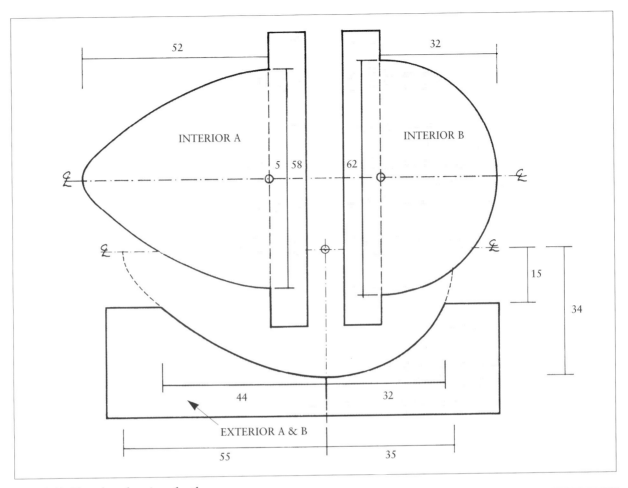

Fig 13.12 *Template drawings for the egg.*

datum marker and push onto Piece B. Apply pressure with the tailstock whilst the glue dries.

◆ Whilst the glue is drying mark and cut out from card the three templates shown in Fig 13.12 as Interior A, Interior B and Exterior A and B.

◆ On the now-exposed but newspaper-covered applewood fixed to B, mark in pencil a 62mm (2⅞in) diameter circle.

◆ On the inside of this pencil line, turn through the applewood and into the sycamore, hollowing out the interior of the blank to match the template 'Interior B'. Turn to a depth of 32mm (1¼in) (*see* Fig 13.13).

◆ Check the shaping regularly with the template and keep the tools sharp (*see* Fig 13.14).

◆ When the internal shaping is exact, clean out, glasspapering smooth, then part off close to the softwood disc.

Fig 13.13 *Turning through the disc into Part B.*

◆ Face off the softwood disc, then drill a 25mm (1in) hole 15mm (⅝in) deep.

◆ Take Part A and glue the 25mm (1in) diameter spigot and the surrounding face. Press the spigot into the drilled hole. Bring forward the tailstock holding the revolving

Fig 13.14 *Testing that the template fits accurately.*

Fig 13.15 *The appropriate applewood disc is glued to Part A, having been turned to accept. A joint is turned on the top surface of the applewood, and Part B is tested against it.*

Fig 13.16 *Testing that the internal shape of Part A matches the template.*

Fig 13.17 *Part B is fitted to Part A and the datum marks are aligned.*

centre to apply pressure.

◆ Once the glue has dried, face off the front of Part A flat and true.

◆ Mark in pencil a 64mm (2½in) diameter circle and cut a 2mm (3⁄32in) deep step on the inside of that line, flat to the centre.

◆ Glue the applewood blank A to the sycamore block, aligning the datum points. Apply pressure whilst the glue sets using the tailstock.

◆ Mark in pencil a 58mm (2⅜in) diameter concentric circle on the newspaper-covered applewood. Turn a step 3mm (⅛in) deep on the inside of that line.

◆ Mark in pencil a 62mm (2⅞in) diameter circle and, on the outside of that, turn a 2mm (3⁄32in) deep step, square and flat.

◆ Try Part B against A and ensure that the fit between the parts is precise (*see* Fig 13.15).

◆ Now the internal shaping of A can continue.

◆ Turn out A to a depth of 52mm (2¹⁄₁₆in) and carefully match the shaping to the template Interior A (*see* Fig 13.16).

◆ Clean up the inside thoroughly.

◆ Fit Part B to Part A aligning datum marks but, more precisely, the walnut veneer and sandalwood dividers (*see* Fig 13.17).

◆ Bring the tailstock forward holding the revolving centre to support the end of B.

◆ Making sure both pieces run true and on centre, turn the outside to a precise 68mm (2¾in) diameter.

◆ Measure from the joint line 32mm (1¼in) towards the tailstock: this is Point X. At that point and on the tailstock side of the line turn down to a 35mm (1⁷⁄₁₆in) diameter.

◆ From the joint line, measure 44mm (1¾in) towards the headstock. This is Point Y. On the headstock side of that line, turn down to a 30mm (1⁷⁄₁₆in) diameter.

◆ Carefully turn from the centre joint line to X and to Y, accurately matching the shape on the card template (*see* Fig 13.18). This will bring the wall thickness of the egg to 3mm (⅛in).

I have often turned thin-shelled walls like bowls and found it straightforward, but turning the outside of a hollow not knowing the exact wall thickness is a little unsettling. Have confidence; it does work. Cut cleanly and carefully using sharp tools.

◆ Withdraw the tailstock and remove B. The wall thickness may now be judged (*see* Fig 13.20).

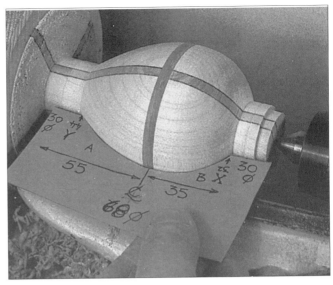

Fig 13.18 The outer profile is turned to match the template.

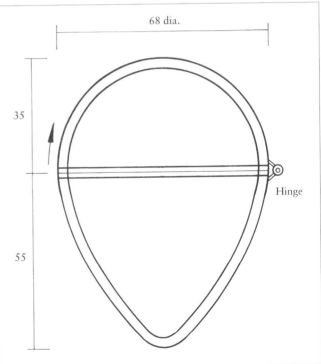

Fig 13.19 A cross section through the egg shell, showing dimensions.

Fig 13.20 The pieces are separated to see how well the wall thickness has been turned.

Fig 13.21 The end of the egg is turned off close to the wood chuck.

Fig 13.22 The top of the egg is turned in a jam chuck.

◆ Carefully turn the rest of A close to the softwood disc and continue the profile of the egg accurately. Part or saw off close to the softwood (*see* Fig 13.21).

The great benefit of the softwood faceplate is that it can be used over and over again. This time, face off the softwood disc and prepare for its next use as a jam chuck.

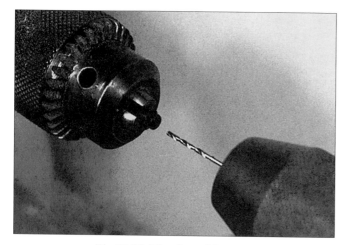

Fig 13.23 The ebony hinge parts are turned and drilled.

◆ Turn a 68mm (2¾in) diameter hollow into the softwood to accept B and A in turn. The ends may be fully turned to shape (*see* Fig 13.22). Remember to take fine gentle cuts. Too heavy a cut could dislodge the part, causing damage.

◆ Glasspaper the piece before removing.

◆ Polish the outside of the egg.

Making the ebony hinge

◆ Fit a drill chuck into the headstock.

◆ Hold a 9mm (⅜in) square of ebony 30mm (1¹⁷⁄₃₂in) long in the chuck, supporting the end lightly with a revolving centre.

◆ Turn a 22mm (⅞in) length to 6mm (¼in) diameter.

◆ Cut three pieces, each 6mm (¼in) long.

◆ Using the drill chuck to hold each piece, face off each end. Drill through using a 1.5mm (¹⁄₁₆in) drill bit or the size to suit the metal rod available (*see* Fig 13.23). (A long panel pin may be satisfactory.)

◆ On the end of two pieces, turn a small finial shape but do not cut into the drilled hole.

◆ Next turn three ebony pieces 9mm (⅜in) long by 2.5mm (just under ⅛in) diameter. These can be turned by holding the ebony in the drill chuck with a 9mm (⅜in) length showing. From the exposed end, turn towards the chuck bringing the outer end to size first.

◆ Mark the centre of each length of the

hinge pieces.

◆ Keep the bar in place through the hinge piece, then drill at the marked centre point using a 2.5mm (just under ⅛in) drill until the centre bar is struck. The hinge piece can be held in pliers to perform this task and a round-ended dental burr can be used to drill the pilot hole.

◆ Wax the metal rod and refit. Glue the 9mm (⅜in) long 2.5mm (just under ⅛in) diameter ebony dowel into each hole using superglue.

◆ Once dry, polish the hinge parts and cut those dowels to a precise 6mm (¼in) from their junction.

◆ Place all three hinge parts with the now-glued ebony dowel in place onto the metal rod – finials at either end.

◆ Hold the hinge against the egg at the joint line and in the centre of one of the quadrants.

◆ Arrange so that the middle hinge dowel faces upwards and the two outer hinge dowels face down.

◆ Using judgement, mark the position for the upper hinge dowel. Remember the angle that the dowel rested on the egg and drill a 2.5mm (just under ⅛in) hole into the egg shell fractionally closer to the joint line than the marked position and at a slightly lower angle. Begin the hole using a round dental burr. If unsure of the technique practise on a piece of scrap wood.

◆ Fit the hinge dowel in place then mark the positions for the lower two dowels. Drill in a similar manner as the first.

◆ With the hinge set in place, open and close the egg. Adjust where necessary.

◆ When satisfied with the hinge movement, glue the dowels into their respective holes with the egg closed.

◆ Mark the length of the metal hinge bar, dead size, to fit across the three hinge knuckles and cut to length. Clean up the ends with a file.

◆ Fit the metal hinge bar in place supergluing the bar into the two outer knuckles only. Do not let the glue run into the centre knuckle.

◆ To complete the hinge, paint the shiny metal ends of the rod with a touch of black enamel paint.

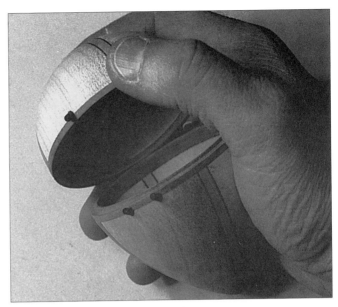

Fig 13.24 The egg and its ebony hinge parts.

THE ROSE

Turning the rose

◆ For the dimensions of the rosebud, refer to Fig 13.25.

◆ Set a 60mm (2⅜in) long by 30mm (1½in) square piece of holly between centres.

◆ Turn fully round as close to full diameter as possible.

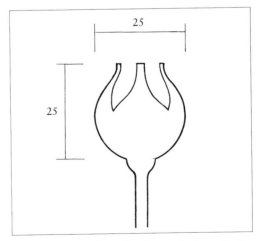

Fig 13.25 The shape for the rosebud sepals. A 9mm diameter hole is drilled out to a depth of 20mm, then hollowed and cut. Wall thickness is approximately 1mm.

Fig 13.26 Turning the holly for the rosebud.

Fig 13.27 Drilling out some waste wood.

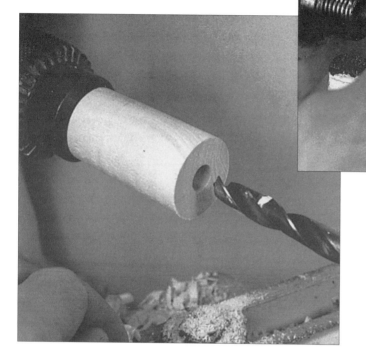

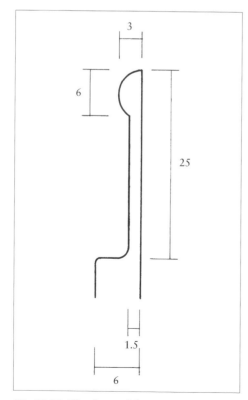

Fig 13.28 The shape of the specially ground tool.

◆ At the tailstock end, turn a 9mm (⅜in) spigot 9mm (⅜in) long (*see* Fig 13.26).

◆ Remove the piece from the lathe. Remove the driving dog and replace with a drill chuck.

◆ Hold the turned spigot in the drill chuck making sure that the piece runs true and on centre. Support the exposed end with the revolving centre. Square off the end.

◆ Using a 9mm (⅜in) drill bit, drill to a depth of 22mm (⅞in). Mark the depth on the drill shank (*see* Fig 13.27).

Turning the rosebud requires some judgement and careful planning. A sketch of the finished shape needs to be produced but it does not have to be rigidly followed. It is a guide. Make sure before starting that the finished shape is fixed in the mind. Have a look at a few rosebuds and see how they are shaped.

◆ Fit the revolving centre into the drilled hole for support whilst turning the outer shape.

◆ Turn the outer shape of the bud down to the start of the stalk – about 25mm (1in) long. Clean up the outer surface for it will be much easier to do this now than later.

◆ Withdraw the tailstock and bring the tool rest across the face of the work.

◆ Using the specially ground tool made from a 6mm (¼in) wood chisel (*see* Fig 13.28), slowly and carefully excavate the

Fig 13.29 *The inner profile being shaped.*

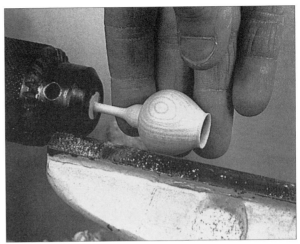

Fig 13.30 *The complete bud turned from holly.*

interior of the bud bringing the wall thickness to about 1mm (¹⁄₂₄in) (*see* Fig 13.29). If you chose holly as your timber you will now be glad that you did.

As you turn the inside, try to visualize where the tool is and how the interior shaping is progressing. Start hollowing from the mouth of the bud and work inwards. Bring the wall thickness to size closest to the opening first and slowly work back. If a light bulb is held against the back of the bud the wall thickness may be judged by the amount of light penetrating.

◆ When satisfied with the bud, turn the stem beneath to a 2.5mm (a little under ¹⁄₈in) diameter and 25mm (1in) long (*see* Fig 13.30). The open end does not need supporting.

◆ Part off carefully close to the chuck.

Turning the petals

There are alternative methods that can be used to hold the bud and petals whilst turning. A simple block of softwood on a faceplate could be drilled out to accept the turned spigot which would be glued in place. A larger three- or four-jaw chuck could be used if there is nothing else available but that, of course, would make the turner far more cautious. For the petals I used a four-jaw chuck to help give confidence to those

who need to use similar equipment and to show that delicate turnery needs only a delicate touch, and the size of the machinery does not matter.

◆ For the dimensions of the petals, refer to Fig 13.31.

◆ Place the piece of pink ivory between centres.

◆ Turn down to a 25mm (1in) diameter.

◆ At the tailstock, turn a 9mm (³⁄₈in) spigot 9mm (³⁄₈in) long.

◆ Remove from the lathe, exchanging the driving dog for the four-jaw chuck.

◆ Hold the 9mm (³⁄₈in) spigot in the chuck. Support the end with a revolving centre.

◆ Face off the end square and true.

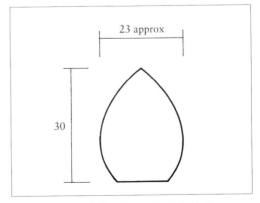

Fig 13.31 *Petals for the rosebud. This is drilled out using a 9mm drill to a depth of 22mm.*

Fig 13.32 Shaping the inside of the petals.

◆ Drill into the end using a 9mm (⅜in) drill to a depth of 22mm (⅞in).

◆ Now judgement comes in again. Measure the outer diameter of the holly – say 25mm (1in), then measure or judge the wall thickness – say 1mm (¼in). Take two wall thicknesses away from the diameter, leaving 23mm (1½in).

◆ Turn the outside diameter to 23mm (1½in).

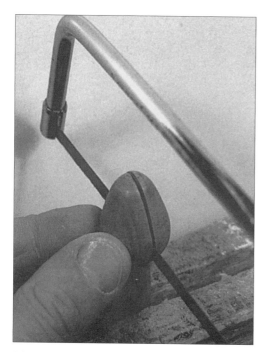

Fig 13.33 Cutting the petals.

◆ Look at the holly bud, and judge or measure its depth. Look at the shaping. Make notes of the internal shape, including the distances between the rise and fall in shape at those points. Then begin to turn the outer shape of the petals.

◆ Turn the whole of the outer shape leaving sufficient attached to give support whilst turning the inner shape.

◆ Remember that the drilled hole end fits into the base of the holly bud. The pointed end close to the chuck will be the tips of the petals.

◆ When satisfied, clean the shape up thoroughly.

◆ Turn out the inside using the specially shaped tool. Keep it sharp. Bring the wall thickness to around 2mm (³⁄₃₂in) this time (*see* Fig 13.32).

◆ When the internal shaping has been satisfactorily completed, shape the outside down to the petal tips parting off smoothly.

Cutting the petals

For months I could not work out how to turn petals for this rosebud. I thought of turning a larger shape and cutting the petals from it using a fret saw. Other methods I considered were equally unsuitable. Nature gave me the answer. Underneath an English beech tree there were scattered hundreds of beech seeds in their pods – beech mast. The prickly outer cases were tightly closed to protect the seeds. The cases were made of four sections which, as they dried, curled back. For several days I passed under the tree kicking aside or crushing a few of these underfoot and then it was suddenly so apparent. I picked up a piece of this beech mast and looked at it carefully, observing how it was arranged: four petal shapes forming the husk which was all but round. Translating this into turning, turn the shape hollow and round and then make two cuts down through the piece; place the cuts at 90° to one another to produce, in a very simple way, four petals.

◆ Take a 9mm (⅜in) diameter piece of dowel. Hold it upright in a vice.

- Place the pink ivory bud onto the dowel.
- Using a junior hacksaw or fine dovetail saw, cut vertically down through the centre of the bud (*see* Fig 13.33).
- Once the piece is cut into two halves, lay each half flat on a cutting board and then cut in half again, producing the petal shape.
- Clean up each petal's edge until well finished.
- Polish each petal.

Cutting the sepals on the holly bud

- In pencil, mark out four sepal shapes on the holly, the deepest part being 15mm (⅝in) from the top.
- Take a fine round burr held in a Dremel tool or a flexible drive shaft and chain drill a series of holes around the outer edge of the shape (*see* Fig 13.34).
- Still using the burr, gently break through the drilled holes so that the waste falls away.
- Clean around the edges using needle files and fine glasspaper.
- The holly can be dyed green using fabric dye but do experiment on a scrap piece first.
- Finally polish the outer surface.

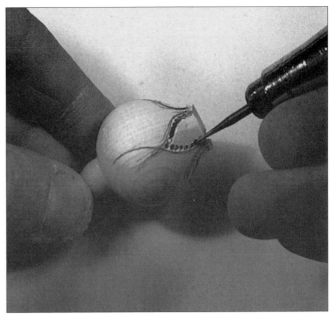

Fig 13.34 The sepals are marked out and chain drilled using a small drill.

Fitting the petals

- Take one petal. Lay it inside against one sepal, and check for a good fit.
- Remove the petal.
- Dab a small amount of PVA glue to the

Fig 13.35 The pink ivory wood petals and holly bud waiting to be assembled.

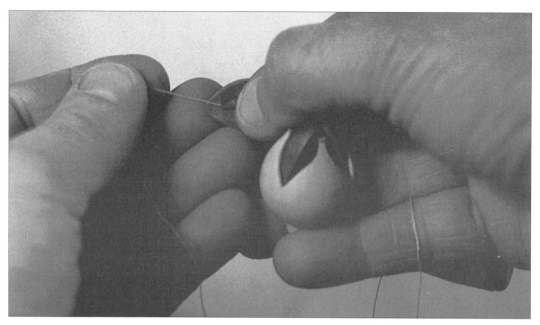

Fig 13.36 A piece of thread is attached to Petal 4 ...

lower edge of the petal.

◆ Refit into the bud positioning as before, making sure that the petal tip appears to be on centre when viewed from above. Also ensure that each petal edge falls equally in

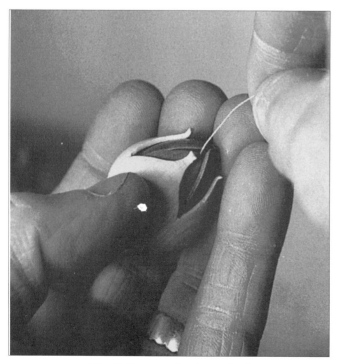

Fig 13.37 ... so that it can be drawn up into place and held whilst the glue sets.

the centre of the hollow between the sepals.

◆ Hold until the glue sets, which should only be a short time, then leave to dry fully.

◆ Fit Petal 2 in the same way, pushing the edges together.

◆ On Petal 3, fix a piece of cotton thread on the inside a third of the way down. Again, PVA glue will hold this in place.

◆ Make sure that the glue has dried on Petals l and 2 and on the thread of Petal 3.

◆ Drop Petal 3 into the bud, *but do not glue this one*; leave the thread hanging out.

◆ Now fit Petal 4 in the same manner as Petals 1 and 2, butting it firmly against the edge of the closest petal (*see* Figs 13.36 and 13.37).

◆ Once the glue has set on Petal 4, Petal 3 may be glued in place.

◆ These last two petals were pushed through the wide opening at the same time, for once three petals are fitted in place the opening is too small for the final one to slip through.

◆ Pull Petal 4 up to check the fit, although it is a little too late to alter much now. Dab a small amount of glue on the lower part of this petal then pull the thread up to hold it in place whilst the glue sets.

◆ When all has set, trim the thread close

Fig 13.38 Turning the rosebud support.

Fig 13.39 Drilling away the wings of the support.

and use a pin to push the last little piece back down into the bud so it is hidden.

Making the rosebud support

◆ Cut a 56mm (2⅜in) diameter disc from 6mm (¼in) applewood or similar close-grained hardwood.

◆ Take that faceplate with the softwood disc still attached and face off flat and true. Drill a pilot hole on centre.

◆ Drill a hole through the applewood disc's centre. Countersink the hole, then screw the disc centrally to the softwood.

◆ Angle the edges of the disc so that it can drop into the base of the egg and sit well against the sloping sides.

◆ Turn a slight hollow towards the centre. Clean up.

◆ Undo the screw, flip it over and turn a slight hollow again towards the centre, but not too deep.

◆ Mark a line 3mm (⅛in) in from the edge and divide the outside of that circle equally into four (*see* Fig 13.38).

◆ Remove the faceplate from the lathe and take it to the drill stand.

◆ Fit a 25mm (1in) drill into the machine and drill each of the four marked positions (*see* Fig 13.39).

◆ Remove the piece from the faceplate, clean up and try in place.

◆ Fit the rosebud into the drilled hole.

◆ Close the top of the egg. If the rosebud prevents the egg closing fully, drill out the hole in the centre of the holder a little larger to allow the bud to drop down.

◆ When the egg closes well the position for the holder is marked.

◆ A slight touch of glue on the edge of the holder will hold it in place.

If the woods are chosen well and the turning executed to a good standard, if the finish is fine and the rose colouring sharp and clean, then Fabergé watch out.

CHAPTER 14

Sovereign Sphere

I REMEMBER ONCE BEING TOLD, 'IF YOU WANT TO HIDE A MISTAKE OR CONCEAL A JOINT, MAKE A FEATURE OF IT,' AND THIS IS EXACTLY WHAT I HAVE DONE HERE TO HELP CONCEAL THE SECRET TUBE CONTAINER HELD WITHIN THE TURNED SPHERE. A SERIES OF CONCENTRIC RINGS, ONE ON THE JOINT LINE, MASK THE TELLTALE SIGNS OF THE FITTED TUBE; A SIMPLE AND STRAIGHTFORWARD METHOD WHICH NOT ONLY RELIES ON INCISED LINES BUT ALSO ON THE CAREFUL SELECTION OF WOOD. THE COLOUR AND GRAIN PATTERN MUST MATCH SO CAREFULLY WITH THE SURROUNDING WOOD THAT IT BLENDS UNNOTICED INTO THE AREA AROUND IT. IT SEEMS SIMPLE ENOUGH SELECTING MATCHING WOOD BUT SOMETIMES WHEN A PIECE OF WOOD IS TURNED AROUND THE LIGHT CATCHING IT ALTERS THE COLOUR, SO BEWARE.

A simpler solution is to make and fit around the sphere a series of false wood plugs of a completely different kind and a matching tube container making an even greater feature of that which is hidden. But the best method I have ever seen was an early Tunbridge stickware ball concealing a tube container large enough to hold sovereigns. On twelve points of the sphere were circular Tunbridge stickware patches. Only one (and its opposite of course) could be pushed out to reveal the hidden secret.

Here I will describe how to make a sovereign sphere using only a single type of wood. If you wish to add different coloured plugs or even be adventurous enough to have Tunbridge stickware ends then I am sure that with a little planning and thought the solutions will present themselves.

The size of the tube container here is large enough to hold four pounds sterling in twenty pence pieces. It is a simple matter to redraw the piece if you wish to make the container smaller or larger.

Having completed my first sovereign sphere and fitted the tube with coins, I handed it to my son who has some experience of my turned tricks. The joint was tight, the wood matched well, he was perplexed. He could hear the coins jangle but could find no way in.

Preparation

◆ Choose a well-seasoned, stable wood because if the piece shrinks, swells or distorts in any way then the joints will become visible, spoiling the illusion. Have sufficient

Fig 14.1 The sovereign sphere with its secret revealed.

wood to make both the sphere and the tube container. I chose good English boxwood, one piece 15cm (6in) long by 75mm (3in) square, and another piece 10cm (4in) by 30mm (1¼in) square.

◆ A three- or four-jaw chuck will be needed.

◆ Have ready a 15mm (⅝in), a 22mm (⅞in) and a 25mm (1in) saw-tooth drill, and also a drill chuck large enough to hold the drills that will fit into the tailstock.

◆ Use the 25mm (1in) and 22mm (⅞in) drills to cut two holes in a small thin scrap of wood to act as a gauge.

◆ For the hemispherical chuck that will be needed, have a piece of elm 110mm (4⅜in) square and 50mm (2in) thick available plus a further piece of elm 110mm (4⅜in) square and 12mm (½in) thick from which to make the collar to fit the chuck.

◆ A simple jig for turning spheres is necessary. The materials for this will be described later in the chapter.

◆ Lathe speed should be 1250 rpm.

Making the hemispherical chuck

◆ For an exploded view of the hemispherical chuck, see Fig 14.2.

◆ From a piece of 50mm (2in) thick elm, cut a 110mm (4⅜in) diameter circle.

◆ Screw this piece centrally and securely to a faceplate and turn it to a 95mm (3¾in) diameter.

◆ Turn the face flat and true.

◆ Draw a 62mm (2½in) diameter circle on a piece of card – cereal packet is ideal. Mark a centre line across the diameter then, using scissors, cut out the circle accurately. This card circle will act as a template and help judge when the exact hemispherical shaping within the elm block is complete (*see* Fig 14.3).

◆ With the lathe running, mark in pencil a circle with a diameter of 62mm (2½in) on the face of the elm block.

◆ Using a 6mm (¼in) gouge, begin turning the hemispherical hollow on the inside of the marked pencil circle. Work slowly and carefully, testing regularly with the card template.

◆ Stop when the hollow is exactly

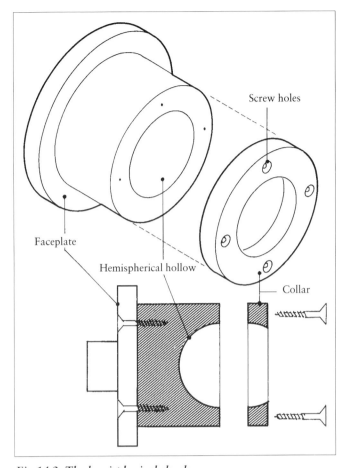

Fig 14.2 The hemispherical chuck.

Fig 14.3 Testing the internal shape of the chuck with a card circle.

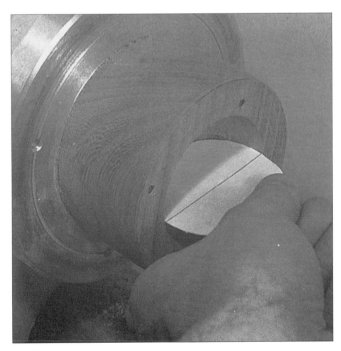

Fig 14.4 Turning through the chuck collar into the hollow beneath.

Fig 14.5 The inner curve of the chuck collar is shaped.

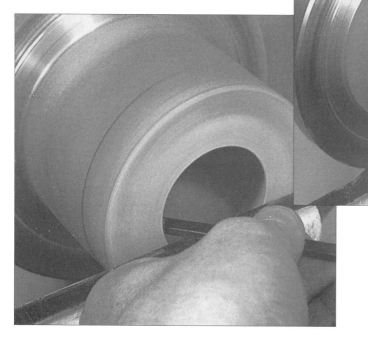

hemispherical. The first part is complete.

◆ Cut a 110mm (4⅜in) diameter circle from the 12mm (½in) thick piece of elm.

◆ Draw a pencil circle of 40mm (1⁹⁄₁₆in) radius concentrically upon the cut disc.

◆ Draw a line across the centre of that circle and a second line at 90° to the first.

◆ The points where the lines cross the drawn circle are positions for screw holes. At these points, drill and countersink to accept a 25mm (1in) No.8 countersunk screw.

◆ Screw the disc centrally upon the hollowed-out block held on the lathe.

◆ Before work progresses draw a 62mm (2½in) diameter circle on paper. Draw a centre line, then a further line parallel to that centre line 12mm (½in) away. Measure the distance across the circle on that second line. It should be 56mm (2¼in). This measurement will be used to produce the correct shape for the collar. Now continue.

◆ Turn the outer edge of the 12mm (½in) thick collar to match that of the main block upon which it is held.

◆ Mark in pencil upon the outer surface a concentric circle with a diameter of 56mm (2¼in) as calculated earlier.

◆ Turn through the disc on the inside of this marked pencil circle, breaking into the hollow beneath. Turn to the pencil circle exactly (*see* Fig 14.4).

◆ Using a round-nose tool and good judgement, turn the underside of the edge without disturbing the exactly turned diameter of the top. Turn underneath so that the cut runs to meet and match that internal joint line.

◆ This collar is turned with an internal curve to match the surface of a 62mm (2½in) diameter sphere and will allow it to be locked firmly in place (*see* Fig 14.5).

◆ Remove and check regularly the internal shaping of the collar against the template but first mark a datum line on the edge of collar and block so that it can be replaced exactly.

Making the spherical jig

◆ The jig I first used was engineer-made but for those not fortunate enough to know an engineer I will describe how a simple but effective jig may be made from wood (*see* Fig 14.6). An exploded view of this jig is shown in Fig 14.7.

◆ The position on your lathe that holds the

tool rest must be adaptable to accept the central pivot hole of the wooden jig; this position must be directly below the central axis of the lathe.

◆ Buy or acquire a square metal turning tool about 9mm (⅜in) square, and grind one end of this tool 60° back with a round fingernail shaping upon its end.

◆ Buy a piece of 9mm (⅜in) plywood (or size to match the tool) of a size to cut three pieces sufficiently large to make a jig that will fit your lathe. The size will depend upon the centre height of the lathe and precise details can be worked out after looking at Fig 14.6.

◆ Have ready a small nut and bolt, four screws and four Rawlplugs.

◆ The top of the tool will have to be set at centre height. The distance from the drilled pivot hole to the point where the tool protrudes must be about 40mm (1⁹⁄₁₆in).

◆ Cut three L-shaped pieces from the ply; the centre piece is 9mm (⅜in) thick, the thickness of the metal turning tool, and shorter than the two outer pieces. Glue and cramp these together.

◆ Mark and drill the centre pivot hole to the size of the fitting that holds the tool rest upon your lathe. Cut a cap piece from the ply to sit on top and bridge the tool slot.

◆ Drill a hole centrally upon this cap piece to allow the small bolt to slip through. The underside is drilled or cut out to accept the nut so that it can be set flush with the surface. The nut may then be glued in place using epoxy resin; do not let the glue enter the screw thread.

◆ Mark and drill four positions, two on either side, on the top of the cap piece. These holes need to be large enough for the screws.

◆ Place the cap on top of the jig so that it covers the tool slot and is flush with the edges. Mark through the holes onto the top edges of the jig on either side of the tool slot.

◆ Drill holes at these points sufficient to take the Rawlplugs; these plugs will hold the screws firmly whereas the bare plywood edge would allow the screws to break out eventually.

◆ Fit the tool in the slot, fit the cap in place

Fig 14.6 The wooden sphere-cutting jig in place.

Fig 14.7 An exploded view of the wooden sphere-cutting jig.

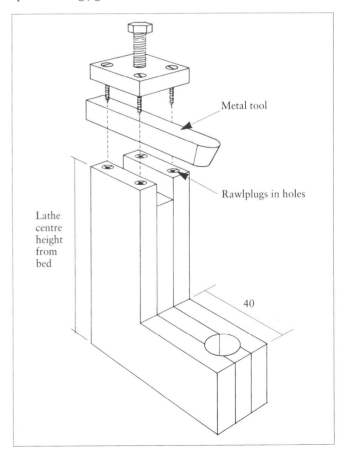

Metal tool

Rawlplugs in holes

Lathe centre height from bed

40

Fig 14.8 Turning the blank from which to turn the sphere.

Fig 14.9 The metal jig set on centre, ready to ...

(once the epoxy glue has set) and screw down. Now fit the bolt into the nut on the underside and lock the tool firmly in position.

Turning the sphere

◆ Set the boxwood block between centres and turn to an accurate 62mm (2½in) diameter (*see* Fig 14.8).

Fig 14.10 ... turn the outer edges of the blank.

◆ Measure 43mm (1¾in) from the headstock. Mark a line. Measure from that line 62mm (2½in) towards the tailstock and mark a line. On the outer edges of these lines, turn down to 15mm (⅝in) diameter.

◆ Measure halfway along the turned block and mark a centre line in pencil around it.

◆ Remove the tool rest and replace it with the spherical jig.

◆ The tool held in the jig must be set right back into the block to begin with.

◆ Set the jig so that the top of the tool is at centre height, and the front middle tip of the tool and the pivot point of the jig are exactly in line with the centre line around the block (*see* Fig 14.9).

◆ Swing the jig to the right. Bring the tool out so that it touches the turned off corner of the block. Lock the tool down firmly, bring the jig back to the central position and turn on the lathe.

◆ Slowly swing the jig to the right, cutting a small amount from the surface of the block; swing to the left, then return to centre. Turn off the lathe and adjust the tool so that it cuts a fraction more.

◆ Repeat the cutting process, swinging right, swinging left and back to centre, adjusting and cutting. Each cut must be slight (*see* Fig 14.10).

◆ The final cut is made so close to the drawn centre line that it almost touches. Do not cut any wood from the centre line.

◆ Once the final cut is made, turn off the lathe, remove the jig and sand up the part-turned sphere. Cut the stubs at either end leaving 6mm (¼in) (*see* Fig 14.11).

◆ Complete the turning of the sphere held between the faceplate hollow and the tailstock cup (*see* Fig 14.12), turning away those ghost images of the stubs until a true sphere remains (*see* Fig 14.13).

◆ Mark twelve equally spaced points on the 62mm (2½in) diameter sphere (*see* Fig 14.14).

Fig 14.11 Sawing off the stubs on either side.

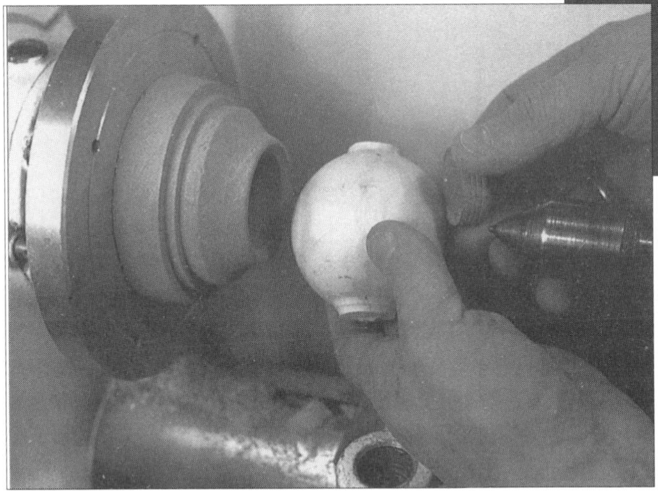

Fig 14.12 The part-finished sphere is held between wooden cup centres.

Fig 14.13 When the lathe is switched on, the stubs form ghost images which can be turned away.

Fig 14.14 The sphere with its twelve equally spaced points.

It must be understood that there may be slight variations in the size of spheres turned and that the intersections may not always fall equally because of these variations and the precise measurements given below (e.g. 32.5mm). Therefore it may be necessary to calculate accurately for the precise size of sphere that has been turned. Below is a formula to use for that calculation.

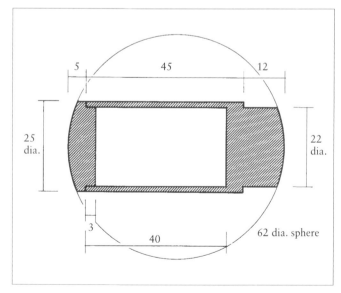

Fig 14.15 A cross section through the sovereign sphere, showing the position and dimensions of the hidden tube box.

◆ Use the ratio figure of 0.526 x diameter to find the distance of vertex separation.

◆ Sphere diameter is 62mm (2½in).

◆ 0.526 x 62 = 32.612mm (0.526 x 2.5 = 1.315in)

◆ Set a pencil compass to 32.5mm (1.3in) radius.

◆ Place the compass point on one end grain end of the sphere and mark a circle about that point.

◆ Place the compass point at any position on that drawn circle. Draw a circle about that point.

◆ Now choose any point where the circles intersect. Place the compass point there and draw another circle.

◆ When all possible intersection points have been used it will be noted that there are twelve intersections all equally spaced.

◆ Locate and mark both end grain positions.

Making the turned tube box

◆ For the dimensions of the tube box, refer to Fig 14.15.

◆ Set the 10cm (4in) by 30mm (1¼in) square piece between centres, turning to a round, leaving as large a diameter as possible.

◆ At the tailstock end, turn a 15mm (⅝in) length to exactly 22mm (⅞in) diameter. Test the size against the hole drilled in the scrap piece of wood. It is better to turn the piece oversize, slowly bringing it down to its correct diameter, than to rush and cut very close to finished size, possibly slipping and ruining the piece. The drilled hole in the scrap of wood ensures that the turned end which fits exactly in it will exactly fit the hole drilled by that particular drill.

◆ From the shoulder just turned, measure 45mm (1¾in) towards the headstock. At that point and for 6mm (¼in) further, turn down to an exact 25mm (1in) diameter (*see* Fig 14.16). Part off leaving a 3mm (⅛in) shoulder on the part closest to the headstock.

◆ Call the part closest to the headstock Part

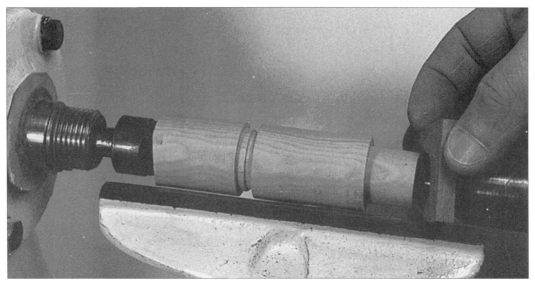

Fig 14.16 Checking the size of the end of the tube blank.

A and the part at the tailstock end Part B.

◆ Remove the driving dog from the headstock and replace it with a three- or four-jaw chuck.

◆ Hold Part B in the chuck with the freshly parted-off face showing to the front.

◆ Bring the tool rest across. Cleanly face off the work square and true.

◆ Remove the tool rest. Into the tailstock, fit a drill chuck holding a 22mm (⅞in) saw-tooth drill. Using white correction fluid, mark on the drill shank a point 40mm (1½in) away from its cutting edge.

◆ Drill the piece in the chuck to the marked depth (*see* Fig 14.17).

◆ Remove the piece from the chuck, replacing it with Part A, making sure that the parted-off face is showing forward.

◆ Bring the tool rest across. Turn the face square and true. Check the fit of the 22mm

Fig 14.17 Drilling out Part B.

Fig 14.18 Drilling out Part A.

Fig 14.19 *Part B is now fitted to Part A, and the body is turned to the correct size and tested with the wooden test piece.*

(⅞in) turned shoulder into the drilled hole in Part B. Adjust where necessary.

◆ When the two parts fit together satisfactorily, leave them fixed together.

◆ Remove the drill chuck from the tailstock and replace with the revolving centre.

◆ Now turn the joined parts down to an exact 25mm (1in) diameter testing it with the gauge hole drilled in the scrap wood (*see* Fig 14.19). Do not turn any part of the smaller turned shoulder.

◆ Part off 75mm (3in) measured from the tailstock end.

◆ Set aside the turned tube box and remove the four-jaw chuck, replacing it with the hemispherical chuck.

Drilling the sphere

◆ Place the pre-turned sphere in the chuck with one of the marked end grain positions facing forward. Bring the tailstock up to the sphere, pressing the revolving centre against the primary point marked at the end grain. The sphere is then held tightly against the back of the chuck whilst the collar is screwed evenly down (*see* Fig 14.20).

It is important that the end grain point is brought to the front, because when the sphere is drilled out this is where the tube container will fit. The tube container has its

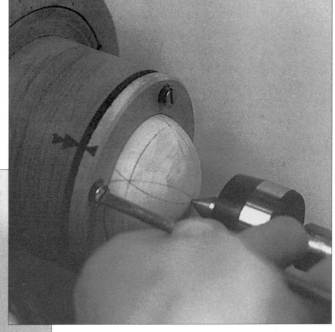

Fig 14.20 *The sphere is fitted into the hemispherical chuck and the collar is tightened.*

Fig 14.21 *Drilling through the sphere.*

grain running through its length showing end grain at its ends. This will match the grain pattern around the hole.

◆ Withdraw the tailstock. Replace the centre with the drill chuck holding a 25mm (1in) saw-tooth drill.

◆ Mark upon the drill shank a point 50mm (2in) away from the cutting edge.

◆ Turn the lathe on and drill into the sphere until the mark on the drill shank is level with the edge of the drilled hole. Withdraw the drill and turn off the lathe (see Fig 14.21).

◆ Replace the drill with the 22mm (⅞in) drill. Mark a point upon its shank 68mm (2¾in) away from its cutting edge.

◆ Turn on the lathe and drill into the sphere until the mark on the drill shank is level with the edge of the drilled hole.

◆ The drill will have cut a little way into the back of the chuck. Withdraw the drill and turn off the lathe.

Completing the sovereign sphere

◆ Take the turned tube box and push it, small turned end first, into the drilled hole. Push it firmly home, tapping it lightly with a mallet if necessary, until the shoulder on the tube box rests firmly on the internal shoulder. It will be clear when this happens.

◆ Bring the tool rest across the face of the work (see Fig 14.22). Carefully turn the protruding end smoothly and fluently into the curved surface of the sphere.

◆ To help this tube box 'disappear' the end must be turned so that there is no change in the curved surface of the sphere, so take particular care at this point.

◆ Place a card alongside the turned end of the tube. Mark the joint line and the centre point. Mark a point 2mm (³⁄₃₂in) from the outside of the joint line, then a series of points 2mm (³⁄₃₂in) apart inside the joint line towards the centre. Holding this card template, turn on the lathe and with a pencil mark these points on the sphere's surface, producing a series of concentric rings (see Fig 14.23). At each of these lines, again

Fig 14.22 The tube box is fitted into the drilled hole, then the top is turned to blend with the curve of the sphere.

beginning with the joint line, using the corner of a square-ended tool, cut a fine groove. This disguises the joint line amongst a series of concentric grooves (see Fig 14.24). Push the revolving centre into the sphere to make a central dimple.

◆ Turn off the lathe and remove the sphere from the chuck.

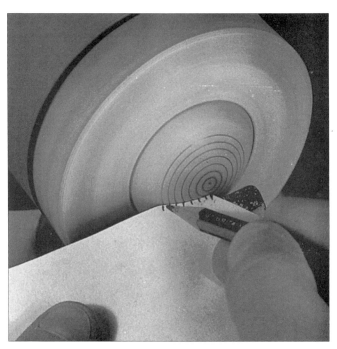

Fig 14.23 Concentric circles are marked using a card template as a guide.

Fig 14.24 Using the corner of a square-end tool, concentric grooves are cut to disguise the joint of the tube box.

Fig 14.25 The stand for the sovereign sphere.

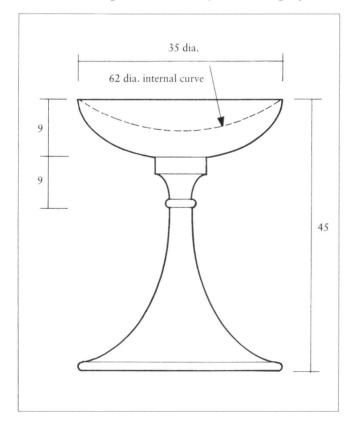

◆ Reposition the sphere in the chuck with the other end of the tube box facing out. Bring the tailstock up fixing the revolving centre against the marked centre of the protruding end. This holds the sphere firmly against the back of the chuck whilst evenly tightening down the collar.

◆ Remove the tailstock. Bring the tool rest across. Turn on the lathe and carefully turn the protruding end so that it blends in perfectly with the spherical surface.

◆ Using the card template again, position the joint line against one of the marks. Draw the pencil circles around with the lathe running (seven circles in all). Using the corner of a square-end tool cut fine grooves beginning at the joint line and working towards the centre, then cut the outer lines. Don't forget to bring the revolving centre up to mark the central dimple.

◆ To complete the sphere, take each remaining primary point, lock in position with the revolving centre, tighten down the collar evenly, then mark and cut the concentric circles.

It will be noticed that the back of the chuck has been drilled into. If you decide to make a few of these sovereign spheres then leave it untouched, but when the job is finished it is best to turn a plug to fit the drilled hole, glue in place, then turn it so that the chuck is hemispherical and whole once again. Don't leave the job unfinished.

◆ Having removed the sovereign sphere from the chuck the tube box can be removed by placing a small scrap of wood or a dowel on the smaller end (if you can find it). Tap with a mallet and out pops the box. After it has been removed a few times it will become quite easy to remove, pushing with the finger or thumb. Fill the box with coins and offer to a friend to puzzle out.

Turning the stand

◆ For the dimensions of the stand, refer to Fig 14.25.

◆ For the stand I used that lovely wood

laburnum and turned from one piece; no joints, just turn and part off.

◆ Cut a piece of square wood, 90mm (3½in) long by 40mm (1⁹⁄₁₆in).

◆ Set between centres and turn to 35mm (1⅜in) diameter.

◆ At the tailstock end, turn a spigot 15mm (⅝in) long and 15mm (⅝in) diameter.

◆ Remove the piece from the lathe and remove the driving dog from the headstock.

◆ Fit a three- or four-jaw chuck.

◆ Hold the turned spigot in the chuck and support the other end with the revolving centre.

◆ Face off the tailstock end flat and square.

◆ Withdraw the tailstock and bring the tool rest across the face of the work. Turn into that face a hollow to match the shape of the turned sphere. Check the sphere in the hollow.

◆ When satisfied, move the tool rest and fit a shaped piece of wood into the hollow bringing the revolving centre against that, supporting the piece. Tighten down.

◆ Now the underside of the stand, the stem and foot, may be turned. Refer to Fig 14.25 for dimensions.

◆ Carefully round under and down to meet the centre stem.

◆ Turn the shaping on the stem, then move to the foot.

◆ Complete the foot, then make an initial parting cut beneath the foot (*see* Fig 14.26).

◆ Clean up the whole stand carefully.

◆ Part off, undercutting the base of the foot so that it stands easily.

◆ Trim off any pip left on the base of the foot, then polish.

With the sphere filled with twenty pence pieces (or any other coins that fit) it becomes very heavy; strangely heavy, with an intriguing rattle. Sit it upon its stand and, if you feel rich, offer the contents as a reward to any who can find their way, non-destructively, into this puzzling piece.

Fig 14.26 Turning the stand.

CHAPTER 15

Lotus Blossom Bowl

T STARTED WITH A BEAD AND FINISHED WITH A BOOK ON LACQUERWARE.

The bead is an old Roman clay object called a melon bead and is supposed to impart luck. Round in shape with a hole through the middle so that it can be strung, it has a series of evenly spaced incised lines running around its surface. Each line starts at one hole and finishes at the other, travelling the whole circumference of the bead.

I have always found this particular bead to have a pleasing shape and it seemed to nag at me to make it from wood. It took some time to work out exactly how it could be turned.

I spent hours working out how to make jigs to hold the piece so that it could be moved on at exactly the correct amount each time before the next turning sequence began. The final method was so simple and practical I had overlooked it from the start.

Once I had decided upon a satisfactory method of turning I forgot about the shape for some while, for what use was it? This is where the lacquerware book came in. On one page was a beautiful lacquer bowl, red

Fig 15.1 The lotus bowl, top and bottom.

on the outside and black on the inside, rounded with fluted sides: a lotus blossom bowl. The two ideas came together. I knew how to cut the fluting and I could see, in theory, how to turn the bowl. That is what makes life so interesting – the challenge of making the theory work in practice.

This lotus blossom bowl, with fluted sides and petal-shaped rim, has worked, turned from start to finish.

With a little care a fully turned lidded box could be made melon shaped, just as it looks with the two halves fitted, before turning out.

Preparation

◆ Select a piece of wood 175mm (6⅞in) long by 90mm (3½in) square.
◆ Make a spherical cutting jig as described below.
◆ Make a hemispherical chuck and collar as described on pages 138–9. For this a piece of 100mm (4in) square by 60mm (2⅜in) thick elm will be needed and a 100mm (4in) square piece of 9mm (⅜in) ply for the locking collar.
◆ Have available a 12mm (½in) wide cheap wood chisel which will be ground to shape.
◆ Make a wooden cup chuck and cup centre as described on page 131. For this a 110mm (4½in) square by 60mm (2⅜in) long piece of elm is required, as well as a 60mm (2⅜in) square by 25mm (1in) thick piece of olive-wood. Any wood will work equally well.
◆ The final supporting plug is made from a 50mm (2in) cube of any available wood.
◆ Lathe speed should be 1500rpm.

Making the spherical jig

◆ This spherical jig is a very simple arrangement (*see* Fig 15.2). The size of wood required to make it will depend upon the size of lathe being used. The jig will fit in and sit upon the tool post.
◆ Remove the tool rest from the tool post and measure from its surface to the centre height.

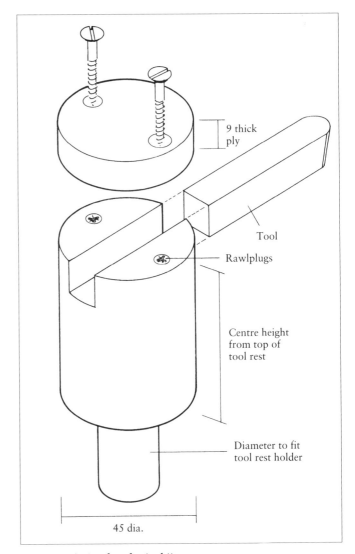

Fig 15.2 A simple spherical jig.

◆ For a Myford ML8 it is 42mm (1¹¹⁄₁₆in). Remove the 2mm (³⁄₃₂in), bringing it down to 40mm (1¹⁹⁄₃₂in). The reason for this is that when the tool is seated in the jig it will sit this distance above the height of the jig to help lock it down.
◆ Add to this measurement 20mm (¹³⁄₁₆in) for the turned spigot which will fit into the tool post.
◆ Take a piece of 60mm (2⅜in) long by 50mm (2in) square hardwood and set between centres.
◆ Turn the boss as close to 50mm (2in) in diameter as possible.
◆ Measure 20mm (¹³⁄₁₆in) from the tailstock towards the headstock and turn this section down to the same diameter as the metal

spigot on the tool rest. This turned section should then drop into the tool post.

◆ Remove the piece from the lathe.

◆ Decide whether a simple round-nose tool or a purchased metal turning tool will be used as the cutter held in this spherical jig. I prefer the metal turning tool for it is less cumbersome.

◆ Whichever tool is chosen, measure its thickness.

◆ On the top of the 50mm (2in) diameter piece, mark a centre line across.

◆ Measure half the tool's width either side of that centre line then mark a line set at this distance parallel to the centre line.

◆ Mark down the sides of the boss a continuation of those lines.

◆ Measure down the sides of the turned boss the thickness of the tool minus 2mm (⅟₁₆in). When the tool is set into this gap, which will shortly be cut out, it will stand proud by this amount. The locking disc on top will press firmly on the tool when screwed down, locking it in place.

◆ Saw on the inside of the marked lines across the top of the boss to the marked depth.

◆ Chisel out the waste wood, then test the tool in place. Make it a good, reasonably tight fit.

◆ From 9mm (⅜in), cut or turn a 50mm (2in) diameter circle for the locking disc.

◆ Mark a 30mm (1½in) concentric circle on its top.

◆ Draw a centre line across, and where this line crosses the marked circle, drill and countersink to accept a No. 8 screw.

◆ Fit the disc on top of the boss with the drilled holes opposing the cut channel. Mark through the holes into the boss.

◆ Drill into the boss at those marked points to accept plastic Rawlplugs. Fit these flush and firm.

◆ Now fit the tool in position and place the locking disc on top. Screw down using two 25mm (1in) long No. 8 countersunk screws.

◆ Fit the spigot into the tool rest.

◆ Two small spacers are cut to fit into the slide in the tool rest (*see* Fig 15.3). The length of these helps to decide on the size of the sphere that may be cut using the jig. The final size of the sphere is decided by the distance which the tool is pushed out from the jig.

Fig 15.3 The spherical jig – showing the spacers.

Making the cup chuck and centre

◆ Fit a 110mm (4½in) square by 60mm (2⅜in) long piece of elm centrally upon a faceplate.

◆ Turn to a 110mm (4½in) diameter.

◆ Turn into the face a 75mm (3in) hollow which tapers at approximately 45° towards the centre. The cut can stop after about 25mm (1in) of depth.

◆ The cup centre is simply made. Take a 30mm (1½in) long by 60mm (2⅜in) square piece of hardwood.

◆ Turn between centres keeping the largest possible diameter.

◆ At the tailstock end a stubby spigot is turned sufficiently large to grip in a three- or four-jaw chuck.

◆ The piece is removed from the lathe. The driving dog is exchanged for a chuck and the stub tenon is held in that chuck.

◆ Draw on card an 84mm (3⅜in) diameter circle and cut it out.

◆ Turn the exposed face of the cup centre to a hollow to match the card template.

◆ Remove the cup centre from the lathe.

Turning the sphere

◆ Fit a 175mm (6⅞in) long by 90mm (3½in) square piece of the chosen hardwood between centres.

◆ Turn to a 90mm (3½in) diameter.

I chose a log of wet hawthorn to turn and streams of cool wet shavings poured off. I sometimes wonder why I even turn dry wood for it is such a pleasure to turn it wet – no dust, clean cutting. Do not leave wet-turned wood on the lathe overnight, always have a polythene bag into which the piece can be placed for storage between work times.

◆ From the tailstock end, measure towards the headstock 75mm (3in), and from that point a further 25mm (1in) again towards the headstock.

◆ Turn that 25mm (1in) wide section down to a 25mm (1in) diameter as an exact match for a drill of that size (see Fig 15.4). Turn both shoulders square and true.

◆ Saw off on the headstock side of that spigot.

◆ With the work still supported on the driving dog, set a 25mm (1in) drill into the drill chuck. Fit the drill chuck into the tailstock, then bring the drill up to the end of the work and drill into it centrally to a depth of 25mm (1in)(see Fig 15.5).

◆ Remove the drill and chuck. Fit the turned spigot into the drilled hole, bring the

Fig 15.4 Turning the hawthorn blank.

Fig 15.5 Drilling out half the blank to accept the turned spigot attached to the other half.

*Fig 15.6 Using the spherical jig to
cut away either side.*

*Fig 15.7 Trimming down to a
pure sphere with stubs.*

tailstock now holding the revolving centre to
the end of the work for support.

◆ Now turn the whole piece to an accurate
84mm (3⅜in) diameter.

*Fig 15.8 Sawing off the stubs close to the
sphere.*

◆ Measure from the joint line 42mm
(1¹¹⁄₁₆in) towards the headstock, then towards
the tailstock. Mark pencil lines around at
these points.

◆ On the outside of those lines, turn down
to a 25mm (1in) diameter leaving the central
part around the joint 84mm (3⅜in) long and
the same diameter.

◆ Now set the spherical jig in position,
locating the pivot point of the tool post
directly under the joint line of the turned
part.

◆ Fix cramps either side of the tool rest slide
to prevent it moving.

◆ Set the tool well back into the jig first of
all, then swing it first to the left, knocking
off the corner of the turned block, then to
the right, trimming that corner off (*see*
Fig 15.6).

◆ Slowly extend the tool until the sphere is
fully turned down to the spigot (*see* Fig 15.7).

◆ Remember when swinging the jig from
left to right and right to left to keep the
pressure constant. If the pressure is down on
the jig, maintain that. If the pressure is
applied any other way, maintain that.

Now hawthorn is a most magnificent,
smooth, clean-cutting wood and creamy
white in colour. If a valuable hardwood is
being used, then to save waste at either end,
instead of turning down to the spigots, turn
them from a cheaper wood and then drill
and fix them into the more expensive piece.

◆ Saw off the spigots leaving a little extra on the side of the sphere (*see* Fig 15.8). Mark a datum across the joint line.

◆ Place the sphere between the cup chuck and centre with the cut stub spigots facing up and down.

◆ Turn on the lathe and a ghost image of the spigots will be seen above the pure surface of the sphere. Turn away these ghost images by hand until a pure sphere is achieved.

Marking out the sphere

The following measurements are purely a guide to help to come close to the required positions. Some adjustments may be necessary. The calculations are based upon a sphere 84mm (3⅜in) in diameter.

◆ To divide the joint line into eight equal parts, first calculate the circumference of the circle using the following the formula:

D or diameter = 84mm (3⅜in)
3.142 x 84 = 264mm
3.142 x 3.375 (3⅜in) = 10.6in

◆ Divide by 8
264 ÷ 8 = 33mm
10.6 ÷ 8 = 1.3in

◆ Set the compass to 33mm (1.3in).

◆ Place the compass point anywhere on the joint line then 'walk' the compass around to mark the eight equally spaced points (*see* Fig 15.9). Mark them clearly.

◆ If the positions are not arranged equally, adjust the compass accordingly.

Marking the sphere for top and bottom points

◆ On paper, draw a sphere the same size as the one turned.

◆ Mark a line across its centre.

◆ Mark a second line across its centre and at 90° to the first.

◆ Set the compass point on the circle where one line touches and stretch the pencil point to touch where the second line cuts the circle: one quadrant.

Fig 15.9 Marking out the sphere.

◆ With the compass still set at this distance, place the point on each of the eight positions around the joint line and mark pencil arcs top and bottom. This will give the top and bottom positions of the sphere. Mark them clearly with long, crossed lines so that they can be relocated later when cuts are made.

◆ Now number the positions around the joint line 1 to 8. Numbers 1 to 4 are marked the correct way up and numbers 5 to 8 are written upside down.

◆ Carefully measure and mark halfway points between 1 and 8.

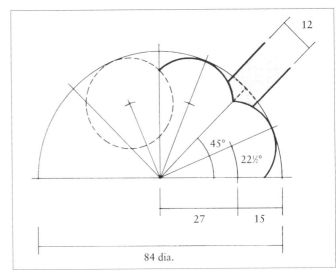

Fig 15.10 Obtaining the shape for the specially ground tool.

Fig 15.11 *Grinding the specially shaped tool. Wear eye protection.*

Grinding the specially shaped tool

◆ Take a 12mm (½in) wide cheap wood chisel.
◆ Paint typist's correction fluid on its end and, when dry, mark the shape upon the end

as shown in Fig 15.10.
◆ Carefully grind away the waste metal until the marked line is reached (*see* Fig 15.11).
◆ Grind a cutting bevel of 35° beneath.
◆ Remember when grinding:
  1. Wear goggles.
  2. Keep loose clothing away from the grinding wheels.
  3. Quench the tool regularly in water.

Setting the sphere ready for shaping

◆ Set the sphere between cup chuck and cup centre so that the joint line is horizontal.
◆ Loosen the cup centre sufficiently to allow the sphere to be moved, bringing Point 1 to the front.
◆ Hold a pencil at Point 1 keeping it precisely positioned whilst the lathe is rotated by hand (*see* Fig 15.12).
◆ The top centre should come down in line with the pencil (if it does not, carefully move the sphere until it does) and Point 8 should line up with the pencil point as it comes around. The bottom centre point should next

Fig 15.12 *The sphere, which is set between chuck and centre, has Point 1 aligned with the top, bottom and Point 5.*

Fig 15.13 The first cut is made.

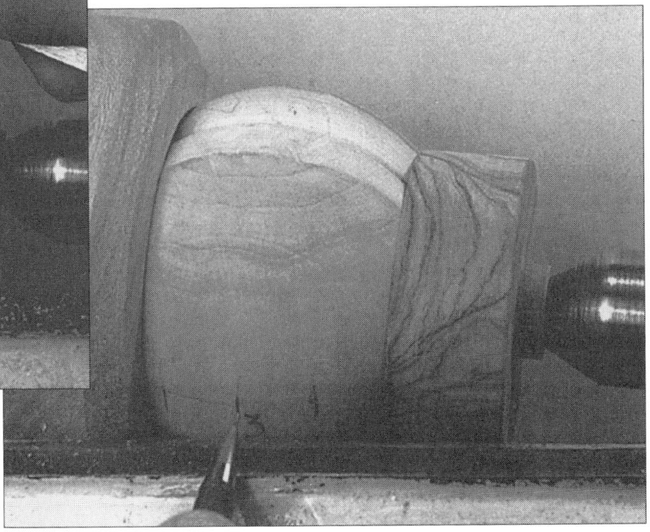

Fig 15.14 Lining up for the second cut.

line up with the pencil point.

◆ Continue adjusting the sphere until all those named four points run around on the same line, then tighten up on the sphere.

◆ When this position is achieved, turn on the lathe and mark a pencil line around those points.

◆ Bring the shaped tool to that marked line and carefully cut to depth.

◆ When the first cut has been satisfactorily finished, clean up, glasspaper and make sure the shaping is good (see Fig 15.13).

◆ Turn off the lathe and loosen the tailstock slightly, allowing the cup centre to loosen on the sphere.

◆ Remark the top and bottom centres.

◆ Bring the joint line to horizontal and rotate the lathe through 180° so that Point 3 comes to the front.

◆ Hold the pencil against Point 3 (see Fig 15.14), rotate the lathe so that top centre, then Point 7, then bottom centre are all in line. Adjust as before until they line up accurately.

◆ Before turning the next line, check the following:

   1. The joint line is horizontal when it comes around to the tool rest.

   2. The first turned cut is horizontal when it comes around to the tool rest. If this is the case then all is O.K.

◆ When satisfied, tighten the cup centre onto the sphere and make the second cut,

checking to see that it is exactly the same depth as the first (see Fig 15.15).

◆ When satisfied, and the cut has been finished well, loosen the cup centre, bring the joint line to horizontal and then turn through 90° to bring Point 4 to the front.

◆ Hold the pencil on Point 4 (see Fig 15.16)

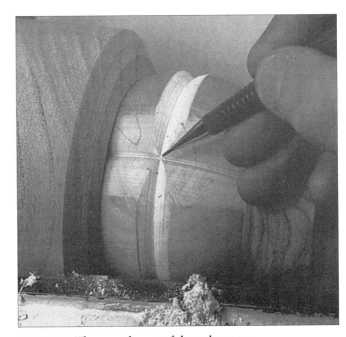

Fig 15.15 The second successful cut, bang on centre.

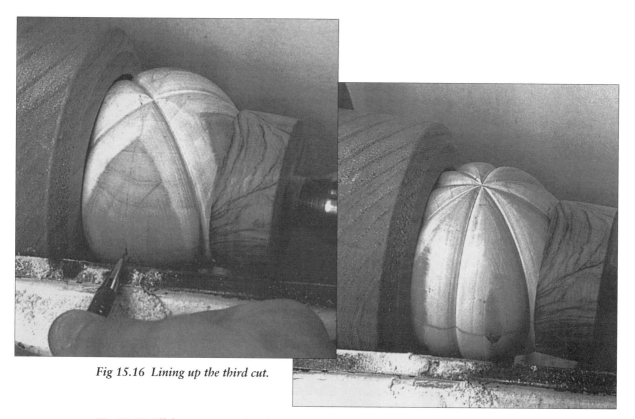

Fig 15.16 *Lining up the third cut.*

Fig 15.17 *All four cuts completed.*

Fig 15.18 *Like a wooden melon, with the
segments cut around the sphere.*

and rotate the lathe by hand. The intersection on top centre, Point 8 and the intersection on bottom centre must all be in line. Adjust to make sure this is correct.

◆ Make the third cut checking that the depth is the same as the first two.

◆ Clean up the cut and, when satisfied, loosen the cup centre moving Point 2, top intersection, Point 6 and bottom intersection all in line.

◆ Complete the fourth and final cut (*see* Fig 15.17). Clean up.

◆ When cutting these lines around the sphere it is best if they are marked in pencil first to ensure accuracy. The shaping tool helps with the initial cut, moving the tool handle left and right, using the point as a pivot. The centre line between the numbered points shows the extent of the cut. The cuts can be cleaned up with gouge and, finally, glasspaper.

◆ When all cuts have been made, remove the piece from the chuck and a wooden melon will have been turned (*see* Fig 15.18). Pull into two halves and the fluting on the edge will clearly be seen (*see* Fig 15.19).

Turning the supporting plug

◆ Take a cube of wood with sides of 50mm (2in) and fit between centres. Turn to the largest diameter possible.

◆ Measure 30mm (1¾in) from the tailstock towards the headstock and turn that section down to 35mm (1⅜in).

◆ Remove the piece from the lathe. Remove the driving dog from the headstock and replace with a three- or four-jaw chuck.

◆ Hold the 35mm (1⅜in) spigot in the chuck.

◆ Turn the outer surface to a convex, rounded shape.

◆ The supporting plug is complete.

Fig 15.19 The two halves separated.

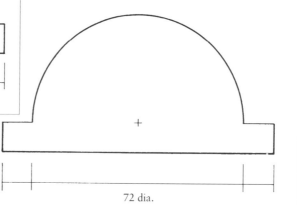

Fig 15.20 The internal chuck template – 84mm in diameter.

Fig 15.21 The internal chuck template – 72mm in diameter.

Turning the hemispherical chuck

◆ Fit the 100mm (4in) square by 60mm (2⅜in) long piece of elm centrally upon a faceplate.

◆ Turn to 100mm (4in) diameter. Turn the face flat and true.

◆ Mark on card an 84mm (3⅜in) diameter circle. Cut out a hemisphere (*see* Fig 15.20).

◆ Mark in pencil on the face of the turned elm block an 84mm (3⅜in) circle.

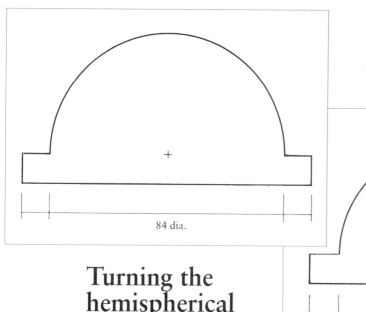

Fig 15.22 One half held in the hemispherical chuck by the collar – the centre can then be turned to shape.

◆ Turn out on the inside of that marked line a hemispherical hollow using the card template to help judge the shaping.

◆ From the 3mm (⅛in) thick piece of plywood, cut a 100mm (4in) diameter disc.

◆ Draw upon that disc in pencil a 90mm (3½in) diameter concentric circle.

◆ Draw a line across that circle followed by a second line across the centre at 90° to the first.

◆ Where these two lines touch the pencil circle, drill and countersink No. 6 screw.

◆ Fit the plywood disc concentrically upon the turned elm block.

◆ Mark upon the plywood surface a 78mm (3⅛in) concentric pencil circle. Cut through on the inside of this line.

◆ Remove the collar.

◆ On the inside of the hemispherical hollow, fit double-sided Sellotape with glasspaper fixed to one side. This will help grip the half-sphere fitted within.

◆ Fit one of the turned half-spheres into the chuck and lock the collar on top.

◆ With a card template marked out to 72mm (3¹³⁄₁₆in) diameter (*see* Fig 15.21) turn out the inside of the hawthorn half-sphere to that diameter hollow (*see* Fig 15.22). Clean the inside perfectly.

◆ Next take the supporting plug and push

Fig 15.23 *The internal shaping complete, a plug is brought up to support the bowl.*

the mushroom-shaped end to the base of the hollow(*see* Fig 15.23).

◆ Bring the revolving centre held in the tailstock forward to support the end of the supporting plug and push it hard into the hollow, tightening down.

◆ Remove the collar and turn over the edge of the bowl (*see* Fig 15.24).

And magically the fluted edge turns away leaving a pleasant petal-shaped rim (*see* Fig 15.25). Even now, every time I turn that edge over and see that petal shaping I find it a stirring moment; real magic to produce a lotus blossom bowl.

Fig 15.24 *The collar is removed from the chuck ...*

Fig 15.25 *... so the bowl rim may be turned to produce that little bit of magic - the scalloped rim.*

CHAPTER 16

Quinfoil Bowl

T SEEMS SO STRANGE THAT TECHNIQUES AND DEVELOPED IDEAS CAN BE LOST FROM THE GENERAL UNDERSTANDING OF A CRAFT. MANY-CENTRED BOWLS, TABLE TOPS AND VESSELS WERE WELL KNOWN TO TURNERS SEVERAL HUNDRED YEARS AGO. A BEAUTIFUL EXAMPLE IS IN THE BRITISH MUSEUM COLLECTION; A GERMAN MADE EIGHT-CENTRED TURNED MAZER, WHICH DATES FROM THE 1500S, FROM BURR MAPLE MOUNTED IN SILVER. IT IS REMARKABLE THAT SUCH AN APPARENTLY COMPLEX FORM OF TURNING WAS BEING UNDERTAKEN SO EARLY. IT SHOWS CLEARLY THAT THESE CRAFTSMEN HAD FULL MASTERY OF THEIR COMPARATIVELY SIMPLE EQUIPMENT.

Here, with the benefit of a modern lathe, a few Allen bolts, plywood and chipboard, the method of turning a five-centred bowl is shown.

Preparation

Holding jig

The following items are required:

◆ Five 6mm (¼in) by 75mm (3in) long Allen bolts and nuts to match.

◆ One piece of 9mm (⅜in) by 200mm (7⅞in) square plywood.

◆ One piece of 20mm (¹³⁄₁₆in) thick by 200mm (7⅞in) square chipboard.

◆ A faceplate on which to fix the holding jig.

◆ Cut a 130mm (5⅛in) diameter piece of good quality hardwood 60mm (2⅜in) thick. I

Fig 16.1 The quinfoil bowl.

chose Australian red gum and was very pleased with the close grain and fine cutting qualities.

◆ Lathe speed should be 500–750rpm.

MAKING THE JIG

◆ Refer to Fig 16.2

◆ Cut a 195mm (7¾in) diameter disc of 20mm (¾in) thick chipboard.

◆ Cut a 195mm (7¾in) diameter disc of 9mm (⅜in) thick plywood.

◆ Fix the chipboard disc centrally upon a faceplate.

◆ Mark concentrically upon the plywood disc, in pencil, a 175mm (7in) diameter circle, a 100mm (4in) diameter circle and an 80mm (3⅟₁₆in) diameter circle.

◆ Reset the compass to 87.5mm (3½in).

◆ Place the compass upon any point on the 175mm (7in) circle. 'Walk' the compass around the circumference marking six equidistant points.

◆ Mark the starting point as Position 1, miss a position, mark the next Position 3, miss a position, mark the next as Position 5.

◆ Draw a line from Position 5 through the centre to the the opposite side. Where it cuts the 100mm (4in) circle on the opposite side, mark Position 2.

◆ Draw a line from Position 1 through the centre to the opposite side. Where it cuts the 100mm (4in) circle, mark Position 4.

◆ Take five No. 8 19mm (¾in) long countersunk steel screws.

◆ At each of the five positions on the plywood disc, drill and countersink holes to accept the screws.

◆ Place the plywood disc centrally on the chipboard disc. Screw the plywood disc onto the chipboard beneath.

◆ Fit the faceplate to the lathe, then turn the edges cleanly.

◆ Carefully turn through the plywood, cutting on the inside of the 80mm (3⅟₁₆in) diameter line. Do not cut into the chipboard beneath.

◆ Remove the faceplate from the lathe and mark a datum line on the plywood and chipboard so that they can be realigned accurately.

◆ Mark a datum line on the faceplate so

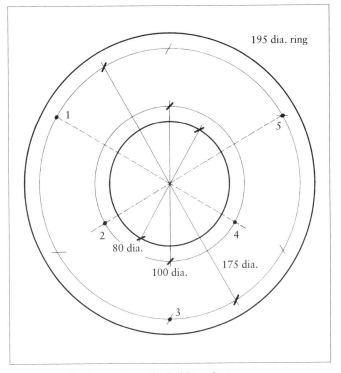

Fig 16.2 *The plywood top for holding the jig, showing the setting for the Allen bolts.*

that can also be accurately realigned.

◆ Remove the chipboard from the faceplate and, of course, the still-attached plywood.

◆ Remove the screw at Position 1.

◆ Fit a 6mm (¼in) drill into the pillar drill. If a hand-held drill is used, make sure that it is held at 90° to the work when drilling.

◆ Drill through Position 1 and through the chipboard.

◆ Drop an Allen bolt into the hole to hold its position.

◆ Repeat the process at each of Positions 2 to 5.

◆ Counterbore the plywood so that the cheese-head of the Allen bolt sinks below the surface or as near as possible without weakening the ply.

◆ Remove the ply from the chipboard.

◆ Counterbore the underside of the chipboard to accept the nuts that fit the bolts. Give sufficient depth to allow for thread movement whilst maintaining strength in the chipboard.

◆ Fit the nuts into the holes. If the nuts need to be glued into place – that is if they are very loose in the holes – use an epoxy glue

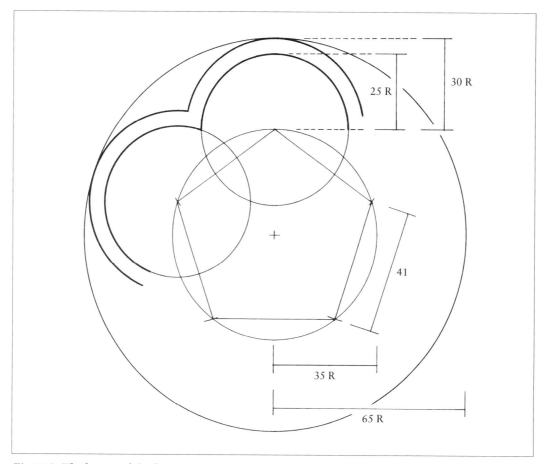

Fig 16.3 *The layout of the five centres on the quinfoil bowl.*

and locate them using the Allen bolts, but be very careful and do not allow any glue to touch the threaded section of the bolt, which could cause the bolt to be glued in place.

◆ When the nuts are fixed in position and the glue has set, replace the chipboard on the faceplate using the datum line to relocate accurately.

◆ Fit the bolts through the holes in the plywood and fit the plywood to the chipboard, again using the datum line to ensure correct location.

◆ Finally a counterweight needs to be cut and fitted, so choose a piece of wood the same thickness and density as that being used to form the bowl.

◆ From that piece, cut a 90mm (3⁹⁄₁₆in) wide by 115mm (4½in) long section.

◆ Measure 57.5mm (2¼in) along the long edge, then measure 15mm (⅝in) in. At that point, drill a 6mm (¼in) diameter hole.

◆ Remove Allen bolts at Positions 2, 3 and 4.

◆ Slide the cut block between the ply and chipboard discs.

◆ Refit the Allen bolts in Position 3 hole through the ply, through the drilled hole in the block and into the chipboard.

◆ Make sure that the block is set equally, showing as much one side of Position 3 as the other. Mark in pencil around the outer edge of the ply marking the curve on the wood block.

◆ Remove the block.

◆ On a piece of card, mark a 130mm (5⅛in) diameter circle. Cut out that circle.

◆ Fit the card circle onto the inner edge – 115mm (4½in) long – of the block until the corners and the curve coincide. Mark around the card circle in pencil on the wood block.

◆ Take the block to the band saw and cut both pencil marked curves.

◆ Refit the block and Allen bolts 2, 3 and 4.

They should all now fit without problems. If No. 2 and No. 4 cannot be fitted because the block is in the way, cut a little more off until the fit is good.

◆ The counterweight is now cut to shape and ready to use.

◆ The final operation. Remove the plywood from the chipboard. Remove the Allen bolts and counterweight.

◆ Glue a sheet of medium glasspaper to the top surface of the chipboard.

◆ Glue a sheet of medium glasspaper to the under surface of the plywood.

◆ Put the two discs together, glasspaper in the middle like a sandwich. Pile some weight on top so that the glasspaper is held firmly whilst the glue dries.

◆ When dry, cut out the glasspaper from the centre hole on the ply and pierce the bolt holes in both the chipboard and the plywood.

◆ This glasspaper surface will ensure an excellent gripping surface when turning the five-centred bowl.

Marking the pentagon

◆ Refer to Fig 16.3.

◆ On the 130mm (5⅛in) diameter blank, mark the precise centre – call it X.

◆ Draw a 35mm (1⅜in) radius circle about that centre.

◆ The block is on the bench directly in front of you, so mark a line through the centre directly away from you.

◆ Where that line cuts the 35mm (1⅜in) radius circle at the top – the point furthest away – mark that as A.

◆ Draw another line, again through the centre but this time at 90° to the first.

◆ Take a protractor and place its centre on the centre of the blank marked X.

◆ Keep the vertical line on the first line drawn and the horizontal line on the second, which was drawn at right angles to the first.

◆ Find a point on the protractor 72° away from the top Point A. Mark this point and join it to the centre. Where it cuts the 35mm (1⅜in) radius circle, mark as B.

◆ The distance A/B is the length of one side of a pentagon marked around a 35mm

Fig 16.4 The blank set out and the holding jig.

(1⅜in) radius circle.

◆ Set the compass to A/B and 'walk' it around the circle marking the other three points, C, D and E.

◆ Reset the compass to 25mm (1in) radius and draw a circle using each of those lettered positions as centres.

◆ Reset the compass, this time to 30mm (1³⁄₁₆in) radius, and draw circles again about each of those five points (*see* Fig 16.4).

◆ The outer circle will form the outer edge of the bowl.

◆ The inner circle marks the area that is to be turned away.

◆ The final part of the marking out process is to continue those first two lines drawn upon the blank – the vertical and horizontal.

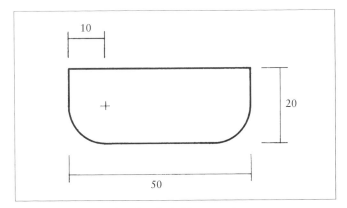

Fig 16.5 The template for the hollows on the five centres.

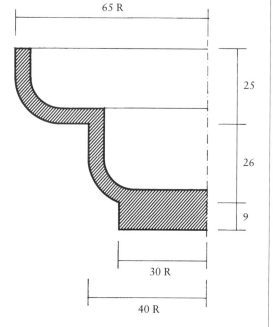

Fig 16.6 Held in the jig, the blank is ready to be turned on the first centre.

Fig 16.7 A cross section through the quinfoil bowl.

Draw them down the edges of the blank at 90° to the top surface. Turn the blank over and join those lines across the base. Where the lines cross will indicate the centre of the underside. Mark this as Z.

◆ Make a simple card template 20mm (¹³⁄₁₆in) deep and 50mm (2in) wide with a 10mm (⅜in) radius curve on the base corners (*see* Fig 16.5). This is the shape that each of the five sections should be turned to.

◆ Fit the faceplate jig onto the lathe.

◆ Bring the tailstock holding the revolving centre towards the jig.

◆ Fit the blank disc into the jig, sliding it across so that point A is in line with the revolving centre.

◆ Push the revolving centre exactly into the centre of point A and tighten down.

◆ Make sure all parts of the blank are held within the shaping of the jig.

◆ Tighten down all the Allen bolts (*see* Fig 16.6). Tighten each one a small way then move onto the next so that none are over-tightened at the expense of others. Tighten the bolts closest to the workpiece first. Tighten the bolt through the counterweight last.

◆ When all are fastened firmly, locking the block in place, rotate the lathe by hand to ensure that nothing catches. When satisfied, withdraw the tailstock.

◆ Bring the tool rest across the face of the work rotating the jig by hand, again ensuring free movement.

Turning the interior

◆ Refer to Fig 16.7 for the dimensions of the quinfoil bowl.

◆ Using a gouge for the majority of the work, turn out a hollow to the outer edge of the marked 50mm (2in) diameter pencil circle to a depth of 20mm (¹³⁄₁₆in)(*see* Fig 16.8). Stop occasionally to check the shaping against the card template (*see* Fig 16.9). It may be necessary to use a round-nose tool to finish the shaping in the corners but use the tool with which you have most confidence.

◆ It is essential that the work is cut cleanly from the gouge or round-nose tool for, as this turnery progresses, it will be extremely difficult, if not dangerous, to sand the

Fig 16.8 Turning out the first centre.

Fig 16.9 Checking the shape using a card template.

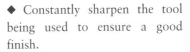

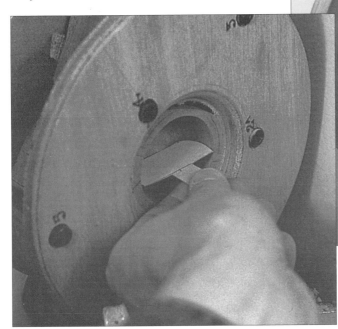

rotating work. Here the use of red gum proved of real benefit. It is a clean-cutting wood which turns crisply with the shavings chipping away leaving a fine surface straight from the tool and, as a bonus, the colour is a wonderful coral red.

◆ When the precise depth and shaping is achieved, stop the lathe, loosen the Allen bolts and move to the next centre. Fit it precisely on that centre and lock down with the tailstock and revolving centre so that the Allen bolts may be tightened.

◆ When all are tightened down, withdraw the tailstock, bring the tool rest across and turn out the next hollow to the precise depth and shape.

◆ When turning this second hollow it will be noticed that the tool will cut into the void of the first hollow, so gentle cuts are needed. The depth of the first hollow may be used as a guide to ensure both hollows are cut equally deep (*see* Fig 16.10).

◆ Continue cutting each of the hollows (*see* Fig 16.11). The final hollow when turned out will break into voids on both sides, so take care.

◆ Constantly sharpen the tool being used to ensure a good finish.

◆ Constantly check that the depth of each hollow is precise and matches those around it.

◆ All cuts must be constant, vertical sides must be vertical, and all bases of hollows

Fig 16.10 The web between two sections can be seen.

Fig 16.11 Setting the next section on centre.

Fig 16.12 Five sections have been turned, leaving a centre column.

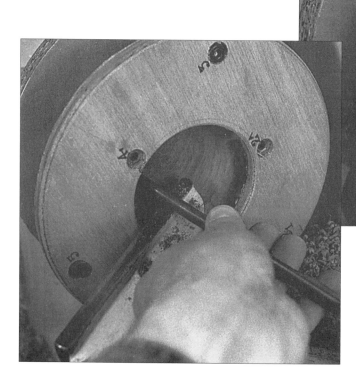

Fig 16.13 The column centred ready to be turned away.

Fig 16.14 Turning the centre hollow.

Fig 16.15 *The internal shaping complete.*

Fig 16.16 *The first cuts on the outer edge.*

must be flat so that they meet evenly.

◆ When all five hollows have been cut (*see* Fig 16.12) move to the centre marked X.

◆ Remove the counterweight, loosen all the bolts, bring X to front centre, lock in place and tighten the bolts (*see* Fig 16.13).

◆ Now turn out the centre very carefully to the points left by the intersection of the turned out hollows and equal to the depth of those hollows.

◆ Continue turning down another 25mm (1in), curving out the base (*see* Fig 16.14). Make clean cuts using sharp tools and the work will finish well from the tool.

◆ The inside of the bowl is now complete. Remove the bowl from the jig and the jig from the lathe (*see* Fig 16.15).

Shaping the exterior

◆ Take the bowl to the band saw and cut the outer edge following the profile of the 30mm (1³⁄₁₆in) radius circles, stopping where they intersect (*see* Fig 16.16).

◆ Fit a 150mm (6in) diameter disc of softwood 35–50mm (1⅜–2in) thick onto a faceplate.

◆ Turn into the softwood a 130mm (5⅛in) diameter 6mm (¼in) deep hollow with straight sides.

◆ Place the shaped bowl into the recess, hollow side against the softwood jam chuck.

◆ Bring up the tailstock holding the revolving centre towards the work. Fit the revolving centre to the position marked Z and tighten down (*see* Fig 16.17).

◆ Measure from the softwood surface

Fig 16.17 *The bowl held on the jam chuck ready for external shaping.*

Fig 16.18 The external shape nearly completed.

19mm (¾in); if the 6mm (¼in) below the rim is included this will mean a full 25mm (1in) is being measured on the body of the bowl, towards the tailstock.

◆ On the tailstock side of this line, turn down to an 80mm (3⅛in) diameter. Turn the bumpy band saw edge in a good curve to meet this turned-down section. Try to remember the internal shaping to avoid turning through.

◆ Measure on the red gum bowl 9mm (⅜in) from the tailstock towards the headstock. This small section is to be turned to a 60mm (2⅜in) diameter and will be the foot of the bowl.

◆ Round over the base of the 80mm (3⅛in) diameter part to meet the foot (*see* Fig 16.18).

◆ Clean up the outside carefully.

Turning the quinfoil shape on the foot

◆ Using the centre marked Z, mark a 30mm (1³⁄₁₆in) diameter circle about that point.

◆ Mark five equally spaced points about that circle using the method shown earlier. Label them 1 to 5.

◆ About each of those centres, draw a 30mm (1³⁄₁₆in) diameter circle (*see* Fig 16.19).

◆ Fit the bowl with the base uppermost into the jig which is now refixed to the headstock.

◆ Bring point 1 to the centre and lock in

Fig 16.19 The layout of the bowl base.

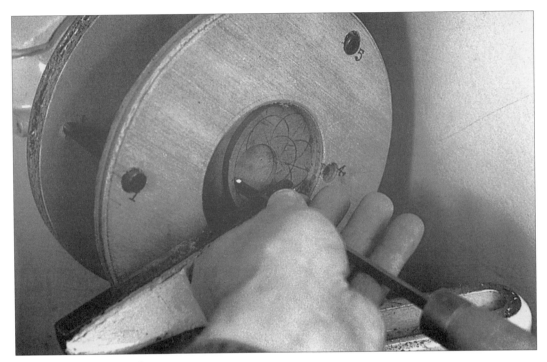

Fig 16.20 *Turning one base centre.*

place using the revolving centre held in the tailstock. Tighten down the Allen bolts.

◆ Turn out the 30mm (1³⁄₁₆in) circle to a depth of 3mm (⅜in), keeping the sides vertical and the base flat (*see* Fig 16.20).

◆ Move to each of the other remaining centres repeating the cut. This should cut out the centre marked Z but if a small pip remains,

clean out with a chisel (*see* Fig 16.21).

◆ Finally clean the band-sawn edges using files and glasspaper until a smooth and fluent shape is achieved.

◆ Glasspaper all parts smooth and finish as required.

A small but interesting quinfoil bowl.

Fig 16.21 *The base turned.*

CHAPTER 17

Facet-sided Box and Vase

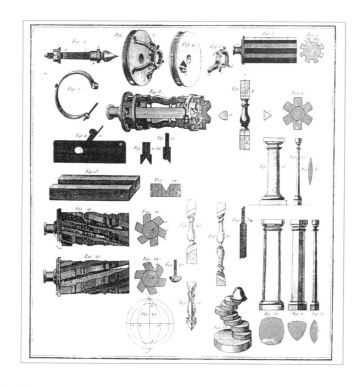

HERE IS AN ENGRAVING IN THAT ANCIENT BOOK *MANUEL DU TOURNEUR* BY HAMELIN BERGERON WHICH SHOWS PIECES FIXED ON THE OUTSIDE OF A DRUM-SHAPED HOLDER. THIS HOLDER CAN BE FIXED BETWEEN CENTRES ON A LATHE AND THE PIECES PROFILE TURNED. BALUSTERS AND COLUMNS ARE SHOWN. ONE COLUMN PRODUCED IN THIS MANNER HAS A CLASSICAL PROFILE BUT WHEN TURNED SIDEWAYS IT IS EXTREMELY THIN.

OTHER COLUMNS AND BALUSTERS ARE TRIANGULAR IN SECTION BUT ALL ARE FULLY TURNED.

Developing this idea and moving it towards faceplate turning, internal curves can be made upon an object. The size of curve, its longitudinal shape, the number of cuts, all may be varied, as well as the axial position of the object. This hints at a pool of ideas so deep that, here, only the surface is touched.

Using the drum method of external or convex cutting of facets, the size of the curve as well as its shape and number may be changed. This is clearly demonstrated in Bergeron's engraving. But in that engraving the number of faces being cut relies upon the

Fig 17.1 A faceted box, vase and oddity.

shape of the hollow into which the piece fits and the initial shaping of the piece itself. As the cuts progress it would become increasingly difficult to hold the complex turned part accurately .

Below I will describe a relatively simple method of indexing the cut so that any number of predetermined sides may be presented to the turner.

A simple faceted box with eight concave cuts into its side and a small vase with six convex-turned sides are shown in Fig 17.1. There is a glimpse of, well, what looks like a wooden sundae glass but that is a mere novelty.

Preparation for the box

◆ Cut two discs of the chosen wood 80mm (3³⁄₁₆in) in diameter, one 25mm (1in) thick, the other 40mm (1⅝in) thick.
◆ Cut a piece of chipboard 200mm (8in) in diameter and 15mm (⅝in) thick, and a piece of 9mm (⅜in) ply also 200mm (8in) in diameter.
◆ Twenty-four 19mm (¾in) long No. 8 countersunk screws are needed.
◆ Have ready a piece of 200mm (8in) square by 64mm (2½in) thick softwood.
◆ A piece of 100mm (4in) diameter by 38mm (1½in) thick softwood will be needed.
◆ A faceplate will be required.
◆ Lathe speed should be 500rpm for the facet cutting and 1250rpm for turning the basic box.

Turning the box

◆ For the dimensions and layout of the box, refer to Fig 17.2.
◆ Fit to the faceplate the 100mm (4in) diameter 38mm (1½in) thick piece of softwood centrally.
◆ Turn the face and edge true.
◆ Fit centrally using a glue and paper joint the 80mm (3³⁄₁₆in) diameter, 25mm (1in) thick piece of hardwood. My choice is padauk.
◆ Once the glue is dry, turn the hardwood face flat and true.
◆ Mark in pencil a 55mm (2³⁄₁₆in) diameter concentric circle on the face of the work.
◆ On the outside of this circle, using a square-end tool, cut a 3mm (⅛in) deep step, flat to the outer edge.
◆ Mark in pencil a 51mm (2in) diameter circle concentrically upon the face of the work.

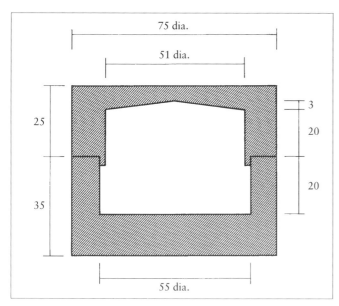

Fig 17.2 A cross section of the facet box.

◆ On the inside of this pencil circle, turn out 20mm (¹³⁄₁₆in) deep (*see* Fig 17.3).

◆ Using a sharp knife, split the top section away from the chuck and set aside.

◆ Clean up the face of the softwood flat and true.

◆ Taking the second disc of wood, which is 40mm (1⁹⁄₁₆in) thick and is the same diameter as the first, fix it centrally upon the softwood surface using the glue

and paper method. Apply pressure using the tailstock.

◆ When the glue has dried, turn off the face flat and true.

◆ Mark a 55mm (2³⁄₁₆in) diameter pencil circle concentrically upon the face of the work.

◆ Turn on the inside of this pencil line to a depth of 20mm (¹³⁄₁₆in).

Whilst I was in Australia a woodturner suggested the following method of holding lids to boxes whilst they are being turned. Unfortunately I did not register the turner's name so he is to remain anonymous. My thanks for the idea go to him. The method of holding is not new but the trick of removal is. It has proved particularly useful in this instance.

◆ Take a hot-melt glue gun and fix the lid to the base. Turn the box fully then remove the piece from the lathe. Place the box in a microwave oven on full power for 25 seconds. This is sufficient to soften the hot-melt glue. Pull the lid from the box.

◆ Hot glue the top onto the base (*see* Fig 17.4) and use the tailstock to apply pressure

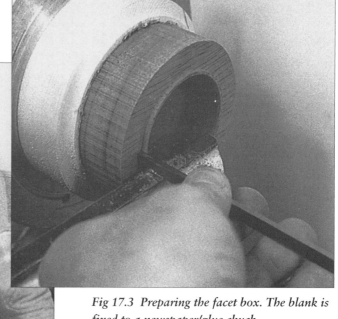

Fig 17.3 Preparing the facet box. The blank is fixed to a newspaper/glue chuck.

Fig 17.4 The base is turned and the top is hot-melt glued to the base.

Fig 17.5 A small locator hole is drilled in the top.

Fig 17.6 The centre of the base is marked once the prepared box blank is removed.

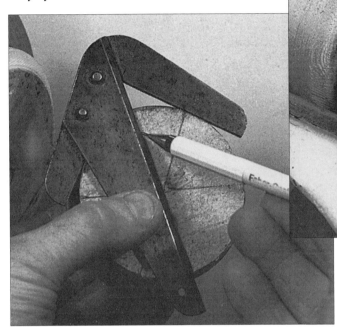

indexing system. These temporarily fixed dowels can be glued in permanently once they have been tested in the jig and are satisfactory.

for the brief moment that it is needed.

◆ Turn the outer edge of the box to a 75mm (3in) diameter.

◆ Round the lid slightly (although this is not strictly necessary).

◆ Fit a 3mm (⅛in) drill into a drill chuck and drill 3mm (⅛in) deep into the centre of the lid as a location point (*see* Fig 17.5).

◆ Using a sharp knife, remove the box from the softwood faceplate.

◆ Take an engineers' centre finder and draw two lines across the base of the work to locate the centre (*see* Fig 17.6).

◆ Set a compass to 50mm (2in) diameter.

◆ Place the compass point on the centre of the base and draw a circle about that point.

◆ Mark any one point on that circle.

◆ Take the work to the pillar drill and, using a 6mm (¼in) drill bit, drill a 9mm (⅜in) deep hole accurately at the marked centre and at the one marked point on the pencil circle.

◆ Take a piece of 6mm (¼in) dowel and cut two 15mm (⅝in) long pieces.

◆ Fit the dowels (do not glue yet) into each of the drilled holes in the base of the box.

◆ This is the start of a dowel-and-hole

Making the chuck

◆ When making the chuck, refer to Fig 17.7 for layout and dimensions.

◆ Fit the 200mm (8in) diameter chipboard centrally to the faceplate and turn down to a 190mm (7½in) diameter.

◆ Mark the centre of the chipboard circle.

◆ Mark a 120mm (4¾in) diameter concentric circle upon the face of the chipboard.

◆ Mark on one side only the position where this line crosses the drawn circle.

◆ Set a compass to a 12.5mm (½in) radius. Place the point on the marked junction and draw a circle. This will be called the indexing circle.

◆ Divide this indexing circle into eight equal parts as follows.

◆ Draw a line at 90° to the first, through the centre of the circle.

◆ Bisect the angles between these two lines on both sides and the indexing circle will be divided into eight.

◆ Take the chipboard disc to the pillar drill.

◆ Fit a 6mm (¼in) drill into the chuck.

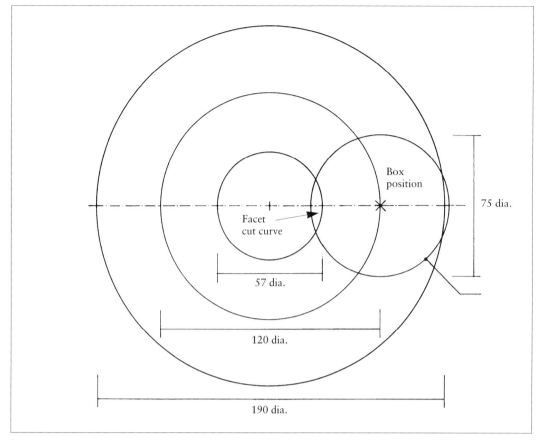

Box
position

Facet
cut curve

75 dia.

57 dia.

120 dia.

190 dia.

Fig 17.7 A layout of the chuck showing the box position.

Fig 17.8 The index holes on the base of the chuck.

◆ At each of the eight division points on the outer edge of the indexing circle, drill to a depth of 12mm (½in) precisely. The indexing circle is now complete (*see* Fig 17.8).

◆ Try the dowel in the base of the box for fit. Adjust where necessary, then glue dowels into box base. Now move on to the thick softwood block.

◆ On the 200mm (8in) square softwood block, mark a 190mm (7½in) diameter circle.

◆ On the same centre, mark a 120mm (4¾in) diameter circle.

◆ Draw a centre line across the circle and mark on one side, where it cuts the 120mm (4¾in) circle, the letter C.

◆ Reset the compass to 37.5mm (1½in).

◆ At the marked point C, draw a circle using the set compass. This produces a 75mm (3in) diameter circle.

◆ Cut on the outside of the 190mm (7½in) diameter circle.

◆ Cut through and around the inside of the 75mm (3in) diameter circle.

◆ Move to the 120mm (4¾in) diameter

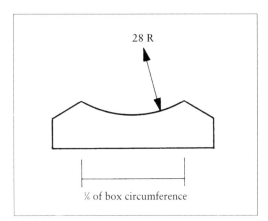

Fig 17.9 *The facet template.*

28 R

⅛ of box circumference

circle, and cut on the inside of that line.

◆ Now return to the chipboard on the faceplate. Mark a datum on the faceplate and chipboard so it can be accurately replaced, then remove the chipboard.

◆ Fit the box blank onto the indexing circle.

◆ Place the chipboard onto the cut-out softwood, fitting the box into the 75mm (3in) cut circle.

◆ Make sure the softwood is accurately and concentrically fitted to the chipboard, then drill and countersink through the chipboard, finally screwing down to the softwood.

◆ Refit the chipboard to the faceplate.

◆ On the 9mm (⅜in) ply, mark a 190mm (7½in) diameter circle.

◆ Band saw the outer edge of the circle.

◆ Place the sawn plywood disc centrally on top of the softwood.

◆ Mark on the ply precisely where the top centre of the box is located. Remove the ply, drill through using a 3mm (⅛in) drill, then replace. This hole should line up with the locator hole in the top of the box. Turn a small 3mm (⅛in) diameter dowel to be fitted into the ply. This dowel should fit dry into the box locator hole.

◆ Remove the box temporarily from the chuck, rescrewing the ply in place.

◆ Fit the whole chuck to the lathe.

◆ Bring the tool rest to the front of the work.

◆ Rotate the work by hand to ensure nothing catches, then mark in pencil a 100mm (4in) diameter circle.

◆ Turn through the ply on the inside of the marked circle.

◆ Chamfer the inner and outer edges of the ply.

◆ The jig/chuck is now complete.

Turning the facets on the box

◆ Before starting to turn the concave facets on the box, the exact width of the cut needs to be calculated.

◆ On paper, draw a 75mm (3in) diameter circle. Draw a centre line followed by a line at 90° to the first, again through the centre.

◆ Bisect the angles between these lines and this will divide the circle into eight equal parts. The distance between each division will be the width of the cut, 29mm (1½in) measured straight.

◆ To save any calculations, draw a 57mm (2⁵⁄₁₆in) diameter pencil circle centred on the chipboard base. If the curved faceted cut on the outside of the box is matched to this marked circle then eight equally spaced, equally wide cuts will be made.

◆ Cut from card a 57mm (2⁵⁄₁₆in) diameter circle with a 29mm (1½in) wide section marked to act as a template (*see* Fig 17.9).

◆ Remove the ply disc from the softwood and fit the box blank onto the indexing ring. Push

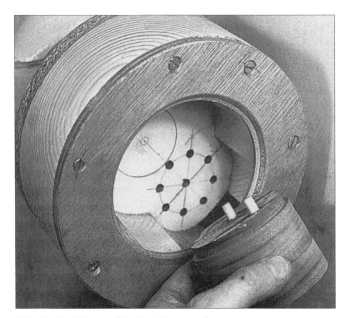

Fig 17.10 *The box blank with an index peg waiting to be fitted into the chuck.*

Fig 17.11 With the box in place and locator peg in position, turning is ready to start.

Fig 17.12 Starting the cut. Note the pencil circle on the chuck base which acts as a guide.

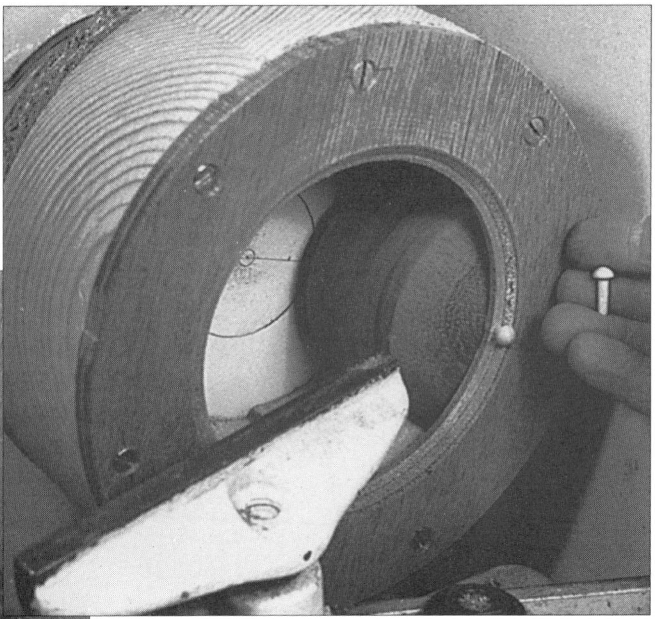

the dowels into the drilled holes (*see* Fig 17.10).

◆ Refit the ply, pushing the small locating dowel into the top of the box blank (*see* Fig 17.11). Tighten the screws. The softwood disc beneath should be a few millimetres (a fraction of an inch) shorter than the box blank, enabling the ply to give a good grip on top.

◆ Bring the tool rest across the face of the work.

◆ Rotate the chuck/jig by hand to ensure nothing catches, then turn on the lathe.

◆ For those used to turning eccentric pieces this experience will be nothing new. For those who lack experience, take care with the first cuts, for a ghosting image is all that can be seen of the work. The first cut must only be taken on the very edge of the ghost image and that same cut must be very light.

◆ Account must be taken of the bevel shape of the tools used because the curve of the cut is very tight. This could cause the lower part of a less steeply angled bevel to rub, keeping

the cutting edge away from the work. Regrind bevels to suit the cut being taken.

◆ This work is not for the inexperienced turner. It is safe if approached cautiously. Care and sensibility is required. When cutting, do not cut too heavily but make fine, light cuts at all times.

◆ Cuts must only be taken on the forward movement. Do not try to cut when the tool is being withdrawn for it is far harder to judge the depth of cut. Keep the tool sharp and take nibbling cuts. Where possible try to arrange to keep the tool rest as close to the work as possible to avoid too much of an overhang. The tool must remain horizontal because if the tip is raised or lowered then a deep cut could inadvertently be made, jarring the box off centre.

◆ Always check that the screws on the plywood disc are tight down.

◆ Continue the cut until it matches the marked inner circle on the base of the chipboard (*see* Fig 17.12).

◆ Do not try to glasspaper the work whilst the lathe is in motion.

◆ The cut is finished when it matches the base circle and its edge runs vertically down the side of the box edge.

◆ Turn off the lathe and check the card template against the cut. If satisfied move on to the next cut.

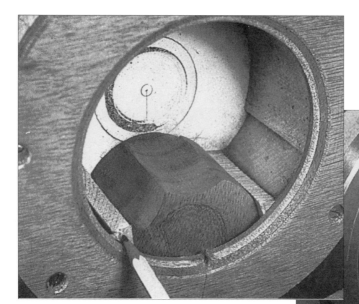

Fig 17.13 Three facets cut. Note the softwood wedges to help hold the box blank even more firmly.

Fig 17.14 Completing the base.

◆ Remove the plywood top.

◆ Lift the box blank out and move the dowel around one position on the index circle.

◆ Replace the plywood top then turn the next facet.

◆ Repeat until all eight facets are cut.

◆ It may be necessary to fit softwood wedges on either side of the box to give added support during some of the cuts (see Fig 17.13). The wedges made of softwood cannot damage the box sides.

◆ For this piece I chose to work with padauk which is an ideal 'mild' timber for this work and that custard powder smell that comes as padauk is worked is an added bonus.

◆ When making the facet cuts it is very tempting to turn the closest edge and then taper down and in, but do be firm with yourself and turn fully down full width – unless you think that a tapered facet would look interesting.

◆ When completely satisfied that all facets are cut well, remove the box from the chuck.

◆ Place the box in a microwave on full power for 25 seconds.

◆ Remove from the microwave. The hot-melt glue holding lid to base should be sufficiently soft to allow the box to be opened.

Turning the top of the lid and bottom of the base

◆ On the softwood faceplate used earlier as a glue chuck, turn a 10mm (⅜in) long 55mm (2³⁄₁₆in) diameter spigot to match the internal diameter of the base.

◆ Saw off the dowels from the base.

◆ Fit the box base onto the jam chuck.

◆ Bring the revolving centre up to support the box.

◆ Turn the base down to 30mm (1⁵⁄₁₆in) thick. This will turn away the dowels.

◆ Turn a 55mm (2³⁄₁₆in) wide, 6mm (¼in) deep foot on the base (see Fig 17.14), then remove from the jam chuck.

◆ Turn the jam chuck to a 50mm (2in) diameter to fit the inside of the top.

◆ Fit the top onto the jam chuck and turn a good domed shape (see Fig 17.15).

◆ Remove the top and fit the two parts together. All that remains is to polish the box.

Fig 17.15 Turning the domed top of the box.

Fig 17.16 The top and bottom of the finished box.

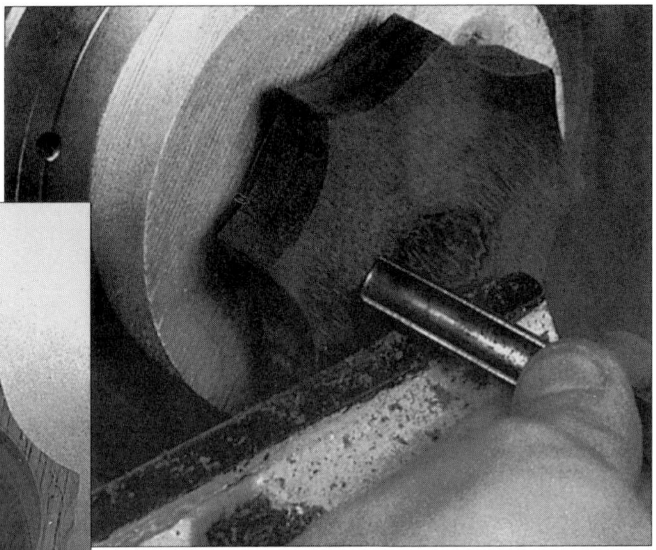

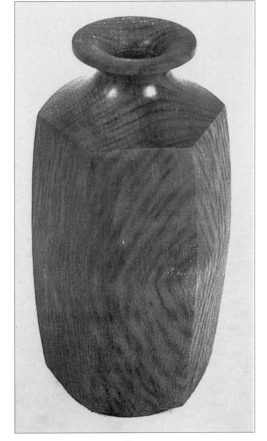

Fig 17.17 The faceted vase.

Preparation for the faceted vase

◆ Have a 200mm (8in) square piece of 15mm (⅝in) thick chipboard and a piece of 200mm (8in) square, 9mm (⅜in) thick plywood ready for the chuck.

◆ Cut four pieces of softwood 144mm (5¹¹⁄₁₆in) long by 50mm (2in) square.

◆ Twenty 25mm (1in) long countersunk steel screws will be needed.

◆ Have ready a piece of hardwood 60mm (2⅜in) long by 30mm (1³⁄₁₆in) square from which to turn a small plug.

◆ Have a piece of good quality hardwood 160mm (6¼in) long by 70mm (2¾in) square from which to turn the vase.

◆ Lathe speed for turning the vase should be 1250rpm and, for turning the facets, 500rpm.

Turning the basic vase shape

◆ For the dimensions of the vase blank, refer to Fig 17.18.

◆ Set the hardwood block between centres.

◆ Turn down to a 62mm (2⁷⁄₁₆in) diameter cylinder.

◆ At the headstock end, turn a 25mm (1in) diameter spigot 15mm (⅝in) long, making sure that the shoulder is turned square and true. Also make sure that the distance from that shoulder at the headstock end is precisely 145mm (just over $5^{11}/_{16}$in) away from the squared-off end at the tailstock.

◆ Remove the blank from the lathe.

◆ Remove the driving dog and replace with a three- or four-jaw chuck.

◆ Take the blank and hold it in the chuck on the turned spigot.

◆ Bring up the tailstock to support the end of the work, fixing the revolving centre into its original hole. This will keep the work accurately centred. Tighten the chuck jaws.

◆ Once the jaws have been tightened, withdraw the tailstock replacing it with a drill chuck holding a 12mm ($\frac{1}{2}$in) drill.

◆ Mark a point on the drill shank 90mm (3½in) away from the cutting edge. Drill into the blank to that depth.

◆ Withdraw the drill. Remove both drill and chuck and replace the revolving centre.

◆ Bring the centre forward into the drilled hole for support, and tighten.

◆ Turn the profile of the vase, measuring 105mm (4⅜in) from the tailstock to mark the position of the vase base (see Fig 17.19).

◆ Remove the vase from the chuck and the chuck from the lathe.

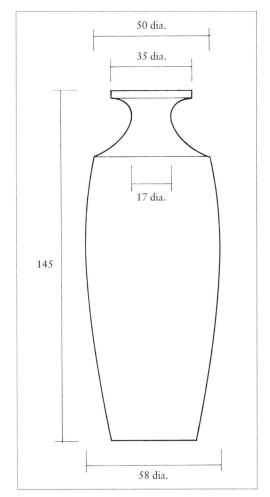

Fig 17.18 The vase blank.

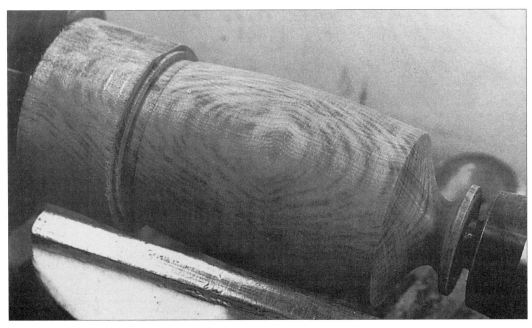

Fig 17.19 The vase blank being turned

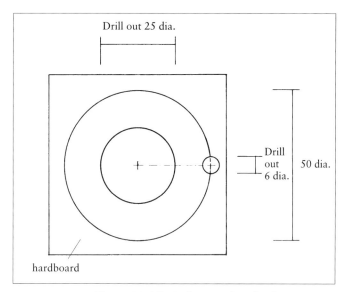

Fig 17.20 *The index template for the vase.*

◆ On a piece of hardboard, mark a 50mm (2in) circle.
◆ Mark a 60mm (2⅜in) square evenly around that circle.
◆ Drill a 25mm (1in) hole at the centre of that drawn circle (*see* Figs 17.20 and 17.21).
◆ Cut out the square shaping around the circle.

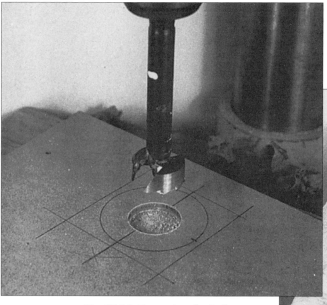

Fig 17.21 *Preparing the index drilling jig for the base of the vase.*

Fig 17.22 *Drilling the index peg hole in the base of the vase blank.*

◆ Fit the piece of hardboard onto the spigot at the end of the vase blank.
◆ Fit a 6mm (¼in) drill into the pillar drill, holding the vase blank with the hardboard piece in place under the drill.
◆ Use masking tape to stick the hardboard in place.
◆ At any one point on that 50mm (2in) diameter pencil circle on the hardboard piece, drill through and into the base of the vase to a depth of 12mm (½in) (*see* Fig 17.22).
◆ Remove the piece from the drill.
◆ Cut a piece of 6mm (¼in) dowel 25mm (1in) long and glue it into the drilled hole in the base of the vase blank. Clean excess glue from the dowel. This will be part of the indexing system.

Making the jig to hold the vase

◆ From the chipboard and ply, mark with a compass and cut 200mm (8in) discs.
◆ Screw the chipboard centrally to the faceplate.
◆ Fit the ply on top fixing firmly with one screw exactly through the centre and one on a 65mm (2⅜in) radius. It is important to mark this accurately.
◆ Turn both discs to a 190mm (7½in) diameter.

Fig 17.23 Assembling the chuck with the vase blank in place.

◆ Separate the discs, both from each other and from the faceplate, having first marked a datum on faceplate, chipboard and plywood so that they may be replaced exactly.

◆ Measure 30mm (1⁷⁄₃₂in) in from the same edge along the centre line on both discs.

◆ On the plywood, drill a 12mm (½in) hole at that point.

◆ On the chipboard, draw a 50mm (2in) diameter circle about that point.

◆ With the compass still set, place the point on the position where the centre line crosses the 50mm (2in) circle, top or bottom – it does not matter which.

◆ 'Walk' the compass around the circle to mark six equally spaced points.

◆ Drill a 6mm (¼in) hole accurately at each of these marked points.

◆ Drill a 25mm (1in) hole precisely on the centre point of the circle.

◆ This produces an index circle to enable six faces to be presented for cutting.

◆ Turn a small plug 30mm (1⁷⁄₃₂in) long, 20mm (¹³⁄₁₆in) of which is 12mm (½in) in diameter, and the remaining 10mm (⅜in) of which is turned to a 20mm (¹³⁄₁₆in) diameter and domed over on top.

◆ Glue this plug into the drilled 12mm (½in) hole in the plywood disc with the domed top on the top surface of the plywood.

◆ Place the vase on the chipboard with the spigot and dowel located in the indexing circle.

◆ Take the six softwood blocks.

◆ Fit one on centre and the other five equally spaced around the disc.

◆ The softwood blocks help balance the work as it rotates, as well as holding the plywood top disc at precisely the right distance away from the back to lock the vase in position.

◆ More than one vase could be turned by replacing these outer softwood blocks with vase blanks, but indexing holes and top plugs would need to be made to accommodate them. Also the centre fixing would need to be strengthened, with maybe a bolt fixed through.

◆ Bring the ply disc down onto the top of these pieces (*see* Fig 17.23) fitting the plug into the top of the drilled opening in the vase (*see* Fig 17.24).

◆ Make sure that the ply is centrally set, then mark positions for drill holes, at least two for each softwood block. Do not fix a screw in the centre of the plywood disc. The revolving centre will fit there for support.

◆ If the screws become loose when constantly fitted and removed, a simple solution is to drill into the softwood at the screw holes and fit plastic Rawlplugs.

◆ When all screw holes have been drilled and countersunk, relocate them ensuring that the ply disc is centrally placed.

◆ Screw into place.

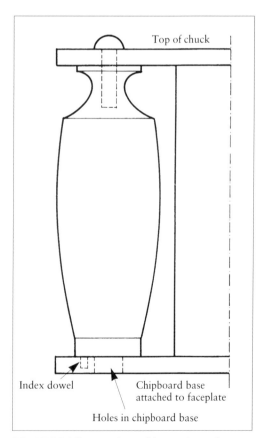

Fig 17.24 *The vase in position to have the facets turned.*

◆ Turn the whole jig over.

◆ Mark positions for the screw holes in the underside of the chipboard – two for each block. Drill and countersink.

◆ Relocate the chipboard and screw firmly in place.

◆ When all screws have been fully fixed, fit the chipboard back onto the faceplate, then fit the faceplate to the chuck.

◆ Bring the revolving centre to support the plywood end of the jig and tighten down.

◆ Bring the tool rest across the face of the work.

◆ Rotate the lathe by hand to make sure nothing catches.

◆ Before work begins the width of the cut made on the edge of the vase needs to be calculated so that equal faces may be turned. It will be approximately one sixth of the circumference of the vase at the widest point – in this case, 32mm (1¼in).

◆ To calculate the facet width of the vase:
  1. Decide how far the centre of the vase is to be offset from the centre of rotation of the lathe.
  2. Set a compass to this distance and draw a circle. This circle's centre is Point 1.
  3. Draw a horizontal line through the centre of this circle.
  4. Place the compass point at the point where this line cuts the left-hand side of the circle, and draw a second circle which is the diameter of the vase. The centre of this circle is Point 2.
  5. Draw a line at 90° to the horizontal line, so that it passes through Point 2.
  6. Where this vertical line cuts the top of the vase circle will be Point 3.
  7. With the compass still set at vase size, place the point on Point 3 and 'walk' it around the vase circle, dividing it into six equal parts.
  8. The position to the left of Point 3 (anticlockwise) will be Point 4. The next anticlockwise position will be Point 5.
  9. Reset the compass so that its point is at the centre of rotation (Point 1) and its pencil end at Point 4.

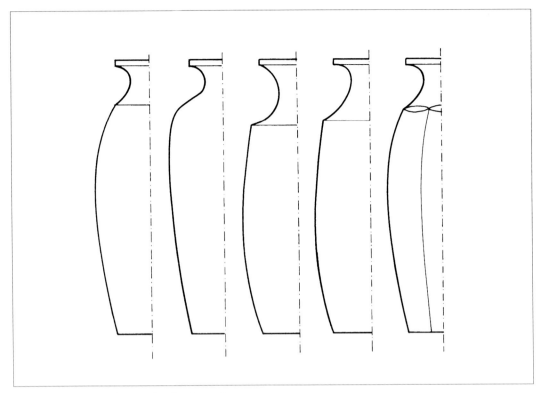

Fig 17.25 Shape selection for the faceted vase.

Fig 17.26 The first facet is cut. Note the heavy
felt-pen guide marks.

10. Draw an arc. This arc will move from Point 4 to Point 5 and will describe the facet cut on the outer edge of the vase.

11. In this case, the facet is approximately 32mm (1¼in) wide.

◆ Decide upon the shape of the face being cut (*see* Fig 17.25). This will relate to the prepared profile of the vase but can be altered even at this stage because more wood can be turned away on each facet cut.

◆ Mark the middle of the cut and the two extremities of the facet cut on the softwood using a thick black felt-tip pen. When the jig is whirring round it is difficult to see these points unless clearly marked.

◆ Using a gouge, make the first cut (*see* Fig 17.26).

◆ Ignore the lumpiness of the cut; be fluent with the gouge. The softwood blocks will be partially turned but this will be of benefit.

◆ Stop and check the shaping regularly and when the cut face reaches the correct width at the centre of the cut, halt.

◆ Clean up the cut face of the work. It may need glasspapering with the grain.

◆ When satisfied with the first cut, remove the ply top and move the vase blank onto the next position.

◆ The following cuts are much easier because the vase shape 'ghosts' above the softwood profile. Stop immediately the tool begins to take shavings from the softwood. Be careful not to turn the softwood too much for it will upset the shaping of the other faces as the softwood profile is used as a guide.

◆ When two faces are cut a really sharp edge should be formed between them. Make sure that this edge is crisp, sharp, even and clean.

◆ Do not be concerned when cutting the third face that the middle face is narrower than the other two for it has been cut on two sides – when each of the others has been cut similarly they will be as wide (or narrow).

◆ Always rotate the jig by hand before turning, and keep the tools sharp.

The wood I chose for this piece of work was superb. It was an Australian wood given as a gift – the most magnificent 'Tasmanian tiger', commonly known as blackheart myrtle. I cannot sing its praises too highly for it cut cleanly, maintained sharp edges

Fig 17.27 Another facet cut.

Fig 17.28 All six faces have been cut. The vase is removed from the chuck.

between faces without chipping, produced a fine surface and the grain patterning on every one of six faces appeared to be different. It had marvellous tiger stripes, leopard spots, blacks and browns with an underlying almost wavering watermark pattern. Besides all that there was an elusive shimmering green flash which could be seen in some lights and not others. 'Tasmanian tiger' – a well-deserved name for the grain

Fig 17.29 The inside of the vase is carefully turned out.

patterning but a kitten to turn.

◆ Once all the sides have been turned and cleaned, remove the piece from the jig (*see* Fig 17.28) and the jig from the lathe.

◆ Hold the piece once more by that 25mm (1in) spigot in a four-jaw chuck.

◆ Bring the centre into the drilled-out end so that when the jaws are tightened the piece remains on centre.

◆ First turn the foot at the base, turning away oddly shaped ends.

◆ Next return to the tailstock end.

◆ Withdraw the tailstock and bring the tool rest across the face of the work.

◆ Turn the top of the vase and into the body, excavating the inside (*see* Fig 17.29). Remember that the outside shape is not regular as in a normal turned vase so make allowance in the wall thickness.

◆ When satisfied with the internal shape the piece can be parted from the lathe, undercutting the foot so that it will stand flat.

◆ If it is felt that the base needs to be fully turned, a simple jam chuck – a deep hollow into which the vase may fit – can be made.

◆ When all the work is finished, polish the vase and consider the shape of the next one based upon this experience.

I would hope that this will just be the beginning, for an interesting variety of turned objects may be made using this technique.

Re-turning a fluted shape can also provide some interesting results as seen in that peculiar if not novel 'sundae' dish (*see* Fig 17.30). Whatever is turned in this way, a little spice is added to a day at the lathe.

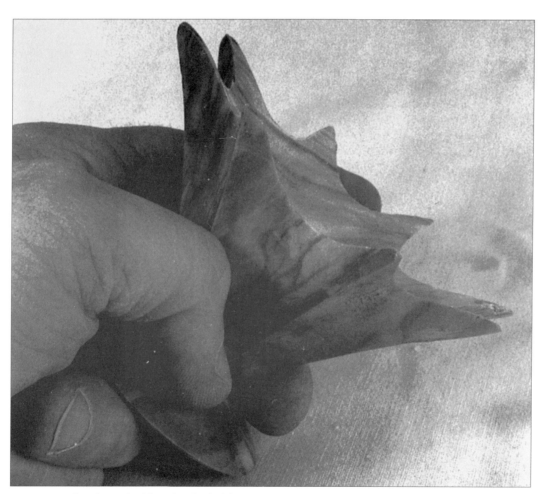

Fig 17.30 That faceted oddity that looks like a sundae glass

CHAPTER 18

Twist-turned Box

AVING TURNED FACETED BOXES AND VASES I BECAME AWARE OF MORE UNUSUAL SHAPES AROUND ME. LOOKING AT CHINA VASES I COULD SEE POSSIBILITIES, BUT IT WAS LOOKING AT ONE VASE IN PARTICULAR THAT REALLY SET ME THINKING. IT WAS FACETED BUT THOSE FACES WERE TWISTED. PICKING UP THE VASE I LOOKED ALONG ONE TWISTED SIDE AND NOTICED THAT IT HAD A CLEAR, ALMOST STRAIGHT DIRECTION AND, AT THAT POINT, I KNEW THAT A TWIST COULD BE TURNED DIRECTLY AND FULLY, REQUIRING NO CARVING.

At first glance this twisted box appears to be impossible as a turned object. At second glance it appears equally impossible, but it has been fully turned.

The prepared blank is held crosswise at an angle in a jig. The turned side is then just a straightforward cut. Using the indexing method shown earlier, any number of predetermined faces can be presented and cut in a regular manner using a normal woodturning gouge.

Tasmanian pink myrtle was used for this piece. Although the sapwood is a little woolly, the wood itself is quite kindly and turns well. The heartwood is a delicate pink moving towards a less interesting brown. The grain pattern can be a wavering pattern crossing through the boundaries of colour or, as in this case, a flame pattern with a strongly bounded pink heart surrounded by a dull brown.

It helps when fitting the lid to the base to choose a wood with a striking grain pattern for, as the box is hand turned, the twist facets may not always match precisely. A striking grain pattern will quickly be aligned and with it the facets.

Preparation

◆ Have ready two pieces of 15mm (⅝in) thick chipboard, each 200mm (8in) square.
◆ Also have ready three softwood blocks 120mm (4¾in) long by 75mm (3in) square and a block 250mm (10in) long by 75mm (3in) square.
◆ A number of 25mm (1in) long No. 8 countersunk screws will be needed.

Fig 18.1 The twist facet box.

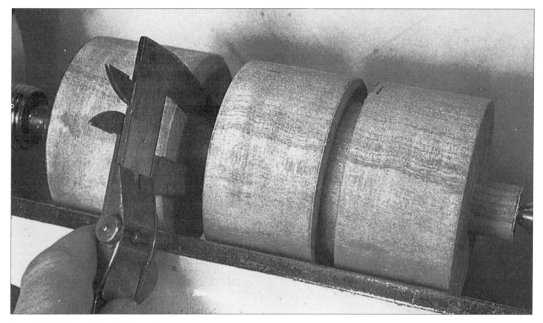

Fig 18.2 Preparing the blank.

◆ A block of the chosen wood 120mm (4¾in) long by 75mm (3in) square will be required.

◆ Lathe speed when turning the box blank should be 1250rpm, and when turning the facets, 500 rpm.

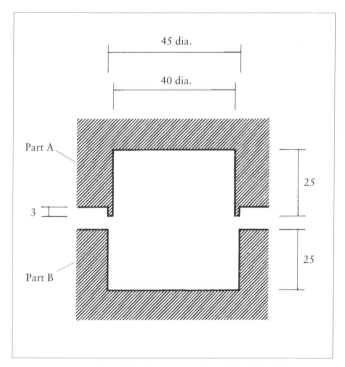

Fig 18.3 A cross section of the blank's interior.

Turning the blank

◆ Take the chosen piece of hardwood and set it between centres.

◆ Turn to a 75mm (3in) diameter.

◆ Measure 15mm (⅝in) from the tailstock towards the headstock.

◆ Turn this end section down to 20mm (¹³⁄₁₆in) in diameter.

◆ From that shoulder, measure 40mm (1⁹⁄₁₆in) towards the headstock and mark in pencil a line around. This section is Part A.

◆ From that pencil line, measure 10mm (⅜in) and turn this part down to 45mm (1¾in) in diameter making sure the shoulders on both sides are square.

◆ From the edge of that turned section, measure a further 40mm (1⁹⁄₁₆in). This is Part B.

◆ The final 15mm (⅝in) is turned down to 20mm (¹³⁄₁₆in) (*see* Fig 18.2).

◆ Cut through the area between Parts A and B leaving most of that 45mm (1¾in) diameter part attached to A.

◆ Remove the driving dog from the headstock and replace with a chuck.

◆ Refer to Fig 18.3 for the inner dimensions of the blank.

◆ Hold the 20mm (¹³⁄₁₆in) diameter spigot of Part A in the chuck, then turn the 45mm (1¾in) section to an accurate size leaving it

3mm (⅛in) high.

◆ Turn its face flat and true.

◆ Turn inside this raised lip at 40mm (1⁹⁄₁₆in) diameter to a depth of 25mm (1in) (*see* Fig 18.4).

◆ Remove Part A from the chuck and replace with Part B, holding on the small spigot.

◆ Turn the face flat and true, then mark in pencil a 45mm (1¾in) diameter concentrically on its face.

◆ Turn on the inside of this marked pencil line to a depth of 25mm (1in).

◆ Check that A fits easily onto B (*see* Fig 18.5).

◆ Take a hot-melt glue gun.

◆ Apply hot glue to the joint between A and B, then press the two parts together making sure the grain pattern of the wood matches.

◆ Bring the tailstock forward holding the revolving centre to apply pressure for the short time it takes for the glue to set.

Making the jig

◆ Cut two chipboard discs each 190mm (7½in) in diameter.

◆ Take a piece of 75mm (3in) square softwood.

Fig 18.4 Turning the inside of the box blank.

◆ Make sure that both ends are cut perfectly square.

◆ On one end, mark pencil diagonals.

◆ Set a compass to a 20mm (¹³⁄₁₆in) radius and place the point where the diagonals cross. Mark a circle on the end of the softwood above that point.

◆ Place the compass point, still set at 20mm (¹³⁄₁₆in) radius, on the marked circle and 'walk'

Fig 18.5 The top and bottom of the box blank complete.

it around marking six equally spaced points.

◆ Fit a 20mm (¹³⁄₁₆in) diameter drill bit into the pillar drill and drill the end of the softwood at the point where the diagonals cross to a depth of 75mm (3in) (*see* Fig 18.6).

◆ Remove the drill, replacing it with a 6mm (¼in) bit.

◆ At each of the six points on the drawn circle, drill to a depth of 15mm (⅝in).

◆ Set the mitre guide on the band saw or table saw to 45°.

◆ Mark a point 3mm (⅛in) down from the drilled end of the softwood and cut across at 45° at that point (*see* Fig 18.7).

◆ Next, cut the remainder of the block at 90° square across from the end of the 45° cut.

◆ Take the two softwood pieces and the prepared pink myrtle blank. Fit the turned spigot of the blank into the squared faces of the drill and cut softwood block.

◆ Set one angled face flat down on the bench and measure the vertical height to the top angled face (*see* Fig 18.8). In this case it is 115mm (4½in), but measure your own piece to arrive at an accurate figure.

Fig 18.6 Preparing the indexing block.

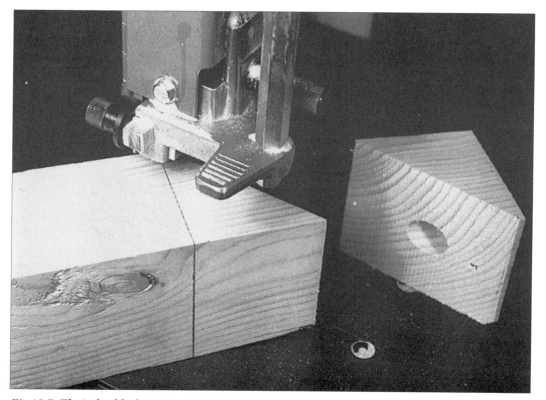

Fig 18.7 The index block cut at 45°.

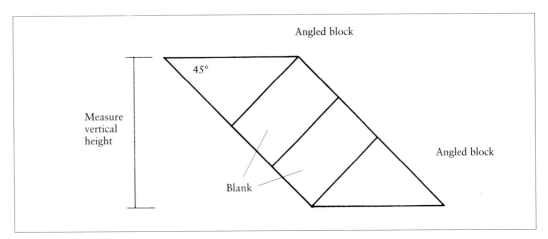

Fig 18.8 The blank positioned between two angled blocks.

◆ Now cut two 75mm (3in) square softwood blocks to that length. Make sure both ends are cut squarely.

Fitting the jig together

◆ Fit one chipboard disc centrally to the faceplate.

◆ The two softwood blocks are used to hold the two chipboard discs apart which will provide space for the angled pink myrtle block to be fixed in place.

◆ Place the faceplate with the attached chipboard disc on the bench.

◆ Stand the two softwood blocks side by side on one half of the chipboard.

◆ Place the angled blocks holding the blank down onto the chipboard next to the blocks with the index-drilled section (*see* Fig 18.9).

◆ The pink myrtle blank must just stay within the bounds of the outer edge of the disc. View from above. The angled blocks may spread over the disc edge.

◆ Arrange the angle blocks in this manner but make sure that neither of them is further over the edge than the other. That is, the lower edge must not be too far back or spread over one side more than the top spreads over its sides.

◆ When the block is arranged satisfactorily place the second chipboard disc on top.

◆ Use a try square to ensure that the top

disc is directly above the lower on all sides.

◆ Mark positions for screws to fix the softwood blocks firmly. Use three screws for each block and avoid the centre of the chipboard.

◆ Mark the positions of the screws to hold the top of the angled block, being aware of the drilled hole through the block. Mark datum lines on the edge of the disc and softwood blocks.

◆ Remove the disc. Drill and countersink those holes.

◆ Replace the disc, realigning it using the marked data and using a try square to ensure accuracy.

Fig 18.9 Assembling the chuck ensuring that top and base are aligned.

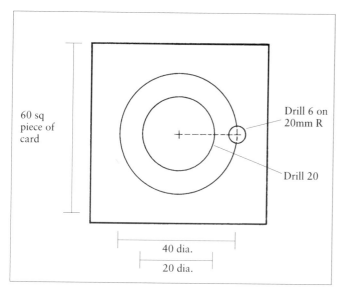

Fig 18.10 The template for indexing.

Drill 6 on 20mm R

Drill 20

60 sq piece of card

40 dia.

20 dia.

◆ Screw the disc in place.

◆ Keeping the pieces together, turn the disc over and mark for screws in the same manner as for the first disc having removed the faceplate first. Mark data as before.

◆ Drill and countersink the screw holes, then return the disc to the blocks.

◆ Relocate accurately using the try square and data as before. Screw down the chipboard disc.

◆ Take the jig to the band saw and very

carefully band saw away any softwood parts which overhang the chipboard edges. Do not cut any of the pink myrtle blank which may (but should not) overhang the edge.

◆ Remove each now shaped, angled block and glue them back in place with epoxy resin, screwing them firmly to their original position. The pink myrtle does not have to be in position whilst these blocks are fixed.

◆ Fix the faceplate back onto the chipboard using the marked datum to relocate accurately.

◆ The index dowel now needs to be fixed to the end of the blank.

◆ On a piece of card or hardboard, draw a 40mm (1⁹⁄₁₆in) diameter circle. On the same centre, mark a 20mm (¹³⁄₁₆in) diameter circle (*see* Figs 18.10 and 18.11).

◆ Drill or cut out on the inside of the 20mm (¹³⁄₁₆in) diameter circle.

◆ Fit the cut-out circle over the 20mm (¹³⁄₁₆in) diameter spigot on the end of the pink myrtle.

◆ Mark any point on the 40mm (1⁹⁄₁₆in) circle and drill a 6mm (¼in) hole at that point through and into the myrtle to a depth of 6mm (¼in).

◆ Cut an 18mm (¾in) length of 6mm (¼in) dowel and, once the piece of card is

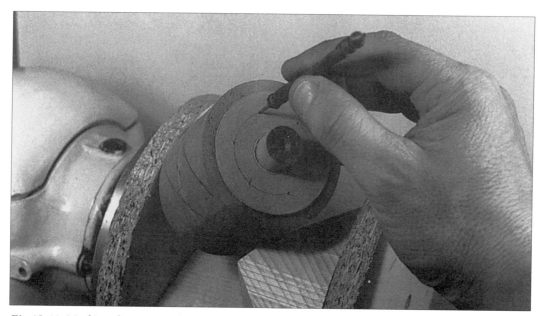

Fig 18.11 Marking the position for the index peg on the base of the box blank.

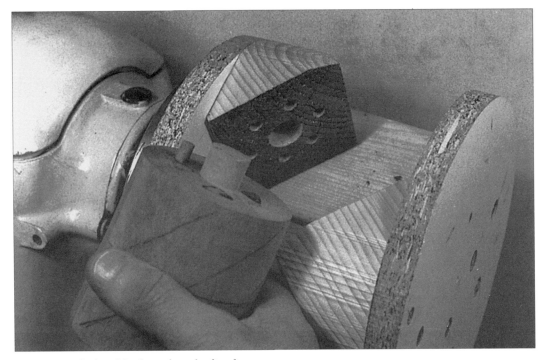

Fig 18.12 *The box blank ready to be fitted into the chuck.*

removed, glue it into the hole.

◆ Clean away excess glue and, before the glue sets, test the piece in the index softwood block making adjustments where necessary.

◆ Remove the pink myrtle and allow the glued dowel to dry in position.

Turning the 'twisted' sides

◆ Fig 18.13 shows the final shape and dimensions of the twisted facet box.

◆ Fit the jig to the headstock and bring the tailstock forward holding a revolving centre to support the end of the jig.

◆ Bring the tool rest across the side of the work.

◆ Rotate the lathe by hand to ensure that nothing catches.

◆ The width of cut needs to be determined before starting. This is calculated quite simply. The cut width is one sixth of the circumference of the work piece. As a very quick guide, when marking out the six equally spaced points on a circle the radius is used. So here for the width of the cut use the

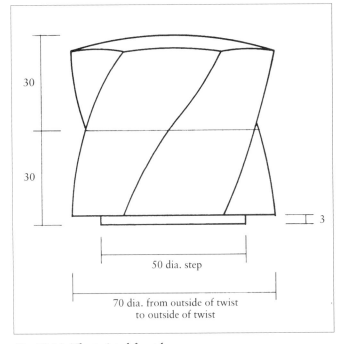

Fig 18.13 *The twisted facet box.*

radius of the piece which is 37.5mm (1½in). *But* this size is straight cuts and this cut is set at 45°, so draw a 45° line and measure 37.5mm (1½in) along it. Mark vertically down from that point and measure the horizontal distance from the start of the angled line to that point. Conveniently it is

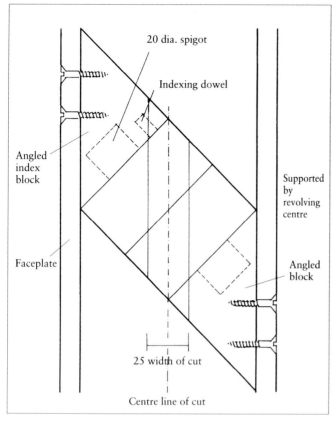

Fig 18.14 *The blank positioned within the chuck, showing the centre line of cut.*

25mm (1in), so this is the true width to cut.

◆ On the blank held in the jig, mark the centre line of the cut (*see* Fig 18.14), then mark half the width of the cut either side: 12.5mm (½in) either side. Mark these three lines with thick black felt-tip above and below on the softwood blocks and in pencil on the blank.

◆ The black felt-pen marks ensure that the cutting area can clearly be seen when the jig rotates and becomes a blur.

◆ The depth of cut must not exceed 12mm (½in) otherwise the internal hollow will be exposed.

◆ Turn the lathe on and, using a gouge, begin cutting the ghost image. Work from the outer marked edges towards the middle.

◆ At the start of the work only a top and bottom cut diagonally opposite will be made, but this is correct for as the cut deepens it will begin to cut on both sides, top and bottom (*see* Fig 18.15). Also, as other faces are cut they will help equal out the shaping.

Fig 18.15 *The first cut only partially made. A little deeper and wider on the next pass.*

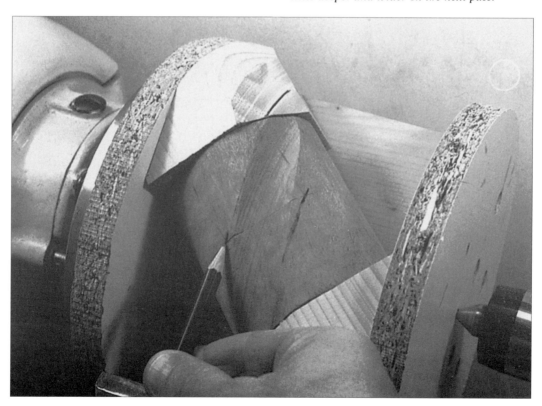

Fig 18.16 The first cut completed.

◆ Turn off the lathe regularly to check progress. When width and suitable depth have been reached, halt (*see* Fig 18.16). Clean up the cut and move to the next position.

◆ Withdraw the tailstock.

◆ Undo the screws on the vertical softwood blocks only. Do not loosen the screws on the angled block – it will be lifted away with the chipboard disc.

◆ Pull out the myrtle blank. Twist it to the next position and refit the top.

◆ Bring the centre back for support. Only

Fig 18.17 All cuts complete.

when the chipboard top is held centrally by the tailstock should the screws be tightened down.

◆ Turn the lathe by hand to make sure that nothing catches, then begin the second cut.

◆ The second and subsequent cuts are much easier because the shape and depth can clearly be seen on the softwood cut areas. The ghost image of the myrtle blank now needs to be cut away.

◆ Cut cleanly from top down to centre until the depth and shape of the softwood profile is reached.

◆ Turn off the lathe and inspect (*see* Fig 18.17). Clean up the cut if the correct size and shape is reached; if not, continue.

◆ Sharpen the tools regularly and make sure that all the screws in the jig are held tight.

◆ By rearranging the angled block position – top right or top left – right- and left-handed twists may be cut.

◆ The shape of the facet does not have to be a U curve; it can be reeded or shaped in other ways – it is worth some experimentation.

Fig 18.18 The lid and base can be finished in a jam chuck.

Fault finding

◆ If when these twisted faces are turned it is found that the face is turned wide at one end and narrow at the other, this shows that one end of the angled blocks was further away from the centre of rotation than the other. The only solution is a new jig; or else to enjoy the form you have turned – make a feature of it.

◆ If the cuts of various faces are uneven or unequal in size, then:

1. The chipboard top may not have been replaced accurately each time. Take more care.
2. The index ring has not been drilled with sufficient care.
3. Uneven cuts can of course be caused by cutting too much away at one face and too little at another. Be consistent.

◆ Chipping out at the edges may be caused by dull or blunt tools or maybe a bad choice of wood.

◆ A chattering cut is most likely caused by a loose jig, so tighten all the screws or fit rawlplugs in worn screw holes.

◆ When all cuts have been made satisfactorily and they have been cleaned up, remove the piece from the jig.

◆ Take the blank to the microwave oven. Set on full power for 25 seconds. The hot glue joint should then be soft enough to be pulled apart.

◆ Clean off any excess glue.

◆ These pieces may be returned to the lathe, their spigots held in the chuck, to allow the centres to be more fully hollowed if needed.

◆ If satisfied, cut off the spigots.

◆ The top face and base may be turned by holding the parts on a jam chuck (*see* Fig 18.18) or fitting them onto the jaws of a chuck which can be expanded to grip the inside. Whichever method is used, turn with care for much work has gone before.

The twist box is now complete. Polish it, then sit and look at it. Then look around and see how many other ways these twisted sides can be used to add excitement to turnery.

PART 3

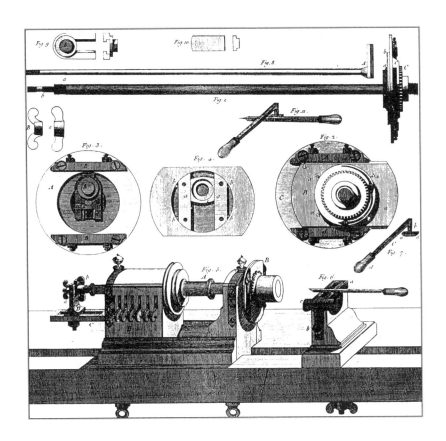

ELLIPTICAL TURNING

CHAPTER 19

Oval Chuck

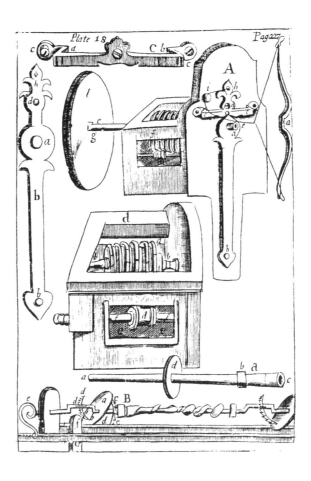

ELLIPTICAL TURNING IS A SKILL THAT HAS BEEN PRACTISED IN EUROPE SINCE BEFORE THE REIGN OF QUEEN ELIZABETH I. IN THE VICTORIA & ALBERT MUSEUM THERE ARE SOME BEAUTIFUL EXAMPLES OF ELLIPTICALLY TURNED LIDDED FRAMES IN IVORY DATING FROM THE SIXTEENTH CENTURY. THE OVAL PROTECTIVE LID LIFTS TO REVEAL A MINIATURE PORTRAIT PROTECTED WITHIN.

This form of elliptical turning was thought to have been produced using an oval cam which was fixed to the central lathe mandrel. The lathe mandrel was set so that it would rock in a controlled manner, constantly pulled by firm springs. A fixed follower was set against the oval cam causing the mandrel to move back and forth, which made the rotating work at the headstock follow an elliptical path. If a tool was held against the work an oval piece would be turned. This form of elliptical turning is described by Joseph Moxon in his book *Mechanick Exercises or the Doctrine of Handy Works*, first published in 1678. At the end of the chapter on elliptical turning he states, 'These oval engines, swash engines and all other engines are excellently well made by Mr Thomas Oldfield at the sign of the Flower-de-Luce, near the Savoy in The Strand, London'. So turners of the day would be well acquainted with the technique; whether they could afford the 'oval engines' was another matter.

In 1812, Peter Nicholson published a work, *Mechanical Exercises,* giving a description of an oval chuck in which the mandrel is 'held' firmly and rotates. The oval motion is caused by an offset circular cam around which parallel followers run. These followers are fixed to runners that move up and down a rotating slide, which itself is fixed directly to the headstock. The whole of this 'oval' lathe is strengthened with many wooden braces and beams fixed to floor and roof in an effort to prevent vibration caused by the eccentric movement of this chuck. This method is again shown in Hamelin Bergeron's book *Manuel du Tourneur* of 1816. Here he describes it as the 'English method'.

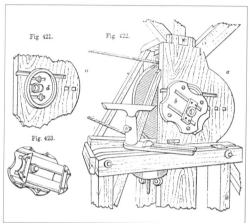

Fig 421. Fig 422. Fig. 423.

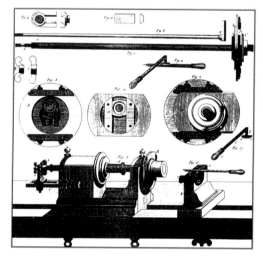

Today elliptical turning is still practised and it continues to develop, but such turnery is produced on more specialist lathes such as those made by Holtzapffel or Evans.

Here, using a basic woodturning lathe with a hollow mandrel and a simply made wooden chuck, I would like to show that elliptical turning can be produced by any turner. The turning skills are virtually the same as those used daily by woodturners.

The skills needed to produce the wooden chuck are basic woodworking skills and the good thing about any piece made by oneself is that it is easily repaired. If anything breaks, is damaged, or wears out, it can be replaced.

The oval chuck described in this chapter is similar to those referred to by Nicholson and Bergeron. It is small and not over engineered or heavy, which helps keep vibration down to a minimum. Being small, the size of piece that can be turned is somewhat restricted, but the aim of this chuck is to teach the basic principles of elliptical turnery. Larger items may require a larger chuck, or for the chuck to be fitted to the outboard end of the lathe. The larger the piece being turned, the greater the throw, and an increase in vibration will follow. It will then be necessary to brace and fix the lathe more firmly to the floor.

There have been many variations and developments of the oval chuck, but the method described here is, I feel, the most direct and straightforward.

If this experience of elliptical turning is an enjoyable one and you intend to continue, it might be sensible to have a simple metal chuck and cam produced from some of the lighter alloys. It could be a valuable addition to the equipment of a turner's workshop; but remember, a wooden chuck can be repaired in your own workshop; it is cheaper, lighter and totally under your control.

THE OVAL CHUCK

Parts

◆ A box is made and fitted over the headstock (*see* Fig 19.1).

◆ The only purpose of this box is to hold the wooden camplate firmly. On the camplate is fitted a circular cam with its elongated central hole.

◆ This wooden camplate can be moved sideways and locked in any given position to offset the circular cam from the main centre of rotation of the lathe.

◆ Fixed directly to the headstock spindle by means of a simple threaded draw-bar through the hollow mandrel, is a specially shaped piece of wood which will act as a slide. This will rotate like a propeller, but will be contained within the runners when the lathe is switched on.

◆ A pair of runners is made to fit onto this slide. These runners move back and forth upon the slide.

◆ The runners are held together by a pair of bearers. These are screwed on the back face of the runners.

◆ The bearers are positioned at right angles to the runners and parallel to each other.

◆ The distance between the inner faces of the bearers equals the diameter of the circular cam. This will ensure that they keep close contact with the edges of that cam as the oval chuck rotates.

How it works

As the slide rotates, the bearers pressing against the edge of the offset cam will cause the runners to move back and forth along the slide. The combined rotation of the slide and the regular movement of the runners cause the faceplate and the work attached to it to move elliptically.

The further the circular cam is set offcentre, the more pronounced the oval

Fig 19.1 The front, top and back of the box fixed over the headstock.

shape becomes. A mark on the camplate can be used as an index to be lined up against specific marks made upon the box front as a guide to the shape of oval that will be produced at any given setting.

Preparation and cutting list

◆ Sufficient wood will be needed to make the box fit tightly around the headstock. As lathe shapes and sizes may vary, the exact amount of wood will have to be calculated according to individual lathe dimensions.

Have available:

◆ Three 40mm (1⁹⁄₁₆in) long 6mm (¼in) pan-headed nuts (with cross slot for screw driver) and bolts.

◆ A 300mm (12in) length of 6mm (¼in) threaded bar and two square nuts. This studding is generally available in hardware stores.

◆ A piece of dense hardwood 75mm (3in) square by 75mm (3in) long, from which to turn the cam.

◆ A piece of dense hardwood 150mm (6in) long by 40mm (1⁹⁄₁₆in) square is needed for the slide.

◆ A piece of oak or similar medium hardwood 300mm (12in) long, 50mm (2in) wide and 25mm (1in) thick will be needed to make the runners and bearers.

◆ A piece of 195mm (7¾in) by 110mm (4⅜in) wide by 6mm (¼in) thick piece of mahogany for the camplate.

◆ A piece of 3mm (⅛in) by 175mm (7in) by 125mm (5in) ply for the faceplate.

◆ A number of 20mm (¹³⁄₁₆in) long No. 6 brass countersunk screws to fix the box together and attach the faceplate to the runners.

◆ Six 25mm (1in) No. 8 brass countersunk screws to fix the bearers to the runners. If oak is being used it is most important not to substitute steel screws because eventually the tannic acid in the oak will cause them to corrode.

◆ A 44kg (97lb) bag of sand to dampen vibration.

Making the chuck

The dimensions used in the following description of constructing this oval chuck assume that the height from the lathe bed to the centre of rotation is 100mm (4in) or more.

◆ The box, which fits over the headstock, has to be made to fit the lathe you are using. It must fit tightly around the headstock. The box shown in the photographs is made from mahogany and is fixed together with brass screws.

◆ The headstock mandrel projects through a hole in the front of the box, which is large enough to allow it to rotate freely (*see* Fig 19.2). There is also a cutout in the front of the box to enable it to fit over the lathe bed. A block is securely fixed to the base of the front so that it can be clamped firmly to the

Fig 19.2 The front in place. Note that the lathe mandrel projects about 10mm beyond the box front.

Fig 19.3 The box is firmly cramped to the lathe bench.

lathe bench (*see* Fig 19.3).

◆ There are three fixing points on the front of the box, besides those that are needed to hold the back and sides together. These fixing points have nuts attached on the inside to accept bolts which hold the camplate in position.

◆ On the inner edges of the front, corner blocks are glued and screwed to allow the top and sides to be screwed on (*see* Fig 19.4). This also allows for the removal of the front when taking the chuck apart.

◆ The top and sides are plain pieces which are permanently fixed to the back.

◆ The back is a similar shape to the front with a hole for the back end of the lathe mandrel. A cutout is made for the lathe bed if it extends through to the back. A block is fixed to the base of the back piece so that it can be clamped to the lathe bench. If it is intended to use the oval chuck on the outboard end of the lathe, fixings must be arranged for the back piece to take the camplate.

◆ If there is no bench to which the box can be clamped, the wooden blocks at the base of front and back can be made to fit under the bed from one side to the other. These can then be screwed to the back on both sides and to the front on both sides, locking the box firmly into place.

◆ It is essential that the box is a tight fit, hugging the headstock casing. This will give additional strength and stability.

◆ IMPORTANT: Try to arrange for the lathe spindle to project 10mm (⅜in) over the front of the box surface. This will ensure that the position of the slide boss is correct. The other parts will then be positioned accurately.

The cam and camplate

◆ Refer to Fig 19.5 for the layout and dimensions of the cam and camplate.

◆ From a very dense piece of hardwood – I used lignum vitae – turn a 12mm (½in) wide 72mm (2¹³⁄₁₆in) diameter disc. The circular face should show end grain so that the edge

Fig 19.4 The underside of the front showing nuts inset into the wooden pieces.

is of constant density, providing even wear. It may be sensible, once the block is turned accurately to size, to make one or two spare cams for eventual replacement.

◆ Cut a 195mm (7¾in) long by 110mm (4⅜in) wide piece of 6mm (¼in) thick mahogany. This will be the camplate.

◆ Draw a centre line along the length of the camplate.

◆ Draw two other lines 12mm (½in) away from the top and bottom edges of the camplate and parallel to those edges.

◆ All measurements will now be taken from the left-hand side of the camplate unless otherwise stated.

◆ Measure 10mm (⅜in) along the centre line, mark that position, then mark a further 20mm (¹³⁄₁₆in) from that point. At these two positions, drill a 6mm (¼in) hole, then join these holes to make a slot.

◆ On the line parallel to the top edge of the camplate (12mm [½in] away from the edge), measure 135mm (5⁵⁄₁₆in) and mark a point. From that point, measure 20mm (¹³⁄₁₆in) along the same line. At those two positions, drill a 6mm (¼in) hole. Join these two holes to make a slot.

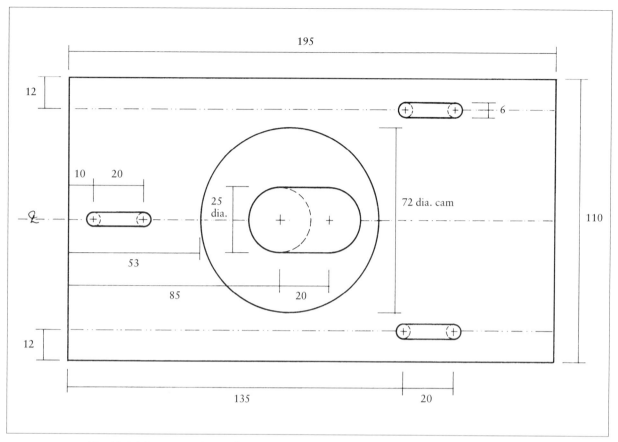

Fig 19.5 The cam and camplate.

Fig 19.6 The back of the camplate showing
elongated hole and screw positions to hold the cam.

◆ For the dimensions of the slide, refer to Fig 19.9.

◆ From a piece of dense hardwood, and here I've chosen cooktown ironwood which was once described as 'organic steel', cut a 150mm (6in) length, 40mm (1⁹⁄₁₆in) square.

◆ Measure along the length 75mm (3in). On both sides of this line measure 12.5mm (½in). This 25mm (1in) section is now centrally located.

◆ Measure 9mm (⅜in) from the top edge down one side and draw a line parallel to the edge. Continue this line all the way round the piece.

◆ Set the fence of the band saw 9mm (⅜in) away from the blade. Run the piece into the blade with one face on the fence, cutting along the marked line, until the start of the 25mm (1in) mid-section is reached. Remove the piece and do the same from the other end. Make sure these cuts are slow, so that a clean surface results.

◆ Remove the band saw fence and then cut along the outer edge of the marked 25mm (1in) central section until it meets the two cuts you have just made. This will leave a T-shaped piece – a central 25mm (1in) block with two long arms.

◆ On the 40mm (1⁹⁄₁₆in) wide flat face, mark a central line down the 150mm (6in) length.

◆ Screw this flat face centrally upon a faceplate using that marked central line to locate it accurately. It is vital that the slide should be positioned centrally at this stage.

◆ Fit the faceplate to the lathe and drill through the centre block using a drill that will cut a hole sufficiently large to allow the 6mm (¼in) threaded bar to fit snugly.

◆ Remove the drill and chuck, replacing them with a revolving centre which is brought forward into that drilled hole to support the work (see Fig 19.10).

◆ Turn the centre block to 25mm (1in) diameter, creating the slide boss (see Fig 19.11). This may need to be smaller or larger according to the size of your lathe mandrel.

◆ Measure 15mm (⅝in) from the tailstock end and turn that section so that it fits the Morse taper of the lathe mandrel. The remaining boss stays at full diameter to butt against the face of the lathe spindle. Remove

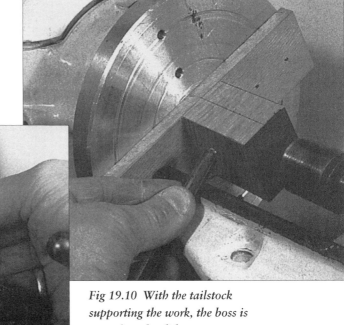

Fig 19.10 With the tailstock supporting the work, the boss is turned on the slide.

Fig 19.11 The turned boss.

Fig 19.12 Planing the angle on the slide edge.

Fig 19.13 A square hole is cut into the slide to accept the square nut.

the piece from the faceplate. The two edges now need to be planed to a slope.

◆ On the top face, measure 7mm (just over ¼in) from the edge and mark a parallel line. Mark a second line the same distance in and parallel to the other edge.

◆ Plane the angled surface between the 7mm (just over ¼in) marking and the bottom edge on both sides (*see* Fig 19.12).

◆ On the top face, around the drilled hole, mark the shape of the square nut that fits onto the threaded bar. Cut out that square

hole to the depth of the nut (*see* Fig 19.13) and fit it in place, testing the threaded bar to ensure accuracy.

◆ Use epoxy glue to stick the nut into the hollow using the threaded rod to hold it in place accurately. At this stage, do not glue the rod in place.

◆ The slide is now complete.

Runners and bearers

For ease, the runners are each made in two parts. They are made from a less dense hardwood, such as oak, because they are easier to make than the slide and it is better for them to wear out first as they are more easily replaced. Both runners and bearers are made from this same wood for that reason.

◆ Two runners are required. They are identical, so here I will describe the making of one only. For their dimensions, refer to Fig 19.14.

◆ Take a piece of hardwood 175mm (6⅞in) long, 20mm (¹³⁄₁₆in) wide and 12mm (½in) thick. Mark on the top face a line 7mm (just over ¼in) away from the edge and parallel to it.

◆ Mark a line parallel to that same edge 9mm (⅜in) down the 12mm (½in) thick side.

◆ Plane this angle between the two marked lines (*see* Fig 19.15).

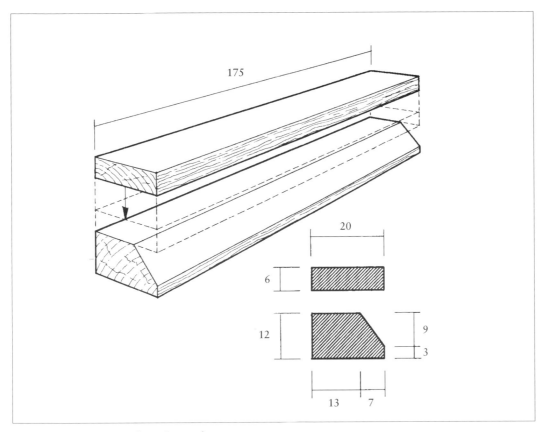

Fig 19.14 *Runners – each made up of two parts.*

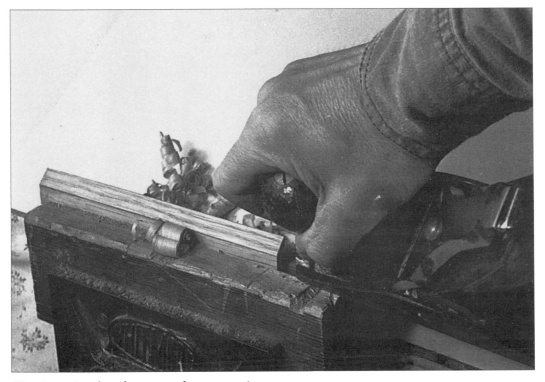

Fig 19.15 *An edge of one part of one runner is planed to an angle.*

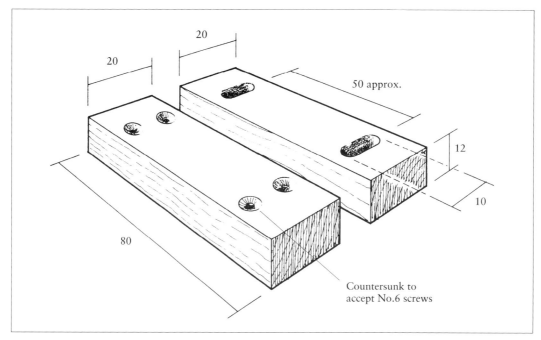

20

20

50 approx.

12

10

80

Countersunk to
accept No.6 screws

Fig 19.16 The bearers.

◆ Take a 175mm (6⅞in) long, 20mm (¹³⁄₁₆in) wide and 6mm (¼in) thick piece and place it on top with the angled edge between.

◆ Using a waterproof glue such as Cascamite, glue the surfaces together. Do not allow the glue to run into the angled part, but if it does, then you must clean it out completely. It is important to have the edges of the top and bottom pieces aligned accurately. Clamp the parts together and leave them to dry.

◆ Once the glue has set, clean away any excess leaving all edges true and square. The runners are now complete.

◆ Cut two bearers from the same wood, each 80mm (3³⁄₁₆in) long, 20mm (¹³⁄₁₆in) wide and 12mm (½in) thick (*see* Fig 19.16).

◆ Fit the slide into the now dry runners and lay the piece on a bench with the slide boss uppermost.

◆ Lay the bearers evenly across the runners and mark on those bearers the position where there is a solid thickness of runner beneath, i.e. a position clear of the angled slide gap which should be approximately 6mm (¼in) in from the inner edge of the runners. On that marked line draw two positions for screw holes.

◆ On one bearer, drill and countersink two

screw holes on the marked line and on the other bearer drill, cut and countersink a 10mm (⅜in) long slot on the line. This will allow that particular bearer to be adjusted. The screw holes should be distanced approximately 50mm (2in) apart across the length of the bearer.

◆ Remove the runners from the slide, placing the angled grooves towards each other and with the ends level. Measure 87.5mm (3⁷⁄₁₆in) from one end and mark a line square across both pieces. Measure half the diameter of the circular cam above and below that line.

◆ Replace the runners on the slide, again with the boss facing upwards. Use a try square to line up the markings on both runners.

◆ Place cramps lightly across the runners, holding them firmly against the slide, but *not* tightly.

◆ Lay the bearer with the screw holes only so that its edge touches the outer edge of one of the marked lines, then screw it into position.

◆ Next, position the second bearer with the slots so that its edge touches the outer edge of the other marked line. The distance between the faces of the two bearers will be

Fig 19.17 The assembled chuck with the bearers fitted. Note the parts of another runner waiting to be fitted flush and glued, and also the plywood faceplate. The threaded rod is fixed into the slide.

the diameter of the circular cam. Screw this second bearer in place with one screw, each side centrally positioned in the slot. This will enable the bearer to be moved to take up slack and wear when necessary.

◆ I chose oak for the runners and bearers because I knew that at one time oak was used as a bearing in water and windmills.

The oak was first soaked in oil or fat which, when in use, was slowly released, lubricating the bearing. So if you soak the runners and bearers in oil and allow them to fully dry, it will help your runners and bearers to move more freely. It is important to glue the parts of the runners together with a waterproof glue before they are soaked in oil.

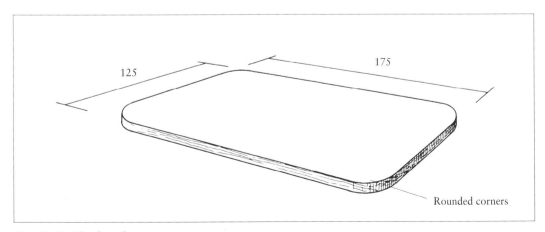

Fig 19.18 The faceplate.

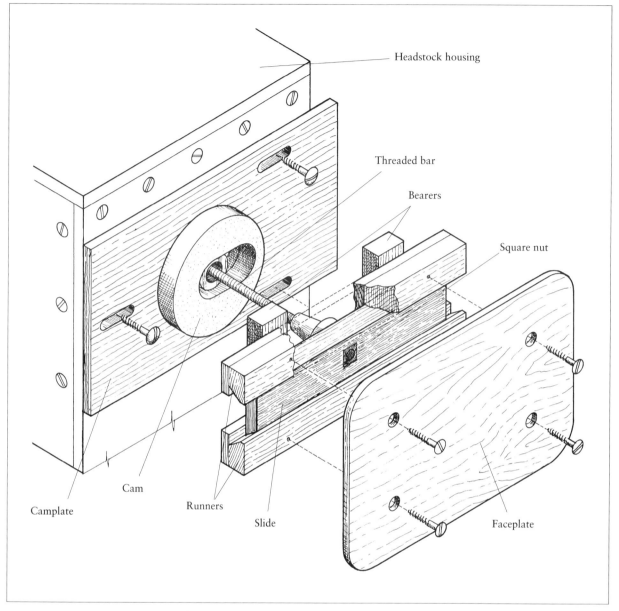

Fig 19.19 Fitting the oval chuck to the lathe.

Faceplate

◆ From 3mm (⅛in) plywood, cut a piece 175mm (6⅞in) long by 125mm (4¹⁵⁄₁₆in) wide (*see* Fig 19.18) and fit it centrally to the runners, but be aware when fixing this faceplate to the runners that the screws must avoid the angled channel in which the slide runs. Round off the corners of the ply faceplate.

◆ Mark a datum (X) on the faceplate and the runners so that if the faceplate is removed it can be relocated accurately.

◆ When adjusting for wear, it may be necessary to reposition the holes in the ply faceplate slightly.

Fitting the oval chuck to the lathe

◆ Fix the box onto the headstock with the front, cam and camplate in position.

◆ Clamp the box firmly to the lathe bench.

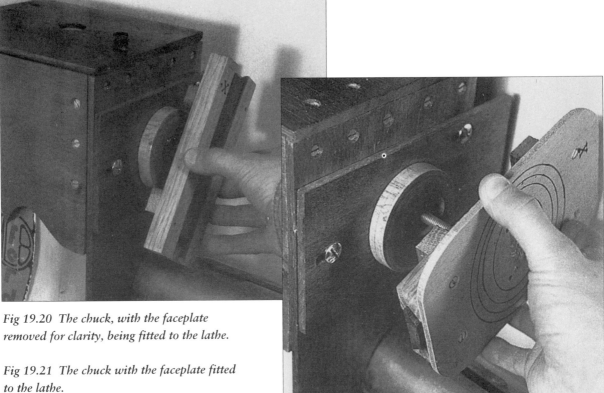

Fig 19.20 The chuck, with the faceplate removed for clarity, being fitted to the lathe.

Fig 19.21 The chuck with the faceplate fitted to the lathe.

◆ Fix the threaded rod into the slide and onto the nut.

◆ Fit the two runners either side of the slide and screw the bearers in position (*see* Fig 19.20).

◆ Screw the faceplate onto the front surface of the runners.

◆ Push the threaded rod through the hollow mandrel, bringing the assembled slide, runners and bearers towards the cam and camplate (*see* Fig 19.21).

◆ Push the bearers onto the cam so that the surface of the bearers rub the rim of the circular cam. Adjust the position of the bearers if necessary to ensure a good fit.

◆ Fix a square nut to the threaded rod as it projects through the back of the headstock mandrel. Tighten this nut and it will pull the assembly onto the cam and hold it firmly as part of the mandrel.

◆ Rotate the lathe by hand to test the chuck, making sure of the following:

1. The faceplate does not strike the lathe bed (adjust if necessary by trimming the corners).
2. The bearers rub evenly upon the cam

Fig 19.22 A view of the chuck rotating. The faceplate has been removed for clarity. As the chuck rotates, the runners move back and forth along the slide creating an elliptical motion.

Fig 19.23 *The elliptical motion shown by holding a pen to the faceplate while rotating the lathe.*

(loosen the screws in the bearer slots to adjust correctly, then retighten – you'll need to remove the assembly from the lathe to do this).

3. The threaded rod does not come loose from the nut in the slide.

◆ When you are completely satisfied that the oval chuck is working well, the threaded rod may be glued with epoxy resin into the slide and the slide nut. Do not allow the threaded rod to project above the surface of the nut. Apply sufficient glue to the rod so that the whole length of the slide boss will be glued. This will strengthen the slide boss enormously. Allow the glue to dry.

Advice

◆ A 44kg (97lb) bag of sand is a tremendous help. Place under the lathe bench on the lathe shelf to dampen vibration.

◆ Do not allow the chuck to run for too long – no more than ten minutes at one time – for like the boy scout rubbing two sticks together, the bearers, cam, runners and slide could begin to smoulder, and it would be a great pity to see all your hard work go up in smoke! In making the projects for this book I have only once noticed some charring. Elliptical turning requires intense concentration and is best done in short bursts.

Fig 19.24 *When tightening bearers or repositioning the faceplate once bearers have been tightened, hold the runners together lightly using a cramp.*

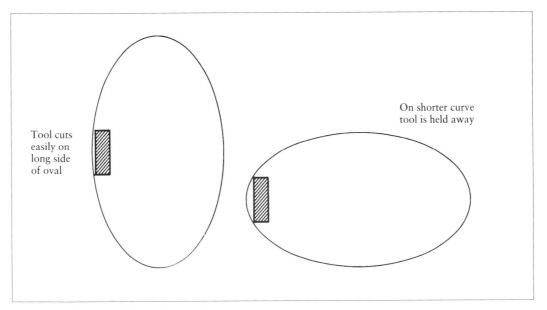

Fig 19.25 *The size of the tool must be considered when turning elliptically.*

◆ Bearers should be adjusted so that they touch the cam but are not tightened against it. When rotated by hand the movements should be easy.

◆ Apply candle wax to the cam occasionally as a lubricant.

◆ Tool shapes and cutting bevels must be considered, because turning an oval involves cutting first in a long sweeping curve, quickly followed by a tighter curve at the end. This tighter curve could easily trap a deep, thicker tool (*see* Fig 19.25). The ground cutting angle needs to be considered for a similar reason. When cutting the tighter curve, the back of the bevel could easily rub, preventing the cutting edge from making contact.

◆ Always rotate the lathe by hand before starting to turn. This will ensure that anything that catches can be trimmed or adjusted before damage is done.

◆ Always mark on the work or faceplate in pencil or felt-tip the line to be cut as a starting guide, for once the lathe is running it is difficult to judge where to make the cut.

◆ When turning normal round bowls, the blank is band sawn circular in preparation. Similarly, when turning oval pieces, first cut the blank close to the required oval shape on a band saw. This oval shape can be drawn out directly onto a piece of tracing paper, fixed to the faceplate and then transferred to the wood. Do not try to turn from square-edged blanks – it makes life difficult and puts tremendous stress on the chuck.

◆ Always make sure all the screws are tight and all locking nuts fixed firmly.

◆ Check the chuck regularly and replace worn parts. Worn parts will cause odd-shaped ovals and inconsistent cuts.

◆ At first, elliptical turning is a little disconcerting, for the wood is revolving off-centre and the chuck is a vibrating, whirring mass. But take heart – after a little while this form of turning becomes as easy as any other.

◆ The faceplate is made of inexpensive ply and can easily be replaced, so replace whenever it appears worn.

◆ Lathe speed should be slow – about 500rpm.

Fault finding

1. Bumpy cuts.
   a) Loose runners. Pull the runners closer together across the slide. Readjust and tighten the screws in bearers and faceplate.
   b) The position of the tool is either too high or too low – it should be at

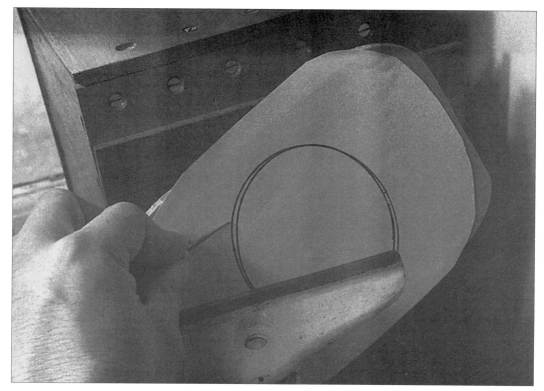

Fig 19.26 Two paths created just by raising and lowering a felt pen.

centre height. N.B. Even if the tool is too high or too low the cut will eventually even out; however this is to be avoided.

2. Oval cut is offset from an earlier cut. This is caused by the tool cutting above or below centre height, the previous cut having been made at centre height. It is vital to cut at centre height at all times.

3. Inconsistent cuts. This is caused by worn parts which will need to be replaced.

4. The axis of the oval cuts progressing from large to small becomes twisted.
   a) The runners and slide are slack and need to be tightened.
   b) The bearer is not set properly upon the cam. Adjust the position of the bearers so that they rest more snugly against the rim of the cam.

5. Smouldering, smoke and flames.
   a) It's all too tight.
   b) In your enthusiasm you have worked for a whole hour non-stop. Rush out and get a cup of water for the lathe and a cup of coffee for

yourself Remember, friction causes heat – allow the chuck to cool.

Safety in oval turning

1. The lathe speed needs to be moderate.
2. Always rotate the lathe by hand before switching it on.
3. All screws and nuts should be tight before starting work.
4. Do not run the chuck for too long.
5. Fix the work piece firmly to the faceplate.
6. Watch fingers and knuckles when working close to the edge of the faceplate. The ghost image may miss, but the true one won't!
7. All basic turning safety measures apply.

Enjoy the experience of turning ovals as any self-sufficient turner of the eighteenth century would have. Appreciate being that little bit closer to your work through the self-sufficiency of building your own chuck.

CHAPTER 20

Oval Frame

A S AN INTRO-DUCTION TO ELLIPTICAL TURNERY THIS SIMPLE FRAME WORKS WONDER-FULLY WELL.

An oval opening is cut through a thin board and the edge is rounded over. A matching piece of wood is fitted to the back with a gap between, leaving a space for glass and a picture. It is a neat little frame which can sit on a desk or table or, with a slight adjustment, be hung on a wall.

The frame shown in Fig 20.1 is made from padauk, that richly red wood which when worked smells of custard powder. Padauk is a kindly wood; it turns and polishes well and is a fine choice for a little elliptical turnery.

Preparation

◆ Cut and plane a piece of wood 400mm (16in) long by 110mm (4⅜in) wide and 6mm (¼in) thick. The whole frame will be produced from this one piece.
◆ A 9mm (⅜in) wide brass hinge and fixing pins are needed.
◆ A small piece of string or cord 100mm (4in) long is required.
◆ The oval chuck with ply faceplate should be set ready to work.
◆ A black felt-tip pen would be useful.
◆ A piece of white card is necessary.
◆ Have some tracing paper on hand.
◆ Offset the cam so that a nicely shaped long oval is produced. Check by holding a pencil against the faceplate.
◆ Lathe speed should be 500rpm.

Turning the oval

◆ Cut a piece of white card 110mm (4⅜in) by 140mm (5½in).

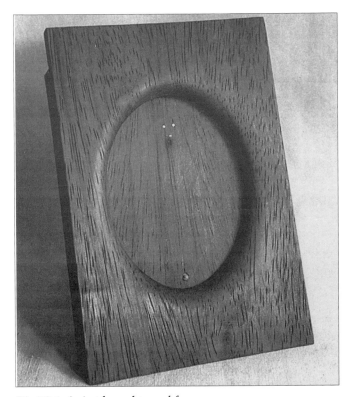

Fig 20.1 A simple oval turned frame.

◆ Fit the card crossways on the faceplate with the longest section overhanging. Use double-sided Sellotape to hold the card to the plywood faceplate of the oval chuck.
◆ Turn the lathe by hand to check that the card does not catch on the lathe bed. Adjust where necessary.
◆ Set the tool rest so that a pencil is at centre height when resting upon it. Check against the revolving centre held in the tailstock.
◆ Bring the tool rest to the face of the chuck and place the pencil against the card fixed to the faceplate.
◆ Rotate the lathe by hand marking an oval on the card (*see* Fig 20.2).
◆ Move the card until the marked pencil oval is positioned so that both card edges are set an equal distance away and the card edge is in line with the perceived centre line of that oval.

Fig 20.2 *Marking the pencil ovals on paper or card fixed to the faceplate*

Fig 20.3 *The size of the oval cut into the frame. This size and shape will vary according to the adjustments made to the oval chuck.*

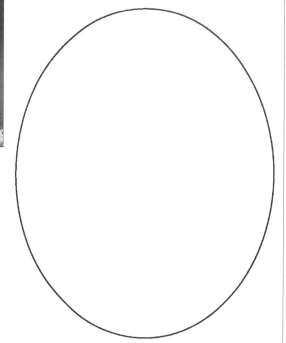

◆ Mark several pencil ovals until one of a satisfactory size is reached – about 70mm (2¾in) wide by 90mm (3½in) long in this case (*see* Fig 20.3).

◆ Mark on the ply faceplate on either side of the card using a black felt pen.

◆ Set the tool rest so that the pen is held at centre height.

◆ Now mark the chosen oval in

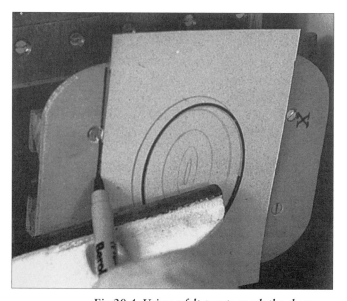

Fig 20.4 *Using a felt-pen to mark the chosen oval and the card edge so that the frame blank can be located in the same position.*

felt pen (*see* Fig 20.4).

◆ Take a tracing of the oval either directly onto tracing paper fixed on top of the card or tracing by hand when the card is removed.

◆ Remove the card and the tracing.

◆ The traced oval helps ensure that a similar size oval is chosen when marking on the piece of wood for the frame.

◆ Cut a 155mm (6⅛in) length of the 110mm (4⅜in) wide, 6mm (¼in) thick padauk for the frame blank.

◆ Measure the width of the plywood faceplate where the frame blank will fit – 125mm (4¹⁵⁄₁₆in).

◆ Take that width away from the frame blank length: 155mm – 125mm = 30mm (6⅛in – 4¹⁵⁄₁₆in = 1³⁄₁₆in).

◆ Divide this size by 2: 30mm ÷ 2 = 15mm (1³⁄₁₆in ÷ 2 = ¹⁹⁄₃₂in).

◆ Mark in pencil two lines at 90° to the width on the front of the frame blank 15mm

($^{19}/_{32}$in) from the top and an equal amount up from the base.

◆ These two lines, with the help of the black felt-pen lines on the faceplate, will help position the frame blank accurately.

◆ The frame blank is now fixed to the faceplate using a newspaper and glue joint.

◆ Spread PVA glue between the black felt-pen lines on the faceplate.

◆ Cut a piece of newspaper of a size to fit the area exactly.

◆ Push the newspaper onto the glue and press down firmly, spreading out wrinkles and bubbles.

◆ Apply glue to the newspaper surface, then fix the frame blank to that glued surface.

◆ Keep the frame blank within the two felt-pen lines and keep the pencil lines on its face lined up with the edges of the plywood faceplate.

◆ Bring a flat block of wood and press it against the frame blank.

◆ Bring the tailstock holding a revolving centre forward to apply pressure to the block, pressing it against the frame blank whilst the glue sets between it and the faceplate (*see* Fig 20.5).

◆ The block spreads the pressure evenly over the frame blank.

◆ Do not try to rotate the chuck whilst held because the oval movement does not have a constant centre. Any movement would cause the joint between blank and faceplate to twist.

◆ Leave to dry.

◆ Once the glue has dried, rotate the lathe by hand to make sure nothing catches. Now is the time to make adjustments.

◆ With a pencil set on a tool rest at centre height, mark on the frame blank a series of ovals judging the size as close to the original as possible.

◆ Use the tracing to choose the correct sized oval and make adjustments to the pencil marking where necessary.

◆ Set the tool rest so that a felt pen marks at centre height, then draw the chosen oval in black felt pen. This heavy black line will clearly be seen, allowing the cut to be made in the correct position.

◆ It is important to keep tools, pens and

Fig 20.5 The frame blank newspaper/glue joined to the faceplate. A wooden block spreads the pressure from the tailstock.

pencils set so they cut or mark at centre height, for an adjustment above or below will cause a different oval pathway to be marked.

◆ Select a square-end tool about 3mm (¼in) thick. This ensures that when the tight curve of the oval is being cut the tool will not bind. This square-end tool will be used to make a parting cut through to the faceplate.

◆ Set the tool rest so that the square-end tool is cutting at centre height. Use the centre in the tailstock as a guide to help with this setting.

◆ Rotate the lathe by hand to ensure nothing catches.

◆ Turn the lathe on and watch how the felt-pen line moves.

◆ Where it passes over the tool rest at the left at centre height, it is a perfect point. Above and below is a wavering line. At this point at centre height the line as it passes is tranquil. Above and below it appears agitated. Always cut at this point of tranquillity which falls at centre height (*see* Fig 20.6).

◆ Ready for the first cut: place the tool rest and gently push it into the rotating work. The sensation is no more than that felt with a normal turning cut, maybe a little similar to work slightly offset but no more, as long as the work is turned at the point of tranquillity.

Fig 20.6 Turning the groove through the frame blank. Note the whirring mass of wood but the clear point of tranquillity where the tool is cutting.

Fig 20.7 The ellipse cut through the frame blank.

◆ The strong black line will be a great help in judging exactly where to make the cut. Use it as you would any tool or guide.

◆ If the lathe vibrates then this movement could upset the accuracy of the cut, so make sure the lathe is well weighed down with bags of sand or bolted to the floor.

◆ Widen the cut to the right, still cutting at centre height.

◆ Turn off the lathe to check the cut (*see* Fig 20.7). At this point also make sure that the runners and bearers of the chuck are good and reasonably tight. Adjust if necessary.

Rub paraffin wax on the cam to lubricate.

◆ Continue until the cut is through to the faceplate and is about 9mm (⅜in) wide.

◆ Next, the edge of the oval can be rounded over using a gouge but this will prove a little more difficult than normal gouge work (*see* Fig 20.8). The cutting line which the gouge takes must remain at centre height and the cutting point on the gouge edge must be decided upon so that the tool rest can be adjusted to maintain that position. The centre portion of the frame is to be discarded, so that may be used to experiment upon with gouge work.

◆ Do try with the gouge for it is a good skill to master but do not be upset or offput if the skill is difficult to achieve. If you are unhappy using a gouge, very light cuts with a round-nose tool will work equally well. Round the inner edge of the oval to a pleasing shape.

◆ When satisfied with the shaping, clean up with glasspaper; this provides a clear example of the point of tranquillity and the agitation that surrounds it. Hold the glasspaper at that point and it is as gentle and easy as glasspapering a round part on the lathe – above or below that point and the shakes begin.

Fig 20.8 Rounding over the edge with a gouge.

The projects

Sovereign sphere and
combination locking box

Folding beaker

Necklace and rattlesnake

Chess set

Chess set showing ring-turned knight

*Balancing egg and egg with (concealed)
rosebud*

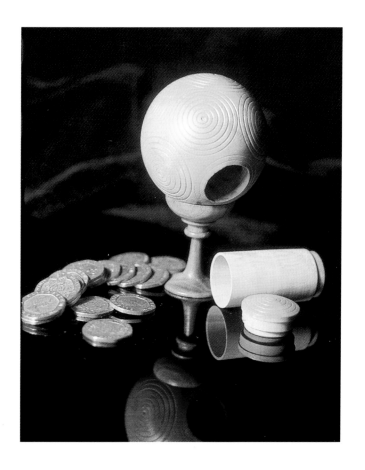

Opening egg and rosebud

Sovereign sphere

*Sovereign sphere
and combination
locking box*

*Lotus blossom
bowls*

Quinfoil bowl with lotus blossom bowls

*Facet-sided box and vase, and twist-turned
box*

Quinfoil bowl, lotus blossom bowls, twist-
turned box, facet-sided box and facet-sided vase

Oval frame and oval frame with moulded edge

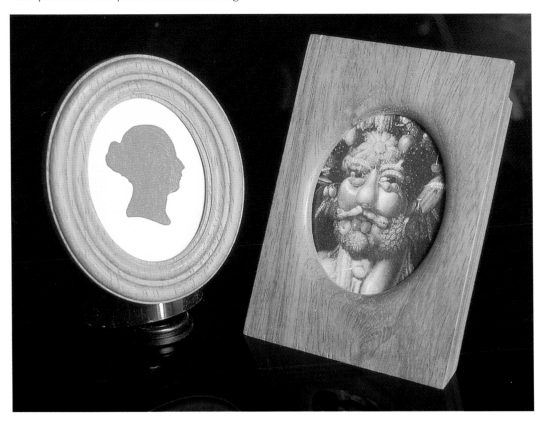

Oval box and oval dish

Oval chuck, oval frames, oval box and oval dish

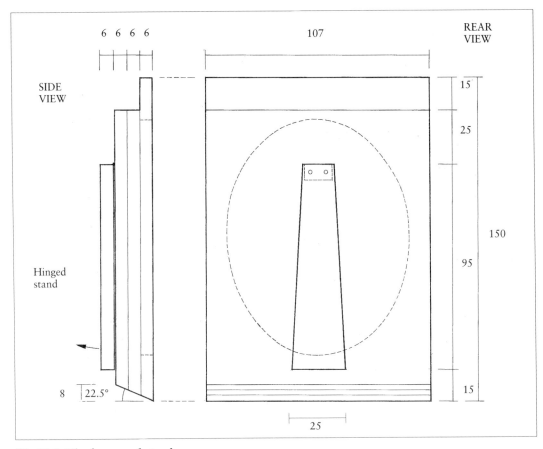

Fig 20.9 The frame and stand.

◆ Switch off the lathe and if the piece is satisfactorily cleaned up take a sharp knife – a sturdy Stanley knife – and push into the newspaper joint, slicing along. This should be enough to begin to shear the newspaper joint and allow the frame to be pulled from the faceplate.

◆ Clean off the faceplate, scraping away glue and paper, leaving it ready for the next job.

◆ Clean off the back of the frame with care.

Making the frame and stand

I have carefully selected this size of frame so that it will not be necessary to have glass specially cut. In many shops there are cheap frames of set sizes. One of these – 90mm (3½in) by 130mm (5in) – holds the size of glass required for this project. Buy the frame and remove the glass. It is cheaper than going to a specialist glass cutter.

◆ Measure the thickness of the glass plus the photograph/picture, then add a little for movement. In this case 2.5mm (3⁄32in) is the total.

◆ From padauk, cut two pieces 137mm (5⁷⁄₁₆in) long by 10mm (⅜in) wide by 2.5mm (3⁄32in) thick – two fillets.

◆ Cut another piece the width of the glass to be used – 90mm (3½in) long by 10mm (⅜in) wide by 2.5mm (3⁄32in) thick – one fillet.

◆ Cut a back piece 137mm (5⁷⁄₁₆in) long by 110mm (4⅜in) by 6mm (¼in) thick.

◆ Lay the frame face down.

◆ Take one of the long fillets and lay it on one edge with its base touching the base of the frame.

◆ Take the other long fillet and lay it on the opposite edge in a similar position.

◆ Lay the third fillet on the bottom edge crossways between them.

◆ Lay a piece of glass between the fillets. Do not worry if it pushes them out slightly; leave enough around the glass to make it easy to slide in and out.

◆ Lay the back piece on top. That was the dry run.

◆ Now remove the parts and replace in the same order with glue between the touching faces.

◆ Leave the glass in place for a short time.

◆ Make sure that the side fillets butt up against the bottom fillet and that the glass is not trapped and has space to move.

◆ Once the back is in place, cramp the whole and allow the glue to dry.

◆ Remove the glass once the cramps have been tightened (*see* Fig 20.10).

◆ When the glue has dried, plane up the edges (*see* Fig 20.11).

◆ Judge the angle at which the frame will lean, then trim the base edge so that it will lie flat when the front is angled.

◆ Cut the support so that it tapers from 25mm (1in) at its base to 12mm (½in) at the top over a 95mm (3¾in) length.

◆ Fit the hinge to the top of the support and drill pilot holes through to take brass pins.

◆ Pin and epoxy glue the hinge in place. Clean off any projecting pins from the opposite side.

◆ Place the support in position on the back using masking tape to hold the hinge in place.

◆ Mark the position for the brass pins through the hinge holes.

◆ Drill through, then remove the masking tape. Pin and epoxy glue the hinge in place. Clean off the projecting pins.

◆ Polish all parts.

◆ Now fit a small piece of string or cord so that the support does not slip open and the frame fall flat.

◆ Measure about 30mm (1½in) up the centre line of the angled back.

◆ Check that this position, if a hole were drilled, would show through in the oval hollow on the front side. If necessary, reposition so that it will.

◆ At that point, drill a hole large enough to take the string.

◆ On the front face, counterbore the hole so that a knot formed in the string will fit flat inside it.

◆ Knot the string and push the string through the hole, pulling the knot into the counterbored hole.

◆ Spread the support to a comfortable distance.

◆ Pull the string across and mark a position where it would naturally fit onto the support.

◆ Drill through the support to accept the string and counterbore on the opposite side.

◆ Knot the string and pull up tight.

The frame is complete. Now search for a suitable picture to put in it.

Fig 20.10 Cramping the frame parts together. The glass has been partially removed.

Fig 20.11 Planing the frame edges.

CHAPTER 21

Oval Frame with Moulded Edge

HIS FRAME IS A LITTLE MORE OF A CHALLENGE THAN THE PREVIOUS ONE. THERE IS MORE TO TURN PLUS THE ADDED PROBLEM OF HOW TO HOLD IT WHILST TURNING.

If a slightly thicker piece than the one described here is used, then this will allow for a deeper moulded section, but care must be taken with the design of the moulding on thicker pieces for they can look extremely heavy.

A recess in the back allows for glass, picture and backing to fit in place and the outer rim on the rear is wide enough to take fixings from which the frame may be hung. This frame is to be wall hung for it will not sit easily on a desk, even with a back support.

If the frame is considered too small for the picture you have in mind then move the chuck to the outboard end of the lathe where a larger throw will allow a larger piece to be turned. But beware, a larger throw means increased vibration and increased wear on bearers and runners, so it may be advisable to start small and let the size of frame grow with the confidence gained from turning.

An increase in confidence and frame size should be accompanied by an increase in chuck size to help spread the wear of many parts and an increase in the bracing and fixings of the lathe. Think and work with caution.

Preparation

◆ Cut a piece of padauk 150mm (6in) long by 110mm (4⅜in) wide by 12mm (½in) thick.

Length and width may vary according to the oval being turned.

◆ Have tracing paper, pencil and felt-tip pen ready.

◆ A 6mm (¼in) thick piece of wood 100mm (4in) square is needed.

◆ PVA glue and newspaper are necessary to form the holding joint between frame and faceplate.

◆ Lathe speed should be 500 to 750rpm.

Turning the frame

◆ Set the tool rest so that a felt-tip pen is at centre height.

Fig 21.1 The moulded oval frame.

Fig 21.2 Tracing the chosen oval from those marked on the faceplate beneath.

Fig 21.3 Marking the oval on wood.

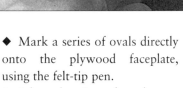

◆ Mark a series of ovals directly onto the plywood faceplate, using the felt-tip pen.

◆ Select the size of oval most suitable for the outside size of the frame. The size chosen here is 100mm (4in) wide by 120mm (4¾in) long.

◆ Trace the shape of the oval onto tracing paper (*see* Fig 21.2).

◆ Transfer this shape from the tracing paper to the piece of 12mm (½in) thick wood (*see* Fig 21.3).

◆ Cut around the outside oval shape on the

band saw keeping the cut constantly a fraction away on the outer edge of the line.

◆ In the same way that, when bowl turning conventionally, a blank is cut out circular to remove the majority of waste wood and to prevent extremes of vibration, when turning elliptically an oval blank is cut out to a convenient size and shape.

◆ Spread PVA glue on the surface of the cut oval blank. This surface will eventually be the face of the frame so if a choice is to be made, now is the time.

◆ Fix newspaper to that glued surface and trim away the excess from around the edge.

◆ Flatten out wrinkles or bubbles in the surface of the glued newspaper.

◆ Spread PVA glue on the inside of the marked oval on the plywood faceplate.

◆ Push the newspaper-glued side of the oval blank onto the newly glued area and line up the outer edge of the blank with the felt-tip line on the faceplate.

◆ Bring forward the tailstock holding a revolving centre.

◆ Place a block of wood against the oval blank and tighten up the revolving centre on it. This will press the blank against the faceplate (*see* Fig 21.4). The block will

Fig 21.4 The sawn oval shape is fixed to the faceplate inside the marked oval upon the faceplate. A newspaper/glue joint is used.

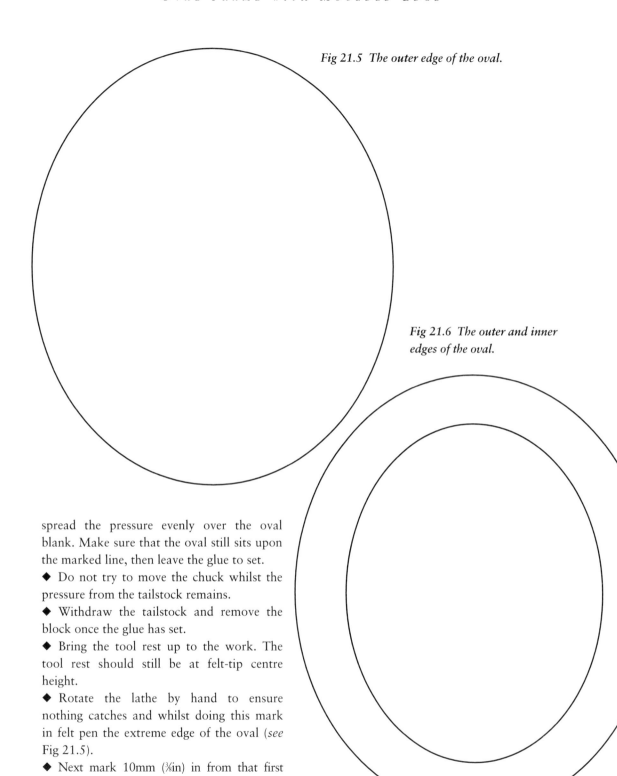

Fig 21.5 The outer edge of the oval.

Fig 21.6 The outer and inner edges of the oval.

spread the pressure evenly over the oval blank. Make sure that the oval still sits upon the marked line, then leave the glue to set.

◆ Do not try to move the chuck whilst the pressure from the tailstock remains.

◆ Withdraw the tailstock and remove the block once the glue has set.

◆ Bring the tool rest up to the work. The tool rest should still be at felt-tip centre height.

◆ Rotate the lathe by hand to ensure nothing catches and whilst doing this mark in felt pen the extreme edge of the oval (*see* Fig 21.5).

◆ Next mark 10mm (⅜in) in from that first marked oval and draw another oval holding the pen still and rotating the lathe (*see* Fig 21.6).

◆ Make a tracing of this inner oval and mark it 'rebate for oval frame' (*see* Fig 21.7).

◆ Reset the tool rest so that a thin (not narrow) square-end tool cuts at centre height.

◆ First turn on the inside of the inner-marked oval using a square-end tool to a

depth of 6mm (¼in).

◆ Turn out the whole of the inside of that inner-marked oval to this depth to make the rebate on what is the back of the frame.

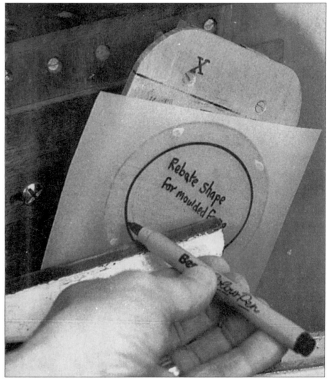

Fig 21.7 *The rebate oval shape is marked and a tracing taken.*

Fig 21.8 *The oval rebate is turned.*

◆ Turning out the inner oval is another opportunity to use a gouge, but remember to set the tool rest to a height that allows the gouge to cut at centre height (*see* Fig 21.8).

◆ It will be noticed that, whatever tool is used, if it is set to cut at centre height the innermost cut, which on circular turning would be a dot or single point, becomes a straight line when turning elliptically.

◆ Turn off the lathe when all of the inside of the marked oval is turned out flat to a depth of 6mm (¼in).

◆ Constantly check the chuck to see if any pieces show wear or have loosened. If they have loosened then tighten. If they are worn, replace or readjust.

◆ Try to make adjustments at the end of a turning process or between procedures, such as now, when removing the oval block from the chuck. This will help keep the oval shape being produced constant.

◆ Between stages is also a good time to rub a little candle wax around the cam to help lubricate.

◆ Using a sharp knife, split the newspaper joint, pulling the oval away from the faceplate.

◆ Clean off the faceplate, scraping the glue and newspaper away leaving the plywood surface as good as new.

◆ On the faceplate, mark in pencil (with tool rest set at pencil-centre height) a series of ovals close to, if not exactly, the size of the rebate traced earlier.

◆ Using the tracing, mark out an oval on a piece of 6mm (¼in) thick wood. Cut generously on the outside of the marked line.

◆ Select the pencil oval marked on the faceplate upon which the cut 6mm (¼in) thick oval most comfortably sits.

◆ Using PVA glue and newspaper, fix this new oval in line with the marked oval on the faceplate.

◆ Use a block to spread the pressure and the tailstock to apply it. Leave whilst the glue sets.

◆ Once the glue has set, withdraw the tailstock and block and mark on the cut blank an oval as close to the tracing oval as possible. Larger is better than smaller.

◆ Turn the oval using a square-end tool set

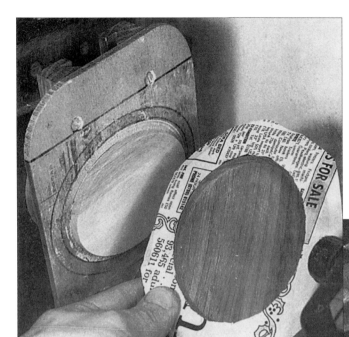

Fig 21.9 *A cut out piece of newspaper is glued to the outer edge of the turned oval. The darker area is the turned rebate which will be fitted over the specially turned oval block fitted to the faceplate.*

Fig 21.10 *The rebate is carefully newspaper/glue joined to the faceplate. A wood block spreads pressure applied by the tailstock.*

to cut at centre height, so that it matches the oval rebate on the back of the frame blank.

◆ When the frame blank fits over the oval fixed on the faceplate, halt.

◆ Make sure that the edge of the frame fits flat against the faceplate.

◆ If the centre oval holds the edges of the blank away from the plywood faceplate then turn a little from its top surface.

◆ To fit the oval frame to the faceplate, use the glue and paper method again. It is very effective. It is simple and leaves no holding marks.

◆ The centre part of the frame, which will be cut out, is drilled and countersunk to accept screws. Make sure these are placed close to the centre.

◆ The rim of the oval frame is the only part to be held using the newspaper/glue joint. Do not let glue stray to the centre oval for if this were to happen they could become permanently fixed together.

◆ Apply glue to the outer edge of the underside of the frame blank – the side with the turned rebate.

◆ Fix newspaper to the glue then trim excess paper from inner and outer edges (*see* Fig 21.9).

◆ Smooth out any ripples or bubbles, then

apply a further layer of glue to the surface of the newspaper. Keep the glue away from the inner edge.

◆ Push the frame blank over the fixed inner oval.

◆ Fit two screws into the holes and screw the blank to the inner oval.

◆ Place a block on top to spread the pressure and bring up the tailstock to apply the pressure (*see* Fig 21.10).

◆ Allow the glue to dry.

◆ When the glue is dry, withdraw the tailstock and remove the block.

◆ Set the tool rest so that the square-end tool will cut at centre height.

◆ Rotate the lathe by hand to make sure that nothing catches.

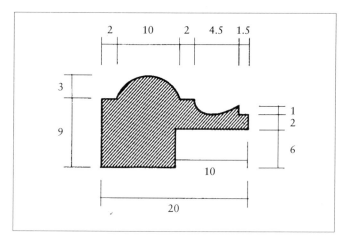

Fig 21.11 A cross section showing the shape of the moulding.

♦ Turn the outer edge of the oval, taking as little off as possible to bring to a clean, oval shape.

♦ Decide the exact shape of the moulding before beginning to turn the frame. A moulding shape is shown in Fig 21.11 and the method of turning that particular one is described below.

♦ Measure 2mm (³⁄₃₂in) from the outer edge.

Mark a line in pencil and cut 3mm (¼in) deep on the outside of that line using a square-end tool.

♦ Measure 12mm (½in) in from the edge. Mark a pencil line and cut down on the inside of that line to a depth of 3mm (¼in) using the square-end tool.

♦ Measure 20mm (¹³⁄₁₆in) in from the edge. Mark a line and cut on the inside of that line using a square-end tool through to the block beneath and into the rebate (*see* Fig 21.13). Cut gently to avoid splintering the inner edge.

♦ The screws through the inner portion will prevent it from flying free once that parting cut is made (*see* Fig 21.14).

♦ Measure 14mm (⁹⁄₁₆in) in from the edge and, from the 3mm (¼in) deep cut on its outside, turn down, cutting a cove (*see* Fig 21.15). Leave a 3mm (¼in) thickness at the centre. A gouge may be used to cut this cove, but whichever tool is used, exaggerate the depth of the cove – go deeper and sweep up to the inner edge because this will improve its shape to the eye (*see* Fig 21.16). Do not forget to adjust the tool rest when changing tools.

♦ On the inner edge of the frame, cut a small 1.5mm (¹⁄₁₆in) deep and wide step to add visual relief.

♦ Turn the outer block – between the two

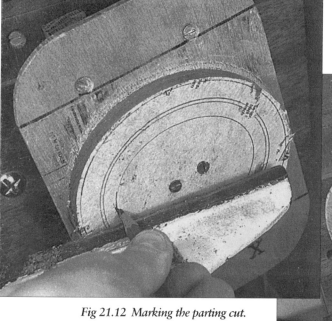

Fig 21.12 Marking the parting cut. The other oval lines show where the moulding cuts will be made.

Fig 21.13 Making the parting cut.

Fig 21.14 Removing the centre.

3mm (⅛in) deep cuts – into a 10mm (⅜in) wide rounded bead. A gouge or round-nose tool may be used for this work.

◆ When turning the frame, stop frequently to check how the work is progressing. Take light cuts to leave as clean a finish as possible. Always cut at centre height as this will be the most tranquil position.

◆ Allow the chuck a little rest time during turning. The work can become so absorbing that longer times spent turning could cause a build up of heat in the chuck. Keep the tools sharp.

◆ Once satisfied with the shape and the finish, glasspaper the work smooth. Do not rub out the sharp edges. It needs to look as if it has been turned, not squeezed into shape.

◆ Always make the cuts at the point of tranquillity to ensure accuracy of shape and ease of turning.

◆ Remove the oval frame from the faceplate, splitting the newspaper/glue joint with a sharp knife (*see* Fig 21.17).

◆ Clean up the back surface of the frame, then polish.

◆ Remove the inner waste piece, unscrewing

it from the inner block.

◆ Returning to the lathe, measure a line 3mm (⅛in) in from the outer edge of the block left attached to the faceplate and mark in pencil.

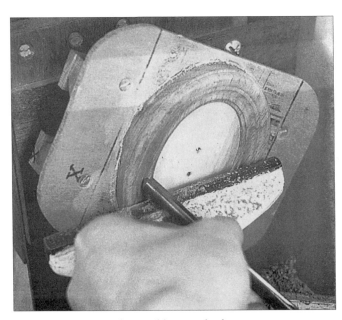

Fig 21.15 Turning the moulding on the frame.

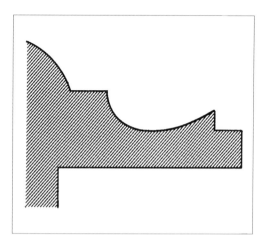

Fig 21.16 Exaggerate the depth of the cove to show its curve to best effect.

Fig 21.18 A picture for your oval frame.

◆ Turn on the outside of that line to a smooth square-edged oval.

◆ Split this piece away from the faceplate using a Stanley knife to break the newspaper/glue joint.

◆ This piece can be used as a template by the glass cutter. The glass cutter will be able to run the cutting tool around the oval edge using it as a guide to produce a perfectly oval glass insert for the frame.

◆ Clean up the faceplate, scraping the surface clean in preparation for the next time

it will be used.

◆ Cut a piece of hardboard or heavy card to fit into the back of the frame. Slip in the glass and the picture (*see* Fig 21.18), pin it all in place, fix eyelets on the outer edges, string up, hang up and enjoy it.

Fig 21.17 The oval moulded frame from the lathe.

CHAPTER 22

Oval Dish

I HAVE A SMALL COLLECTION OF MAUCHLINE WARE, WOODEN SOUVENIR WARE MADE IN THE MIDDLE OF THE LAST CENTURY IN THE TOWN OF MAUCHLINE IN AYRSHIRE, SCOTLAND. THE PIECES WERE MOST FREQUENTLY MADE OF SYCAMORE AND HAVE ENGRAVED TRANSFERS APPLIED TO THEM. THESE ENGRAVINGS COVER A WIDE VARIETY OF SCENES AND WERE RELATED TO THE AREA IN WHICH THE SOUVENIR WAS PURCHASED.

The variety of pieces produced was very wide, ranging from boxes to sewing tools, brooches, frames, egg cups, whistles and many other turned items. In fact any wooden piece that could be sold was produced.

At the height of production, Smiths of Mauchline employed over four hundred people, many of whom would have been turners. It must have been a fascinating sight watching production turners working day after day, efficiently turning out piece after piece.

By chance I came upon a most interesting piece of Mauchline ware – an oval dish. It was interesting for two reasons. The first point of interest I discovered when I turned the dish over; the turned foot was twisted slightly off centre. This was a problem I had encountered when turning elliptically and is caused by slackness in the bearers and runners. It was good to know that production turners faced similar problems. The second and more interesting point was that they were actually using an oval chuck and felt that it was worthwhile to take the trouble to produce oval pieces. Having discovered that there were oval Mauchline pieces I have looked further, but have found few. However, that is the pleasure of collecting!

Fig 22.1 The oval dish (left) and my Mauchline ware oval dish.

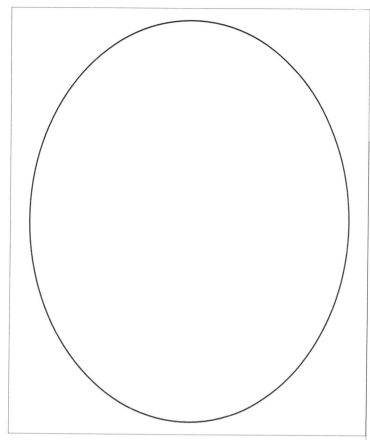

Fig 22.2 An outline of the outer edge of the dish.

Fig 22.3 An outline of the foot of the dish.

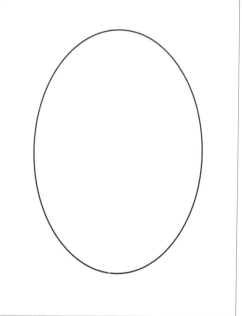

The oval dish that I decided to turn was to be a little deeper than the one I had bought, and I attempted to maintain a far more even and thinner section than was found in the Mauchline ware piece, which was quite heavy where the sides met the base.

The choice of wood for this oval dish was decided for me; during my visit to Australia I had been given a splendid piece of West Australian sandalwood and I needed an excuse to use it. It cut sweetly on the band saw. The perfume blown off whilst cutting was rich and delicate, clinging to clothes, so that for days afterwards it could still be enjoyed! The wood proved to be a perfect choice. It was close grained, clean cutting, and-finished well from the tool.

Preparation

◆ Cut a piece of wood 120mm (4¾in) long by 100mm (4in) wide by 20mm (¹³⁄₁₆in) thick.
◆ Cut a piece of softwood 75mm (3in) long by 60mm (2⅜in) wide by 12mm (½in) thick.

This will be used to raise the dish blank from the surface of the faceplate.
◆ Have some PVA glue and newspaper available to produce paper and glue joints.
◆ Check the oval chuck, making sure that all parts are properly adjusted and that it is ready to use.
◆ Lathe speed should be 500rpm

Turning the dish

◆ Set the tool rest so that a pencil point is at centre height. Turn the lathe by hand to make sure nothing catches.
◆ Mark a large oval (*see* Fig 22.2) which will be the size of the outer edge of the dish and will fall inside the size of the prepared sandalwood blank.
◆ Inside that, mark a smaller oval (*see* Fig 22.3) which will be about the size of the foot of the dish.
◆ Readjust the tool rest so that a felt pen

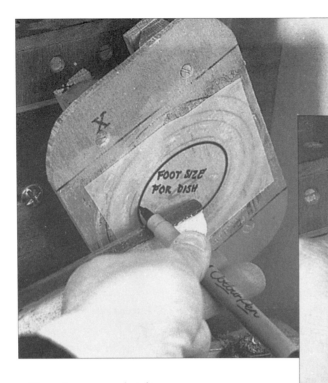

will mark at centre height.

◆ Rotate the lathe by hand and mark in those two chosen ovals in black felt pen.

◆ The reason for marking in pencil first, followed by felt-tip, is that the pencil markings, being much lighter, are less obvious when the lathe is switched on, so several may be marked and the best chosen. The chosen oval can then be fully defined in felt pen and that guide mark will be clearly seen above all others when turning.

◆ Take a tracing of both ovals and mark on those tracings exactly what they are, e.g. 'outer edge of oval dish', so they can be identified and used again in the future (*see* Figs 22.4 and 22.5).

◆ Transfer the shape of the smaller oval to the piece of softwood.

◆ Transfer the shape of the larger oval to the thicker piece of sandalwood.

◆ Cut out both pieces on the band saw. If you are fortunate enough to be cutting sandalwood, think of all those poor unfortunates who are not!

◆ Take the oval piece of softwood and spread PVA glue upon one flat face.

◆ Fix newspaper to that surface, smoothing out all wrinkles and bubbles. Trim the surplus paper from around the edge.

◆ Spread PVA glue onto the smaller marked oval on the faceplate.

◆ Push the softwood oval newspaper-covered surface onto the glued area (*see* Fig 22.6).

Fig 22.6 The foot-raiser newspaper/glued to the faceplate.

Fig 22.7 The sandalwood oval blank newspaper/glued to the foot-raiser. The block spreads the pressure applied by the tailstock.

◆ Line up the oval with the felt pen markings.

◆ Press a block of wood on top of the softwood, bringing the tailstock forward to add pressure whilst the glue dries. The block helps spread the pressure applied by the tailstock. Check that the softwood oval is still accurately located within the oval markings on the ply faceplate before leaving it for the glue to dry fully.

◆ Once the glue has dried, withdraw the tailstock and remove the wooden block.

◆ Apply PVA glue to the top surface of the softwood oval, covering it with a piece of newspaper. Smooth out wrinkles and bubbles.

◆ Apply more glue to that newspaper surface, then press the sandalwood oval onto the glued surface. Now it becomes a little tricky because the cut edge of the sandalwood oval has to be lined up with the felt pen oval on the ply faceplate 12mm (½in) beneath.

◆ By eye carefully line up the oval blank with the felt pen marking. Press a wood

block on top of the oval blank and bring the tailstock back to add pressure (*see* Fig 22.7).

◆ Tighten the tailstock onto the blank only when satisfied that the oval blank is precisely located. Do not try to rotate the lathe for, as the oval chuck has a wandering centre, this will cause the blank to be twisted out of position.

◆ Leave the glue to dry.

◆ The softwood piece is needed to raise the oval blank away from the faceplate to allow the underside of the dish to be turned. It would be possible to turn the underside without this foot-raiser, but there would always be the increased danger of the faceplate being struck or of the faceplate striking the turner.

◆ Once the glue has dried, rotate the lathe to make sure nothing catches.

◆ Mark in felt pen (at centre height) the largest complete oval on the outer edge of the sandalwood blank.

◆ Carefully turn the edge to the full oval shape, having set the tool rest so that the tool

Fig 22.8 The oval sandalwood blank ready to be turned.

Fig 22.9 The underside profile.

cuts at centre height.

◆ Bring the tool rest to the side of the work so that the gouge cuts at centre height.

◆ Rotate the lathe by hand to ensure that nothing catches and that the tool rest is positioned so that the tool may reach all parts necessary (*see* Fig 22.8).

◆ Begin the cut, turning the underside first.

◆ Watch the work and the faceplate flashing round. Keep the tool on the tool rest and do not overextend it towards the faceplate. This will help to prevent contact with the faceplate. It might be more comfortable to turn left handed, which will keep your hands further away from the faceplate.

◆ The deeper the gouge cuts into the underside of the dish, the more the back hand holding the handle of the tool needs to be raised to keep the cut at the point of tranquillity. It will be clear when the cut moves from this point, because the cut will become more bumpy. If unhappy or uncertain using a gouge, try a sharp, round-nosed tool.

◆ When cutting on centre height the cut will be even and tranquil. If the cut is moved above or below centre, it will become a little jarring. The easiest and most efficient point at which to cut is at centre height and this position I call 'the point of tranquillity'.

◆ So often, when turning round work, the progressive shaping of the cut can be viewed on the back profile. In elliptical turning, the back image is a muddled ghost. To view the progress of the shaping you must look at the profile from directly above (*see* Fig 22.9).

◆ Sharpen the tools, wax the cam, and tighten the runners and bearers if necessary.

◆ Have a clear idea of the shaping of the underside of the dish. Have a drawing fixed close by for reference and look at it frequently, relating it to the cut (*see* Fig 22.10).

◆ Finishing straight from the tool is more difficult than with round work, but experience improves performance.

◆ Using a narrow, square-ended tool, cut a 3mm (⅛in) wide foot, cutting part of this into the softwood foot-raiser. This will leave about a 2mm (³⁄₃₂in) foot on the base of the dish.

◆ When completely satisfied with the shaping beneath, remove the tool rest and glasspaper

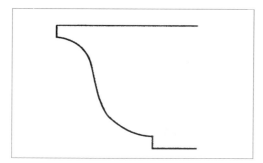

Fig 22.10 The oval dish profile.

the underside smooth. Keep to the point of tranquillity which will be very apparent.

◆ The next stage is to start turning the inside, so move the tool rest to the face of the work.

◆ Set the rest so that the tool cuts at centre height.

◆ Rotate the lathe by hand.

◆ Switch on the lathe and begin turning out the inside of the dish (*see* Fig 22.11).

◆ Constantly check the wall thickness. This is not so easy with the work rotating, so switch off now and again to feel the wall, or

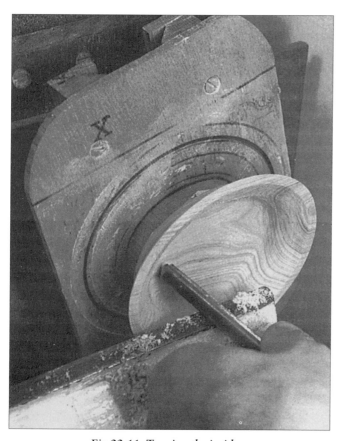

Fig 22.11 Turning the inside.

use callipers to check on the thickness. Remember that it will be virtually impossible to rechuck the work so it must be satisfactorily finished first time.

◆ Tighten the bearers and runners when necessary and keep the tool sharp.

◆ Turning ovals with a gouge is a skill that requires plenty of practice. Do not feel a sense of guilt or failure if the skill that you commonly practise on round work does not come immediately and you have to complete the piece using a round-nosed tool. Just enjoy the technique of elliptical turning; it is a new skill that will take a little time to get used to.

◆ Once the shape and the wall thickness are considered to be perfect, remove the tool rest and glasspaper the inside, again at the point of tranquillity. It is quite interesting that this point of tranquillity is even more evident when glasspapering with the hand than when turning with the tool.

◆ Using a sharp knife, split the dish away from the softwood raiser and set the dish aside (*see* Fig 22.12).

◆ Split the foot-raiser away from the faceplate and scrape the faceplate clean.

◆ It will be noticed that I always insist that the faceplate is cleaned before the work is fully finished. This will ensure the chuck will always be ready for use and that the glue and paper which may still be a little soft is removed more easily.

◆ Clean off the base of the dish immediately for the same reason.

◆ Now look and see if the axis of the foot of your dish is in line with the main shape, or if it is twisted as in the Mauchline example shown in Fig 22.13. If it is twisted then you need to keep the bearers and runners a little tighter. If it is in line, well done!

◆ Polish the dish.

If this experience of turning a dish has been a pleasant one, then maybe a larger but not necessarily much thicker dish would be worth considering for your next project. In which case it may be necessary to move the whole chuck to the outboard end of the lathe and increase the bracing.

Fig 22.12 Splitting the dish away from the
faceplate using a sharp knife.

Fig 22.13 The slightly twisted foot of the
Mauchline dish.

CHAPTER 23

Oval Box

F ALL THE ELLIPTICAL TURNING I HAVE DONE, THIS BOX PROVIDED THE MOST EXCITEMENT – A LITTLE BIT OF SMOKE FOLLOWED BY SLIGHT DAMAGE TO THE SLIDE CLEARLY DEMONSTRATED THE LIMITS OF A WOODEN CHUCK OF THIS SIZE.

With careful preparation of the blank, reducing weight where possible by drilling out much of the centre, this chuck can be used successfully. But if several boxes of this size are required it would be advisable to increase the size of the chuck, enlarge the boss size on the slide, and increase the width of the slide, providing a wider-angled area between itself and the runners. Besides this, a wider area of contact between cam and bearers would be needed. The above improvements would certainly enable boxes to be turned easily and confidently and would increase the life of this type of wooden oval chuck considerably.

Wooden oval chucks can satisfactorily compete with the more sophisticated engineer-produced metal variety. After all, much if not all of the early elliptical turning was produced on chucks made wholly of wood.

This oval box is made of Australian grey gum burr. I cannot praise this wood highly enough for the use to which it was put. For turning oval boxes it is excellent – the burr is tight, with no pieces falling or breaking out, and of course there is no grain direction to worry about since it is in all directions, and this proved to be of great benefit.

Fig 23.1 The oval box.

Preparation

◆ Mark out on the oval faceplate the size of the box to be produced. Here it was approximately 100mm (4in) long by 65mm (2½in) wide (*see* Fig 23.2). It is best not to be overambitious with your first box, so don't make it too large.

◆ Cut two pieces of grey gum burr, one 20mm (¹³⁄₁₆in) thick for the top, the other 30mm (1⅞in) thick for the base. The length and width of both must be sufficient to cut the required oval.

◆ Have a piece of 12mm (½in) thick softwood ready as a spacer, so that when turning the lower edge of the box it can be fully turned without interfering with the faceplate.

◆ PVA glue and newspaper are needed.

◆ Tighten the bearers and runners, oil the slide and wax the cam, but be careful when turning on the lathe after having oiled the slide – you may have a spray of oil thrown off. Protect anything of importance in the immediate spray area.

◆ Lathe speed should be 500rpm.

Turning the box

◆ For the dimensions of the finished box, refer to Fig 23.3.

◆ Having drawn the chosen shape in felt pen on the faceplate, make a tracing.

◆ Transfer the shape to the thinner piece of wood for the lid of your box.

◆ Band saw the oval shape.

◆ Apply PVA glue to the flat surface of the oval and apply a piece of newspaper, smoothing out wrinkles and bubbles.

◆ Apply PVA glue to the inside of the marked oval on the faceplate.

◆ Press the newspaper side of the wood oval onto the glued area of the faceplate, matching its shape to the felt pen markings.

◆ Bring forward a block of wood and press it against the wood oval. Use the tailstock to add pressure whilst the glue sets.

◆ Once the glue has dried, withdraw the tailstock and remove the pressure block.

◆ Bring the tool rest forward, setting it so that the gouge cuts at centre height.

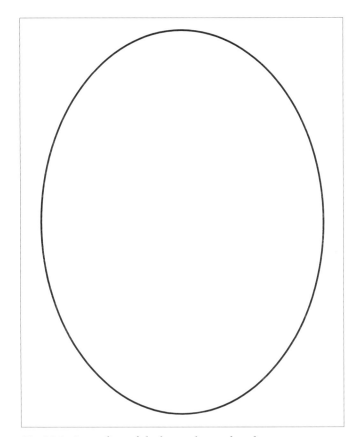

Fig 23.2 An outline of the box to be produced.

◆ Rotate the lathe by hand to make sure nothing catches.

◆ Turn the face of the oval flat, bringing it to 15mm (⅝in) thick.

◆ Mark a felt-pen line (having reset the tool rest) 9mm (⅜in) in from the edge of the oval

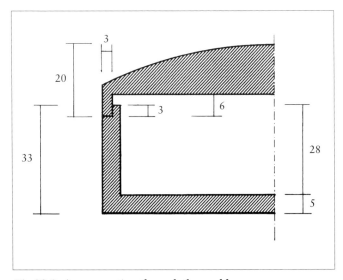

Fig 23.3 A cross section through the oval box.

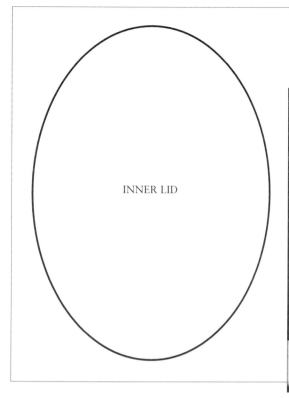

INNER LID

Fig 23.4 *An outline of the inner lid.*

Fig 23.5 *The oval lid blank fitted to the chuck. The outer oval and rebate line are marked.*

(*see* Figs 23.4 and 23.5).

◆ Take a tracing of that oval and mark it 'Inner Lid' (*see* Fig 23.6).

◆ Reset the tool rest so that the square-end tool will cut at centre height.

◆ Make sure that you select a square-end tool with an end section that will allow you to cut the tight curve of the oval without its lower edges rubbing and preventing the top edge from cutting.

◆ Rotate the lathe by hand.

◆ Cut on the inside of the marked line to a depth of 9mm (⅜in), widening the cut out a

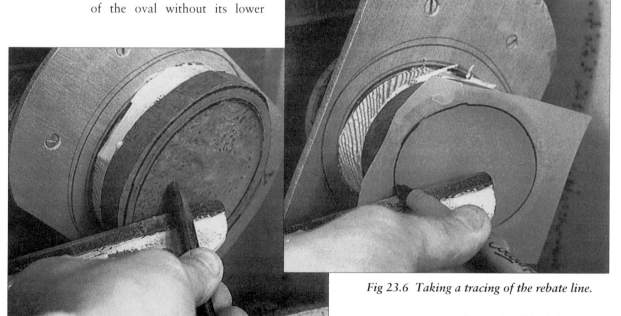

Fig 23.6 *Taking a tracing of the rebate line.*

Fig 23.7 *Turning the inside of the lid.*

Fig 23.8 Turning the rebate so that it is square edged.

Fig 23.9 Checking that the edge is flat across the width of the lid.

little towards the centre (*see* Fig 23.7).

◆ Switch off the lathe and readjust the tool rest so that the gouge will cut at centre height.

◆ Rotate the lathe by hand before beginning the cut and, when satisfied, turn out the inside of the lid to a depth of 9mm (⅜in).

◆ Make sure before finishing that the top face of the rim is flat and true to ensure a good fit between top and base (*see* Figs 23.8 and 23.9).

◆ Use a Stanley knife to split the newspaper and glue joint, so that the lid may be removed from the faceplate.

◆ Clean off the faceplate.

◆ On a piece of 12mm (½in) thick softwood, mark the large oval shape and cut out on the band saw.

◆ Spread PVA glue on one side of the softwood oval, fixing newspaper to that glued surface. Smooth out all wrinkles and bubbles.

◆ Spread PVA glue to the inside of the felt-pen oval on the faceplate.

◆ Press the softwood oval onto the glued area with the newspaper surface down.

◆ Make sure that the edge of the softwood oval lines up with the marked oval on the faceplate. Press firmly into place using a block and the tailstock to add pressure. Leave whilst the glue dries.

◆ Once the glue has dried, remove the tailstock and block.

◆ On the thicker piece of grey gum, mark out the larger oval shape using the tracing, then cut out on the band saw.

◆ Use a large saw-tooth or Forstner bit to remove the majority of the waste wood from the centre, drilling to a depth of 20mm (¹³⁄₁₆in) and leaving a wall thickness of about 12mm (½in). On my first box I did not do this and detailed on page 222 are some of the problems I encountered. I hope you will avoid these problems by drilling out at least some of the waste wood before you start.

◆ Fix this cut oval to the softwood using a newspaper and glue joint as before. Make sure that the oval is fully aligned before clamping it in place to dry.

◆ When the glue is fully dry it is time to begin turning.

◆ Adjust the tool rest so that a pencil will mark at centre height, then mark a series of ovals on the face of the burr. Choose the one that matches the shape of the tracing marked 'Inner Lid'.

◆ Mark the correct size oval in felt-pen, having adjusted the tool rest.

◆ Readjust the tool rest so that the square-end tool will cut at centre height.

Fig 23.10 Turning the rebate on the box base to accept the lid.

Fig 23.11 Turning inside the box.

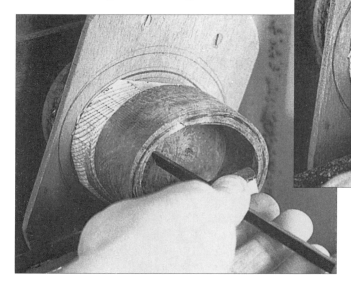

inside of the marked 'Inner Lid' oval. Deepen that cut to 25mm (1in), cutting the whole centre out to that depth ensuring the base is flat and true (*see* Figs 23.10 and 23.11).

◆ The lid can now be fitted using hot-melt glue applied to the step.

◆ Now this becomes a most exciting turning experience. You are constantly aware of the cuts being made and the necessity to cut upon the precise centre line with the large, off-centre whirring mass causing the heart to pound!

◆ The whole of the top surface of the lid can now be turned to a gentle domed shape.

◆ Switch off the lathe, bring the tool rest round to the side of the work and set the tool at cutting height. Begin to turn the side of the box. Because this larger piece extends further away from the faceplate, more twisting forces are applied to the boss on the slide when cuts are made. These cuts therefore need to be smaller and finer to prevent damage to the boss.

◆ When turning the side you need to be aware of the internal hollow; the only guide you have to assist in judging the thickness of the wall is the tracing of the 'Inner Lid'. If you think that the wall may be getting dangerously thin, measure the width and length of the tracing and test against the outer measurements of the box. At this point you may like to turn a small recessed foot at the junction of the softwood spacer and the base of the box.

◆ When satisfied with the outer shaping, glasspaper the whole piece smooth, always working at that point of tranquillity.

◆ Cut a 3mm (⅛in) deep step on the outside of that oval and make sure that it is square, flat and true.

◆ Test the lid on the step and make adjustments until the fit is precise.

It was here that problems arose on my first box. The bearers were overtightened on the cam and I should have corrected this before continuing to turn the inside of the box base. With my larger, heavier solid oval blank the vibration increased, but once I began to turn away the centre and reduce the weight the vibration decreased; however, it was too late, the damage had been done. The tightness of the bearers and the increased weight caused the bearers to smoulder, which was first apparent from the smell of smoke. I turned off the lathe and found that the chuck was sloppy and loose. A closer examination of the bearers revealed charring and severe wear, but the lignum vitae cam was still in perfect condition, for the slightly softer, more easily replaceable bearers had worn first. The bearers have two faces, so I unscrewed them, turned them round and refixed and readjusted them before continuing.

◆ To turn out the centre of your box you must make a cut 3mm (⅛in) away on the

◆ Use a Stanley knife to split the box from the softwood spacer and the spacer from the faceplate (*see* Figs 23.12 and 23.13).

◆ Clean up the faceplate thoroughly.

◆ Clean the glue and newspaper from the bottom of the box.

◆ Take the box to the microwave oven and set on full power for 15 seconds. Remove and the lid should lift free. If you don't have a microwave oven you can use a hot-air paint stripper for a short period.

◆ Clean off any remaining glue from the box joint.

This wooden chuck held up almost to the end. At the final sanding, there was a cracking sound which was the boss of the slide beginning to break away from it. This was caused by turning a larger and heavier solid piece, and could have been avoided by drilling away the majority of the centre before the turning began. The good news was that it was easily repairable and soon after, and indeed ever since, it has been working as well as ever. This is the great advantage of using a chuck made in one's own workshop.

I would hope that this introduction to elliptical turning has been a happy experience and that you have been encouraged to continue either using wooden chucks or developing and using a metal chuck. See page 226 for the address where you can obtain drawings of a metal chuck, which works on similar principles to the wooden chuck described here. It fits the lathe in the same manner and could be made using light alloys with sections drilled out to reduce weight.

As a thought towards experimentation in this form of turnery, consider the following:

Constant diameter odd-sided cams

◆ The cam that the bearer follows in the chuck described above is circular and obviously has a constant diameter.

◆ A British fifty-pence piece has seven sides and also has a constant diameter.

◆ The Rotary or Wankel engine has a three-sided moving part that is of constant diameter.

◆ I have seen the constant diameter of odd-sided pieces clearly demonstrated using a ruler and a fifty-pence piece. The coin is placed upon its edge on a flat work surface;

Fig 23.12 *Having fitted and turned the lid and box sides, it is removed from the raising block attached to the faceplate.*

Fig 23.13 *A view of the box top.*

Fig 23.14 Fitted to the camplate is the three-sided cam of constant diameter. The slot has yet to be fully cut.

Fig 23.15 The oval chuck fitted over the three-sided cam.

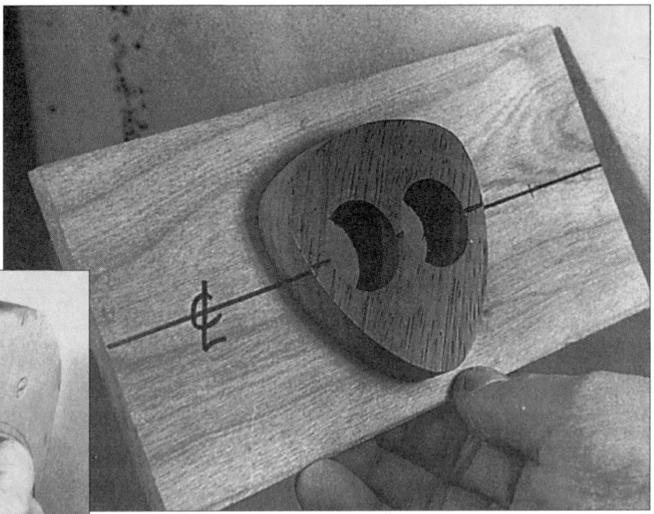

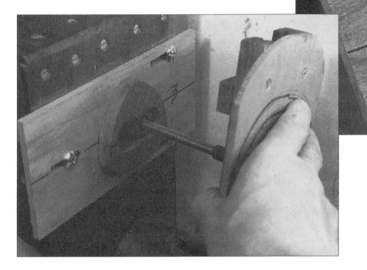

Fig 23.16 The twisted oblong.

the vertical sides of the coin are held lightly between thumb and forefinger. The ruler is placed on top of the coin so that it runs between the thumb and finger supporting the coin. The coin is rolled gently along the works surface keeping the ruler in contact with the top of the coin. The ruler will stay at a constant height above the work surface, riding smoothly upon the coin beneath, and will not jolt up and down, thus proving that the shape has a constant diameter.

◆ A seven-sided cam, I felt, would have little real effect on the shape being turned on the faceplate, but a three-sided constant diameter cam might. So I made a three-sided cam with the same diameter as the circular cam used in the oval chuck (*see* Figs 23.14 and 23.15).

◆ When the lathe was rotated by hand the bearers followed the cam and the shape produced on the faceplate was a slightly twisted oblong (*see* Figs 23.16 and 23.17).

◆ I tried the wooden chuck on this cam with the lathe switched on, but the throw was too much to make progress. A more substantial metal chuck is needed if oblong frames, dishes, or even oblong boxes are to be turned.

◆ Below is the method used for marking out a three-sided constant diameter cam:

1. Draw a triangle. It doesn't have to be a regular triangle, but for the cam to be evenly shaped, draw an equilateral triangle (one with three equal length sides and 60° angles). You may like to experiment with irregular-shaped triangles; they may produce some interesting results.
2. Extend the sides of the triangle.
3. Set the compass to a radius greater than the longest side of the triangle.
4. Place the point of the compass upon one point of the triangle (Point 1).
5. Strike an arc until it touches two extended sides of the triangle.
6. Place the point of the compass on one of

the other two points of the triangle (Point 2).

7. Reset the compass so that it reaches and touches where the first arc cut the extended side close by.

8. Now strike that arc across to the next closest extended side; where the arc crosses that extended side will be Point A.

9. Now place the compass on the third point of the original triangle and extend it to Point A.

10. Strike an arc from Point A across to the next untouched extended side. Where it cuts this line will be Point B.

11. Now return to Point 1 and place the compass point there.

12. Extend the compass to touch Point B and strike an arc around to the next extended side. This will be Point C.

13. Now place the compass on Point 2 and extend it to touch Point C.

14. Strike an arc around to the next extended side, where the arc cuts this line will be Point D.

15. Finally place the compass on the third point of the triangle and extend it to meet Point D. Strike an arc to the final extended side which will join the first arc. The shape is now complete (*see* Fig 23.18).

If a precise 72mm (2¹³/₁₆in) constant-diameter three-sided cam is required, follow the above instructions starting with an equilateral triangle with a side length of 51mm (2in). Set the compass to 62mm (2.875in) and use this as the measurement in step 3 above. The rest will follow. An alternative method is to use the magic of photocopy reduction and enlargement, having drawn the desired shape to any convenient size first.

This cam has a roving centre. The constant diameter is measured through this centre, but just try finding it!

One final consideration. When cutting the slot for this cam, to allow it to be offset it has to be either aligned parallel to one side or on a vertical line bisecting one angle. I have only produced a cam with a vertical bisecting slot. I am not sure whether it would

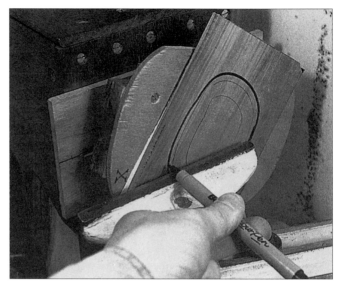

Fig 23.17 The twisted oblong drawn upon a blank piece of wood.

cause any variation in shape if the slot were to be cut parallel to one side.

I hope that experimentation along these lines will be as fruitful and exciting as full elliptical turning.

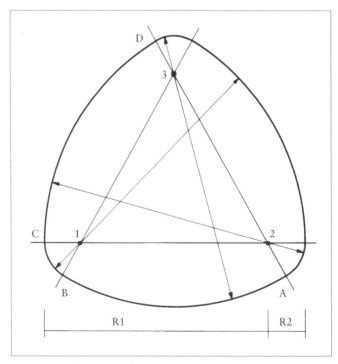

Fig 23.18 The three-sided cam of constant diameter, 72mm (2⅞in), based on a 52mm (2in) equilateral triangle. Chosen radius (R1): 62mm (2⁷/₁₆in).

Useful Addresses

For miscellaneous tools, metal lathe tools, gauge plates and general bits of hardware write to:
Proops Brothers
34 Saddington Road
Fleckney
Leicestershire

For Vitex abrasive paper:
Lincolnshire Woodcraft Supplies
13 All Saints Street
Stamford
Lincolnshire

For details of plans for the metal oval chuck, send a SAE to:
Frank Dutton
8 Redruth Close
Horeston Grange
Nuneaton CV11 6FG

A new Elliptical Turning Association has been formed. For those with an interest in elliptical turning, please write to:
Professor Volmer
Salzstrasse 94
09113 Chemnitz
Germany
or
Bill Newton
5 Beacon Brow
Horton Bank Top
Bradford
West Yorkshire BD6 3DE

Bibliography

Joseph Moxon, *Mechanick Exercises or the Doctrine of Handy-Works*. First published 1678; reprinted by the Astragal Press.

Hamelin Bergeron, *Manuel du Tourneur*. First published 1816; reprinted by Inter-livres.

John Jacob Holtzapffel, *The Principles and Practice of Ornamental or Complex Turning (Volume V)*. First published 1884; reprinted by Dover Publications.

Metric Conversion

Inches to Millimetres and Centimetres
MM – millimetres   CM – centimetres

Inches	MM	CM	Inches	CM	Inches	CM
⅛	3	0.3	9	22.9	30	76.2
¼	6	0.6	10	25.4	31	78.7
⅜	10	1.0	11	27.9	32	81.3
½	13	1.3	12	30.5	33	83.8
⅝	16	1.6	13	33.0	34	86.4
¾	19	1.9	14	35.6	35	88.9
⅞	22	2.2	15	38.1	36	91.4
1	25	2.5	16	40.6	37	94.0
1¼	32	3.2	17	43.2	38	96.5
1½	38	3.8	18	45.7	39	99.1
1¾	44	4.4	19	48.3	40	101.6
2	51	5.1	20	50.8	41	104.1
2½	64	6.4	21	53.3	42	106.7
3	76	7.6	22	55.9	43	109.2
3½	89	8.9	23	58.4	44	111.8
4	102	10.2	24	61.0	45	114.3
4½	114	11.4	25	63.5	46	116.8
5	127	12.7	26	66.0	47	119.4
6	152	15.2	27	68.6	48	121.9
7	178	17.8	28	71.1	49	124.5
8	203	20.3	29	73.7	50	127.0

Index

About the Author

David Springett is lucky enough to spend his work days doing what he most enjoys, which is turning. To be precise, he turns highly decorated East Midland lace bobbins in bone and wood, for which he has gained an international reputation.

In the evenings, David maintains his turning interest by experimenting with unusual and improbable forms of turnery, seeking inspiration amongst neglected early turning techniques. The fruits of this activity may be seen in this book, as well as in his previous book, *Woodturning Wizardry*.

David and his wife Christine live in Rugby, Warwickshire, where they run weekend lacemaking courses at the British College of Lace.

TITLES AVAILABLE FROM
GMC PUBLICATIONS LTD

BOOKS

Woodworking Plans and Projects	GMC Publications	Making and Modifying Woodworking Tools	Jim Kingshott
40 More Woodworking Plans and Projects	GMC Publications	The Workshop	Jim Kingshott
Woodworking Crafts Annual	GMC Publications	Sharpening: The Complete Guide	Jim Kingshott
Woodworkers' Career and Educational Source Book	GMC Publications	Turning Wooden Toys	Terry Lawrence
Woodworkers' Courses & Source Book	GMC Publications	Making Board, Peg and Dice Games	Jeff & Jennie Loader
Green Woodwork	Mike Abbott	The Complete Dolls' House Book	Jean Nisbett
Making Little Boxes from Wood	John Bennett	The Secrets of the Dolls' House Makers	Jean Nisbett
The Incredible Router	Jeremy Broun	Furniture Projects for the Home	Ernest Parrott
Electric Woodwork	Jeremy Broun	Make Money from Woodturning	Ann & Bob Phillips
Woodcarving: A Complete Course	Ron Butterfield	Members' Guide to Marketing	Jack Pigden
Making Fine Furniture: Projects	Tom Darby	Woodcarving Tools, Materials and Equipment	Chris Pye
Restoring Rocking Horses	Clive Green & Anthony Dew	Making Tudor Dolls' Houses	Derek Rowbottom
Heraldic Miniature Knights	Peter Greenhill	Making Georgian Dolls' Houses	Derek Rowbottom
Practical Crafts: Seat Weaving	Ricky Holdstock	Making Period Dolls' House Furniture	Derek & Sheila Rowbottom
Multi-centre Woodturning	Ray Hopper	Woodturning: A Foundation Course	Keith Rowley
Complete Woodfinishing	Ian Hosker	Turning Miniatures in Wood	John Sainsbury
Woodturning: A Source Book of Shapes	John Hunnex	Pleasure and Profit from Woodturning	Reg Sherwin
Making Shaker Furniture	Barry Jackson	Making Unusual Miniatures	Graham Spalding
Upholstery: A Complete Course	David James	Woodturning Wizardry	David Springett
Upholstery Techniques and Projects	David James	Adventures in Woodturning	David Springett
Designing and Making Wooden Toys	Terry Kelly	Furniture Projects	Rod Wales
Making Dolls' House Furniture	Patricia King	Decorative Woodcarving	Jeremy Williams

VIDEOS

Dennis White Teaches Woodturning		
Part 1	Turning Between Centres	
Part 2	Turning Bowls	
Part 3	Boxes, Goblets and Screw Threads	
Part 4	Novelties and Projects	
Part 5	Classic Profiles	
Part 6	Twists and Advanced Turning	

Jim Kingshott	Sharpening the Professional Way
Jim Kingshott	Sharpening Turning and Carving Tools
Ray Gonzalez	Carving a Figure: The Female Form
David James	The Traditional Upholstery Workshop Part I: Stuffover Upholstery
David James	The Traditional Upholstery Workshop Part II: Drop-in and Pinstuffed Seats

GMC Publications regularly produces new books and videos on a wide range of woodworking and craft subjects, and an increasing number of specialist magazines, all available on subscription:

MAGAZINES

WOODCARVING   WOODTURNING   BUSINESSMATTERS

All these publications are available through bookshops and newsagents, or may be ordered by post from the publishers at 166 High Street, Lewes, East Sussex BN7 1XU, telephone (0273) 477374, fax (0273) 478606.

Credit card orders are accepted. Please write or phone for the latest information.